# Geographic Information Systems:
# Defence Applications

# Geographic Information Systems:

## Defence Applications

Edited by

## Desmond Ball and Ross Babbage

Strategic and Defence Studies Centre
Research School of Pacific Studies
Australian National University

Brassey's Australia
A Division of Pergamon Press Australia

Member of Maxwell Macmillan Pergamon Publishing Corporation

Brassey's has imprints in London, Washington and Sydney. The companies' origins lie in *Brassey's Naval Annual*, first published in 1886. Brassey's now specialises in books on international relations, defence, foreign policy, strategy and tactics, military history, military affairs and military technology. Brassey's (UK) also publishes the annuals, papers and journal of the International Institute for Strategic Studies. All three Brassey's companies welcome English language publishing proposals from authors and institutions throughout the world.

Brassey's Australia is a division of Pergamon Press Australia and a member of the Maxwell Macmillan Pergamon Publishing Corporation.

| | |
|---|---|
| AUSTRALIA | Pergamon Press (Australia) Pty Ltd, 19a Boundary Street, Rushcutters Bay, NSW 2011, Australia |
| UK | Pergamon Press plc, Headington Hill Hall, Oxford OX3 0BW, England |
| USA | Pergamon Press, Inc., Maxwell House, Fairview Park, Elmsford, New York 10532, USA |
| PEOPLE'S REPUBLIC OF CHINA | Pergamon Press, Room 4037, Qianmen Hotel, Beijing, People's Republic of China |
| FEDERAL REPUBLIC OF GERMANY | Pergamon Press GmbH, Hammerweg 6, D-6242 Kronberg, Federal Republic of Germany |
| BRAZIL | Pergamon Editora Ltda, Rua Eça de Queiros, 346, CEP 04011, Paraiso, São Paulo, Brazil |
| JAPAN | Pergamon Press, 8th Floor, Matsuoka Central Building, 1-7-1 Nishishinjuku, Shinjuku-ku, Tokyo 160, Japan |
| CANADA | Pergamon Press Canada Ltd, Suite 271, 253 College Street, Toronto, Ontario M5T 1R5, Canada |

First published 1989

Chapters 1, 7, 9 and 11 Copyright © 1989 Strategic and Defence Studies Centre, Australian National University
Chapters 2, 3, 5 and 8 Copyright © 1989 K. J. Lyons, O. F. Moss and P. Perrett
Chapters 4, 6 and 10 Copyright © 1989 The Commonwealth of Australia

Cover design by Hand Graphics
Typeset in Hong Kong by Graphicraft Typesetters Limited
Printed in Australia by Macarthur Press

National Library of Australia Cataloguing in Publication Data

Geographic information systems.

Bibliography.
Includes index.
ISBN 0 08 034444 5.

1. Military geography — Australia — Data processing.
2. Information storage and retrieval systems — Geography.  I. Ball, Desmond, 1947– .
II. Babbage, Ross, 1949– .

025'.0691

# CONTENTS

# FIGURES

# COLOUR PLATES

# ACRONYMS AND ABBREVIATIONS

| | |
|---|---|
| AACLI | Australian Advisory Committee on Land Information |
| ABS | Australian Bureau of Statistics |
| ACSM | American Congress for Surveying and Mapping |
| ACT | Australian Capital Territory |
| ACTEA | ACT Electricity Authority |
| ADF | Australian Defence Force |
| AGSTATS | Database of Agricultural Statistics |
| AID | Automatic Interaction Detection |
| AII | Australian Infrastructure Information |
| AIS | Airborne Imaging Spectrometer |
| ALIC | Australian Land Information Council |
| ALS | Australian Landsat Station |
| AMG | Australian Map Grid |
| AO | Area of Operations |
| AODC | Australian Oceanographic Data Centre |
| AOSI | Army Office Staff Instruction |
| AP | Aerial Photography |
| ARC | Applied Research of Cambridge |
| ARDB | Australian Resources Data Bank |
| ARIS | Australian Resources Information System |
| AS | Airborne Scanner |
| ASC | Atherton Shire Council |
| ASO | Australian Survey Office |
| ASPRS | American Society of Photogrammetry and Remote Sensing |
| ASSTASS | Australian Surface Ship Towed Array Sonar System |

| | |
|---|---|
| AURISA | Australian Urban and Regional Information Systems Association |
| AUSSAT | Australian Domestic Satellite System |
| AUSTACCS | Australian Army Command and Control System (automated support system) |
| Autocad | Automatic CAD (graphics package) |
| AUTOCHART | RAN computerised charting system |
| AUTOMAP | RA Svy computerised mapping system |
| AVHRR | Advanced Very High Resolution Radiometer |
| BDE | Brigade |
| BTEC | Brucellosis and Tuberculosis Eradication Campaign |
| BUP | Building Unit Plan |
| CAD | Computer-Aided Design Computer-Aided Drafting |
| CALMIS | Conservation and Land Management Information System (WA) |
| CAM | Computer-Aided Mapping |
| CARIS | Spatial analysis and mapping software |
| CART | Software package for producing classification trees |
| CCAE | Canberra College of Advanced Education |
| CCD | Census Collection District |
| CCM | Cross-Country Movement (ETL graphics) |
| CCT | Computer Compatible Tape |
| CD | Compact Disc Collection District (census) |
| CGS | Chief of the General Staff |
| CIR | Cone Index Rating |
| CLISG | Commonwealth Land Information Support Group |
| CNES | Centre National d'Etudes Spatiales (France) |
| COBOL | Common Business-Oriented Language |

| | |
|---|---|
| CODASYL | Conference on Data Systems Language |
| CONVERT | Database converter |
| CPU | Central Processing Unit |
| CSE | Central Studies Establishment (DSTO) |
| CSIRO | Commonwealth Scientific and Industrial Research Organisation |
| CSIRONET | CSIRO computer communications network |
| CWM | Corporate Working Map |
| CYBER | Cybernetics |
| CZCS | Coastal Zone Colour Scanner |
| DARSO | Division of Administrative Responsibility of the Services in Operations |
| Datatrieve | Data retrieval system |
| DBMS | Database Management System |
| DCCS | Director of Command and Control Systems |
| DCDB | Digital Cadastral Database (Qld) |
| DDAS | Divisional Deployment Area Study |
| DEC | Digital Equipment Corporation |
| DFIS | Distributed Facilities Information System (WA) |
| DID | Department of Industry Development (Qld) |
| DIESO | Maritime diesel oil |
| DIV | Division |
| DLI | Defence Land Information |
| DLP | Director of Logistic Plans |
| DMA | Defense Mapping Agency (USA) |
| DMS | Department of Mapping and Surveying (Qld) |
| DoD | Department of Defence |
| DOLA | Department of Land Administration (WA) |
| DoT | Department of Transport<br>Department of Territories |
| DPI | Department of Primary Industries (Qld) |

| | |
|---|---|
| DRCS | Defence Research Centre Salisbury |
| DSS | Decision Support System |
| DSTO | Defence Science and Technology Organisation |
| DTDB | Digital Topographic Database |
| DTM | Digital Terrain Model |
| DXF | Drafting Exchange Format (Autocad) |
| ECDIS | Electronic Chart Display and Information System |
| EDE | Engineering Development Establishment |
| EEZ | Exclusive Economic Zone |
| EIGHT | Eighth-degree grid cell database |
| ELECT | Federal electorate database |
| ERS-1 | European Space Agency Resource Satellite 1 |
| ESRI | Environmental Systems Research Institute (USA) |
| ETL | Engineering Topographic Laboratory (USA) |
| FD SVY | Field Survey |
| FFO | Furnace Fuel Oil |
| FIG | Fédération Internationale de Géometres |
| FIS | Facility Information System |
| FMS | Facility Management System |
| FNQEB | Far North Queensland Electricity Board |
| Fortran | Formula translation |
| GAZETTEER | Database of NATMAP 1:250 000 series |
| GBRMPA | Great Barrier Reef Marine Park Authority |
| GDB | Graphics Database Geographic Database |
| GDBMS | Geographic Database Management System |
| GDP | Gross Domestic Product |
| GDTA | Groupement pour le Développement de la Télédétection Aérospatiale |

| | |
|---|---|
| GEM | Geographic Expert system |
| GFIS | Geo-Facilities Information System (IBM) |
| GIS | Geographic Information System |
| GISMO | General Integrated Survey Model of the Ocean |
| GMS | Geostationary Meteorological Satellite |
| GPG | Graphics Program Generator (format of GFIS) |
| GRID<br>GRIDLIST | Regional identification software package |
| GRIDO | Grid cell database |
| GRIP | Geographically Referenced Information Processing |
| GRIPS | Grid from Polygon System |
| GTP | Group Title Plan |
| HIS | Hydrographic Information System |
| HQ | Headquarters |
| HUB | SGCC computer information pool system |
| IBM | International Business Machines |
| ICL | International Computers Limited |
| IDC | Interdepartmental Committee |
| IFOV | Instantaneous Field of View |
| IHO | International Hydrographic Organisation |
| IMO | International Maritime Organisation |
| INT | Intelligence |
| IPB | Intelligence Presentation of the Battlefield (ETL graphics) |
| LADS | Laser Airborne Depth Sounder |
| LAIS | Land Administration Information System (NT) |
| LAN | Local Area Network |
| LANDACT | ACT LIS |
| LANDATA | Vic LIS |
| LANDSAT | Earth Land Resources Satellite series (USA) |

| | |
|---|---|
| LANDSEARCH | LIS Directory (Commonwealth) |
| LATIS | Land Tenure Information System |
| LFC | Large Format Camera |
| LGA | Local Government Area |
| LICRS | Land Information Cross Reference System |
| LIDS | Logistic Infrastructure Data System<br>Logistic Infrastructure Directory Study |
| LIM | Land Information Management |
| LIMS | LIM System |
| LIS | Land Information System |
| LISC | Land Information Steering Committee |
| LISSC | LIS Support Centre (WA) |
| LISST | LIS Support Team (NT) |
| LOTS | Land Ownership and Tenure System (SA LIS) |
| LUPLAN | Land Use Planning software package |
| MAPNET | NT LIS |
| MAPPER | Tasmanian LIS database |
| MAPROJ | Mapping software package |
| MAPVIEW | Access station for MAPNET |
| MAS | Map Accuracy Standard |
| MATAS | Major Army Training Area Study |
| MCM | Mine Countermeasure |
| MD | Military District |
| MGI | Military Geographic Information |
| MGIS | MGI System |
| MHE | Mechanical Handling Equipment |
| Minitab | Statistical software package |
| MRD | Main Roads Department (Qld) |
| MSC | Mareeba Shire Council |
| MSS | Multispectral Scanner |

| | |
|---|---|
| NASA | National Aeronautics and Space Administration (USA) |
| NATMAP | Division of National Mapping |
| NATO | North Atlantic Treaty Organisation |
| NATPK | Database of conservation reserves |
| NCDC | National Capital Development Commission |
| NDO | Natural Disasters Organisation |
| NIMBUS | Atmospheric observation satellite series |
| NOAA | National Oceanic and Atmospheric Administration (USA) |
| NPWS | National Parks and Wildlife Service |
| NSW | New South Wales |
| NT | Northern Territory |
| NTP/PATN | Numerical Taxonomy Package |
| PC | Printed Circuit Personal Computer |
| Pixel | Picture element |
| PMR | Perth Metropolitan Region |
| POL | Petrol, Oil and Lubricants |
| Polyvrt | Computer mapping package |
| PREPLAN | GIS software package |
| psi | Pounds per square inch |
| QEC | Qld Electricity Commission |
| Qld | Queensland |
| Q-NET | Qld satellite communications system |
| QNPWS | Qld NPWS |
| QWRC | Qld Water Resources Commission |
| RAAF | Royal Australian Air Force |
| RAE | Royal Australian Engineers |
| RAMS | Topographic data software package (Geovision) |
| RAN | Royal Australian Navy |

| | |
|---|---|
| RA Svy | Royal Australian Survey Corps |
| RBV | Return Beam Vidicon (satellite camera) |
| REGION | Regional identification software package |
| REGIS | Regional GIS (Qld) |
| ROM | Read-Only Memory |
| SA | South Australia |
| SAR | Synthetic Aperture Radar |
| SCDB | Spatial Cadastral Database |
| SDB | Subdivision Database |
| SEASAT | Early oceanography satellite (USA 1978) |
| SES | State Emergency Service |
| SGCC | State Government Computer Centre (Qld) |
| SIR | Shuttle Imaging Radar<br>Synthetic-aperture Imaging Radar |
| SIS | Spatial Information System |
| SLAR | Side-Looking Airborne Radar |
| SLIC | State Land Information Council (NSW) |
| SLISE | Selected Land Information Extraction program |
| SO1 | Staff Officer Grade 1 |
| SPOT | Satellite Probatoire de l'Observation de la Terre (France) |
| SQN | Squadron |
| SSNP | Sun-Synchronous Near-Polar |
| SWIM | Shallow Water Imagery Mapping |
| TACTERM | Computerised terrain-matching navigation system |
| TCIRS | Texture/Cone Index Rating/Season |
| TEWT | Tactical Exercise Without Troops |
| TIMSS | Thermal Infra-red MSS |
| TM | Thematic Mapper |
| UK | United Kingdom |
| UNIGKS | Graphics software package |

| | |
|---|---|
| UNIRAS-GEOPAK | Graphics software package |
| UNISURV | Research Report series (University of New South Wales School of Surveying) |
| URISA | Urban and Regional Information Systems Association (USA) |
| URPIS | Urban and Regional Planning Information Systems |
| USA | United States of America |
| Valtax | Valuation and Taxation |
| VAX | Virtual Address Extension; computer company |
| VDU | Visual Display Unit |
| VG | Valuer General |
| Vic | Victoria |
| WA | Western Australia |
| WALIS | WA LIS |
| WASLUC | WA State Land Use Coding |
| 4WD | Four-Wheel Drive |
| WORM | Write Once, Read Many |
| XCTR | Cross-Country Trafficability Rating |

# CONTRIBUTORS

**Dr Ross Babbage** is Deputy Head of the Strategic and Defence Studies Centre at the Australian National University, Canberra. Dr Babbage commenced his tertiary education in the later 1960s, studying for his bachelor's and master's degrees in economics at the University of Sydney. In 1975 he joined the Australian Department of Defence in Canberra and worked in what is now the Strategic and International Policy Division and then the Joint Intelligence Organisation. In the mid-1970s, Dr Babbage researched his Ph.D. thesis in the Department of International Relations at the Australian National University. An edited version of his thesis was subsequently published under the title *Rethinking Australia's Defence* (University of Queensland Press, St Lucia, Queensland, 1980). In 1978, Dr Babbage returned to the Australian Public Service, working in the Office of National Assessments and then in a series of positions in the Department of Defence. In his most recent departmental appointments he led the ANZUS and United Nations Branch and then the Force Development Branch. Dr Babbage took up his present position in February 1986. He is engaged in two major research projects. The first concerns the problems of planning for the defence of Australia. The second is an investigation of the security planning of the major powers in the north-west Pacific.

**Professor Desmond Ball** is Head of the Strategic and Defence Studies Centre at the Australian National University, Canberra. He has previously been a Lecturer in International Relations and Military Politics in the Department of Government at the University of Sydney, a Research Fellow in the Center for International Affairs at Harvard University, and a Research Associate at the International Institute for Strategic Studies in London. He is the author of more than 120 academic monographs and articles on nuclear strategy, nuclear weapons, national security decision-making, and Australia's defence policy. His major books include *Politics and Force Levels: The Strategic Missile Program of the Kennedy Administration* (University of California Press, Berkeley, 1980), *A Suitable Piece of Real Estate: American Installations in Australia* (Hale & Iremonger, Sydney, 1980), *A Base for Debate: The US Satellite Station at Nurrungar* (Allen & Unwin, Sydney, London and Boston, 1987) and *Pine Gap: Australia and the US Geostationary Signals Intelligence Satellite Program* (Allen & Unwin, Sydney, 1988). He is the co-author of *The Ties That Bind: Intelligence Cooperation Between the UKUSA Countries* (Allen & Unwin, Sydney, London and Boston, 1985); co-author of *Defend the North: The Case for the Alice Springs-Darwin Railway* (Allen & Unwin, Sydney 1985); co-author of *Crisis Stability and Nuclear War* (American Academy of Arts and Sciences, and Cornell University Peace Studies Program, Ithaca, New York, 1987); editor of *The ANZAC Connection* (Allen & Unwin, Sydney, 1985);

editor of *Strategy & Defence: Australian Essays* (Allen & Unwin, Sydney, 1982); editor of *The Future of Tactical Air Power in the Defence of Australia* (Australian National University, Canberra, 1976); co-editor of *Problems of Mobilisation in the Defence of Australia* (Phoenix Defence Publications, Canberra, 1980); co-editor of *Strategic Nuclear Targeting* (Cornell University Press, Ithaca, New York, 1986); co-editor of *A Vulnerable Country? Civil Resources in the Defence of Australia* (Australian National University Press, Canberra, 1986); co-editor of *The Future of Arms Control* (Australian National University Press, Canberra, 1986); and co-editor of *Civil Defence and Australia's Security in the Nuclear Age* (Strategic and Defence Studies Centre, Australian National University, Canberra, and Allen & Unwin, Sydney, 1983).

**The Honourable Kim C. Beazley, MP**, was sworn in as Minister of State for Defence on 13 December 1984. He has served in Parliament since 1980, when he won the Perth metropolitan seat of Swan in a general election. In the first Hawke Labor Government he was Minister for Aviation and Minister Assisting the Minister for Defence. Mr Beazley also served as Special Minister of State from 14 July 1983 until 20 January 1984. He holds Master's degrees from the universities of Western Australia and Oxford, where he studied as a Rhodes Scholar from 1973 until 1976. Mr Beazley's Oxford thesis dealt with the strategic significance of the Indian Ocean region. He later co-authored the book, *Politics of Intrusion: The Super Powers and the Indian Ocean* (Alternative Publishing Cooperative, Sydney, 1979). During his first term in Parliament, from 1980 to 1983, Mr Beazley took part in a number of debates on aviation, defence and foreign policy matters. He was secretary of Caucus Foreign Affairs and Defence Committee and a member of the Joint Parliamentary Committee on Foreign Affairs and Defence. Mr Beazley was born in Perth on 14 December 1948 and was the youngest member of the Ministry at the time of his appointment. He is also the youngest Defence Minister and the sixth West Australian to serve in the position.

**Mr John Blackburn** is a Senior Surveyor in the Information Management Unit of the Surveying and Land Information Group, Department of Administrative Services. He was previously the Assistant Director of the Commonwealth Land Information Support Group, where he was responsible for the development of the Commonwealth's land-related information directory, LANDSEARCH. In 1987 he was the project manager for a Regional Geographic Information System (GIS) covering the Jervis Bay region of NSW and developed jointly with other government, academic and private organisations. He was also a member of a Working Group planning the implementation of an Integrated Land Information System (LIS) for the ACT. He has published several papers on LIS/GIS development in Australia, including two with Professor Ian Williamson. His previous work experience includes systems design and surveying in private industry. He has graduate qualifications in surveying from the Western Australia Institute of Technology (now Curtin University), and has post-graduate study in business administration in progress at the Canberra College of Advanced Education.

**Mr Kenneth G. Burrows** is Deputy Director of the Royal Australian Navy Hydrographic Office, responsible for Cartography, Distribution and Information Resources. He has also been responsible for the concept and development of the Hydrographic Information System through the adaption of computer systems technology to meet the information management and technological requirements of Geographic Information Systems. He is the Australian member on various international committees, under the auspices of the International Hydrographic Organisation, including committees on the Electronic Chart, Digital Information Exchange Standards and the subcommittee on data qualification standards to support future user applications of GIS.

**Dr Doug Cocks** Ph.D. (Calif.) M.Agr.Sc. (Melb.), is a Senior Principal Research Scientist and Leader, Decision Support Systems Program in the CSIRO Division of Wildlife and Ecology. Prior to joining CSIRO in 1968 he taught regional and production economics at the universities of Cambridge and California. His current areas of professional interest include environmental planning, land use policy and the application of geographic information systems to the allocation and management of natural resources.

**Dr Richard Davis** is a Principal Research Scientist with the Division of Water Resources, CSIRO. He is leader of the Division's Knowledge System Group. His broad interests lie in developing improved methods for planning and managing natural resource use; in recent years he has concentrated on developing management advice programs based on artificial intelligence techniques. These programs have now been applied to problems of wildfire management, pest control, shrub regrowth and soil loss. His recent publications include chapters in P.W. Newton and M.A.P. Taylor (eds), *Microcomputers for Local Government Planning and Management* (Hargreen Publishing Company, Melbourne, 1986) and C. Cocklin, B. Smit and T. Johnston (eds), *Demands on Rural Land: Planning for Resource Use* (Westview Press, Boulder, Colorado and London, 1987), and papers in the *Journal of Environmental Management, Environment and Planning* and the *International Journal of Ecological Modelling*. He is on the editoral board of the journal *AI Applications in Natural Resource Management*.

**Colonel A.W. Laing** is Director of Survey (Army) and Head of the Royal Australian Survey Corps. He is a graduate of the Royal Military College, Duntroon and the Royal Melbourne Institute of Technology (Associate Diploma in Land Surveying) and has attended the Royal Engineer Long Geodesy course at Oxford University and a Joint Services Staff College course. Colonel Laing's survey and military management experience includes postings to Vietnam, Papua New Guinea and Indonesia as well as to the School of Military Survey, Army Headquarters and the Defence Science and Technology Organisation. In Indonesia he worked on the first Australian Army projects in which satellite receivers were used to establish mapping control. Colonel Laing has held his present appointment since 1983.

**Dr Peter Laut** is a Senior Principal Research Scientist with the CSIRO Division of Water Resources. Dr Laut was appointed to the Geography Department, Australian National University in 1965, moved to the University of Manitoba in 1969 and returned to Australia to the CSIRO Division of Land Research in 1973. He has led numerous projects involving land inventory and land capability since then. From 1980 much of his work has been in the north of Australia, first evaluating the degree of difficulty for livestock mustering as part of the bovine tuberculosis eradication campaign, and later assessing land resources for military purposes. His current research is in catchment management. Since joining the CSIRO his major publications have been: co-author, *Australian Biophysical Regions*, Urban Paper (Department of Urban and Regional Development, Canberra, 1975); co-author, *Environments of South Australia*, Report in 7 vols (CSIRO Division of Land Use Resources, Melbourne, 1977); co-author, *Provisional Environmental Regions of Australia*, 2 vols, (CSIRO, Melbourne, 1980); co-author, 'Hydrologic Classification of Sub-basins in the Macleay Valley, N.S.W.', *Transactions*, Australian Institute of Engineers, Vol. 26, 1984; and co-author, *Landscape Data for Cattle Disease Eradication in Northern Australia*, Technical Paper No. 47 (CSIRO Division of Water and Land Resources, Melbourne, 1985).

**Professor Ken Lyons** graduated from the Royal Military College, Duntroon, in 1962 and served as a Lieutenant and Captain in the Royal Australian Survey Corps, Australian Regular Army, until December 1969. During that time he was awarded a Bachelor of Surveying degree with Honours and a Master of Surveying Science degree from the University of New South Wales. He had extensive field experience in Field Survey Units, serving in New South Wales and Western Australia, and commanded the Survey Unit of the Task Force in South Vietnam. From 1972 to 1979 he served as Captain and Major in the Army Reserve. He has held appointments as Lecturer and Senior Lecturer in the Department of Surveying at the Western Australia Institute of Technology (now Curtin University) and obtained his Ph.D. at Murdoch University. He was head of the Department of Surveying and Land Studies, Papua New Guinea University of Technology, and is currently Professor of Surveying and Land Information at the Department of Geographical Sciences, University of Queensland. He is also a Director of the Queensland Centre for Surveying and Mapping Studies and the Australian Key Centre in Land Information Studies. His interests in Land and Geographic Information Systems include military applications, remote sensing, and terrain evaluation and shallow water mapping using remote sensing techniques.

**Captain Owen Moss** graduated from the Officer Cadet School, Portsea, into the Royal Australian Survey Corps in 1977. He subsequently studied at the University of New South Wales and completed a Bachelor of Surveying degree in

1981. From 1982 to 1983 he was posted as a Troop Officer managing photogrammetric and catographic production and several mapping control operations in the Northern Territory and Western Australia. In 1984 he served as a Personnel Staff Officer to a Military District Headquarters and in 1986 he was posted to the University of Queensland to study for a Master of Mapping and Surveying Science degree, which he completed in 1987. His primary fields of study have been Remote Sensing and Geographic Information System applications for military use.

**Mr Paul Perrett** is a Registered Surveyor with a wide range of experience in the public, private and academic sectors of the surveying and mapping industry. He obtained a Bachelor of Applied Science (Surveying) degree from the Queensland Institute of Technology in 1980 and is currently undertaking the Master of Mapping and Surveying degree at the University of Queensland, researching various aspects of Geographic Information Systems. He is employed by the Queensland Government's Department of Mapping and Surveying in their GIS/LIS Applications Sub-program and is involved in activities of the Australian Key Centre in Land Information Studies.

**Mr Michael Phillips** is the Director of the Commonwealth Land Information Support Group (CLISG), established in 1984 to carry out an interdepartmental initiative aimed at increasing coordination and cooperation in the collection, storage, use and dissemination of Commonwealth land-related data. Mr Phillips has an honours degree in Surveying from Melbourne University, professional registration as a surveyor and a post-graduate diploma in computing from the Canberra College of Advanced Education. His working experience (public and private sector) has included work on the technical side of surveying and computing systems and administrative and policy positions. Recently he has concentrated on policy and applications in land information management. He is Secretary to the Australian Land Information Council, the Commonwealth's representative on the Council's technical subcommittee and a Federal Councillor to the Australian Urban and Regional Information Systems Association (AURISA).

**Major Dennis Puniard** is a graduate of the Officer Cadet School, Portsea, and the Royal Military College of Science, Shrivenham, UK. He is a Royal Australian Survey Corps officer whose areas of special interest have included the provision of geographically based information to the Australian Defence Force and the use of remote sensing to that end. His military postings have included Officer Commanding Print Troop, Army Survey Regiment; Operations Officer 8 Field Survey Squadron, Papua New Guinea; Adjutant and 2IC Air Survey Squadron, Army Survey Regiment; Senior Instructor, School of Military Survey; Officer Commanding 1 Division, Topographic Survey Troop; Officer Commanding 1 Field Survey Squadron; Staff Officer to the Scientific Advisor Army and Officer Commanding Technical Services Army Survey Regiment. He holds a Bachelor of Applied Science (Surveying) degree from the Royal

Melbourne Institute of Technology (RMIT), a Diploma of Cartography (RMIT) and a Master of Surveying and Mapping Science degree from the University of Queensland, and has previously published in the areas of surveying and cartography. His present posting is a Staff Officer at the Headquarters Australian Defence Force, Canberra, with specific responsibilities for environmental intelligence.

**Mr Paul Walker**, M.A. (Canterbury), is a Senior Research Scientist in the CSIRO Division of Wildlife and Ecology, Canberra. Prior to joining CSIRO in 1975, he worked as a transport research officer in New Zealand. He has been an adviser to a number of state and federal government departments on geographic data processing and has lectured at Geography departments in both Australian and New Zealand universities. His areas of professional interest include the design and construction of geographic information systems and their use for large-area land and resource evaluation.

# FOREWORD

The Government's Defence policy and program is comprehensively covered in the Policy Information Paper, *The Defence of Australia*, which I tabled in Parliament on 19 March 1987.

At the core of that policy is the concept of defence self-reliance and a strategy of defence in depth. Defence self-reliance in Australia's strategic and unique geographic circumstances is achievable. Self-reliance as a goal is based on a realistic assessment of our strengths, as well as on a rigorous appraisal of our weaknesses. It draws on the skilful harnessing of Australia's national resources in the defence of Australia and its interests.

The remoteness and harsh environment of the most likely areas of entry to Australia would pose considerable difficulties for a would-be enemy as indeed it would for the development and operations of our own forces. To ensure that the balance is tilted in our favour we need to know, understand and make use of our environment and our infrastructure.

The knowledge and judicious exploitation of resources, both natural and man-made, will play a vital role in any contingency.

While it is true that the importance of geographic information has long been recognised, little has been done in Australia to develop a comprehensive geographic information system. Quite simply, until now, Australia's defence policies have not accorded priority to geographic information on Australia. The Policy Information Paper on defence clearly corrects that deficiency.

The question now is how are we to establish and maintain a system which will meet the comprehensive needs of defence planners. Much of the information is already there. It has been compiled by various governmental and private bodies concerned with, for example, land use and resource applications. What is required is good management to exploit this information and to fill any gaps in the particular requirements of defence.

Recent developments in technologies and systems relevant to geographic information systems show promise. Advances in data collection and storage technologies as well as transmission and display systems point the way to defence planners having access to accurate and detailed geographic information in the near future and at relatively low cost.

A comprehensive geographic information system is vital to the development of a national defence capability and consequently this book is a welcome contribution to this area of Australia's defence effort. I hope it will provide stimulus for further research and discussion.

Kim C. Beazley
November 1987

# PREFACE

In 1985–86, the Strategic and Defence Studies Centre decided to intitiate a project on Geographic Information Systems (GIS) and the defence of Australia. The project was designed to identify and assess the potential contribution which GIS could make to defence planning and operations, and to bring the subject to broader public attention. We were persuaded that, notwithstanding some important limitations that also required explication, the promise of GIS was compelling. We had been interested for more than a decade in the ability of modern electro-optical sensor systems to provide in digital form imagery of extraordinary resolution. In the mid-1980s, during the course of a major study of infrastructure information and terrain intelligence in the Northern Territory and Kimberley region, we became aware of the progress that had been made in the establishment of cadastral and other land-related information systems in Australia. In October 1985, we were apprised of the work and holdings of the Land Information Systems (LIS) Branch of the Northern Territory Department of Lands — for which we are grateful to Mr John Pinney, Deputy Secretary of the Northern Territory Department of Lands and Mr Vic Stephens, Head of the LIS Branch of that Department.

It seemed to us, however, that there was a general lack of appreciation of the relevance and potential of GIS within the Defence community, and in early 1986 we decided to organise a workshop on the subject.

The Working Group established to prepare the workshop program consisted of Professor Ken Lyons, Head of the Queensland Centre for Surveying and Mapping Studies at the University of Queensland, and Colonel Alex Laing, the Director of Survey (Army), Royal Australian Survey Corps, in addition to Dr Ross Babbage and myself. We are very grateful to Professor Lyons and Colonel Laing for their assistance. Colonel Laing's participation in the working group and subsequent workshop was formally endorsed by Lieutenant General Peter Gration, then the Chief of the General Staff, and we wish to thank General Gration for this support.

We also wish to thank Mr John Sleep, Commonwealth Surveyor-General, Mr Wal Lamond, Deputy Surveyor-General, and Mr Michael Phillips, Director of the Commonwealth Land Information Support Group, who introduced us to the work of the Australian Survey Office (ASO) with respect to Land Information Systems (LIS) and the efforts of the ASO to coordinate LIS activities throughout the Commonwealth and state/territory governments; and to Lieutenant Colonel John Winzar, Directorate of Survey (Army), who briefed us in May 1987 on the development of terrain analysis within the Australian Army.

The workshop was held at the Australian National University on 20–21 August 1987. Its agenda was to discuss the current state of the art and the potential of GIS in Australia; the requirements of the Department of Defence and the Australian Defence Force (ADF) for GIS; and the ways in which the Department of Defence and the ADF might make efficient and effective use of GIS. The chapters in this volume were originally prepared for the workshop, but in all cases they have been extensively revised for publication.

The workshop involved some 50 experts in various aspects of GIS theory, technique and application. Some particular government departments and agencies represented included the Department of Housing and Construction, the Australian Survey Office, the CSIRO, and various elements of the Defence establishment — including the Defence Science and Technology Organisation (DSTO), the Military Geography and Social Research Branch of the Joint Intelligence Organisation (JIO), the Navy's Hydrographic Service, the Directorate of Army Development, the Directorate of Survey (Army), the Directorate of Accommodation and Works (Army), the 1 Division Intelligence Unit, and the Army Survey Regiment. The contributions of these workshop participants are reflected throughout the volume, and we acknowledge a collective thanks to them for this.

Finally, we would like to thank the members of the support staff of the Strategic and Defence Studies Centre who assisted with the organisation of the workshop and the preparation of this volume — Colonel J.O. Langtry, Mr Richard Q. Agnew, Mrs Billie Dalrymple, Mrs Elza Sullivan and, most particularly, Mrs Helen Hookey, who prepared the list of acronyms and abbreviations, the bibliography, and the index.

Desmond Ball

Canberra

December 1987

# CHAPTER ONE

# Introduction

## Desmond Ball

A radical change has taken place in the focus of Australian defence planning since the late-1960s.[1] In contrast to the previous policy of 'forward defence' and dependence upon 'great and powerful friends', a policy of defence self-reliance has now been officially adopted which 'gives priority to the ability to defend ourselves with our own resources'.[2] The environment for future Australian military operations is the Australian continent, Australia's island territories, the 200-mile Exclusive Economic Zone (EEZ), and the air and maritime approaches. Effective and efficient operations in the defence of Australia would be critically dependent upon familiarity with this environment and its physical characteristics.

Given the vast area of Australia, its territories and its maritime approaches, and the necessarily limited capabilities of the Australian Defence Force (ADF), the policy of self-reliance demands extensive utilisation of all national assets — including the civil infrastructure.[3] However, the maintenance of comprehensive directories of civil assets and their capacities, with current information concerning the more remote areas of the country, is a quite daunting task.

Over the same period that this radical transformation has taken place in Australian defence policy and planning, an equally dramatic revolution has occurred in the discipline of geography. Beginning with the development of computer-assisted mapping and map analysis in the mid-1960s, spectacular developments proceeded in remote sensing and automated data collection, data storage and retrieval, data analysis, and techniques for the display of spatial data from the real world for numerous and varied purposes. These developments collectively constitute a Geographic Information System (GIS).[4]

A GIS offers a unique and invaluable solution to the demand for geographical information, both physical and human, generated by the new focus of Australian defence planning. Indeed, it is likely to prove indispensable to effective and efficient planning.

A GIS can be defined as a system which facilitates the storage and intelligent use of geographic data — that is, data about land and water resources and human activities which use these resources. For the purposes of this volume, GIS has been interpreted quite broadly to include: infrastructure information as well as terrain and hydrographic information; digital imagery produced by satellites as well as cadastral information collected by local and state government authorities; and the methodological frameworks and assumptions employed in GIS as well as the applications of the models and techniques.

The essential feature of GIS is the use of sophisticated computer hardware and software to collate, store, manipulate, and process this geographic data. A GIS thus consists of:

**(1)** An extensive database of geographic information involving both positional data about land and/or hydrographic features as well as descriptive/non-locational data about those features; and

**(2)** Suites of programs or applications which enable the data to be input, accessed, manipulated, analysed and reported.

The output may be in textual and/or graphical form (i.e., reports or maps, charts, diagrams, etc.).

The Australian Survey Office (ASO) has described the utility of GIS as follows:

> A GIS can be a powerful tool to assist decision making, such as evaluating funding alternatives. Furthermore, having made a decision to proceed with an activity — a GIS can help in the process of monitoring the effect of that activity on the surrounding environment. Therefore the creation of a geographic database addressing all the various factors involved in a project serves as a basis for initial planning, implementation and finally for long term monitoring....
>
> The new generation of computerised GIS provide efficient data input, database management, analysis and presentation. Maps and graphics can be displayed on screens or plotted on paper, providing immediate visual output of analysis. They are flexible, allowing compilation of a geographic database from data derived from several sources, and providing output to suit a wide range of purposes.[5]

The Strategic and Defence Studies Centre became persuaded of the potential of land-related information systems for Australian defence planning in 1983–85, while engaged in a major study of infrastructure information and terrain intelligence in the Northern Territory and the Kimberley region. This project involved the collection of an enormous amount of information — including information on all bridges and river crossings; water sources; land usage; transportation and communication systems; soils and cross-country trafficability; terrain and vegetation; coastal information (such as tides, sea fauna, landing points); manoeuvre areas; etc. The information came from a wide variety of sources and was provided in a variety of forms including: official government reports and documents; interviews with officials, station lease-holders and other local people; conventional maps and hydrographic charts; photographs; and personal observation and 'ground truthing'. We were eager to find a means of efficiently storing this information, and to compare our collection with those of other instrumentalities in order to check for errors and lacunae. At this point we were apprised of the work and holdings of the Land Information Systems (LIS) Branch of the Northern Territory Department of Lands, and became persuaded that the promise of GIS for Australian defence planning was compelling.

During our subsequent acquaintance with GIS, we have been impressed with several things. First, there are many important ways in which GIS can contribute to defence planning and military operations. There are in fact no other approaches which can provide any similar capabilities with respect to the efficient collection, storage, manipulation and retrieval of geographic data across the whole of north Australia and down to tactical requirements. The specific applications which relate to defence planning and operations are myriad and include the following:

- The provision of comprehensive regional, continental, hydrographic and oceanographic databases to assist decision-making, such as cost-effectiveness evaluations of alternative projects.

- The provision of terrain, infrastructure and environmental information for use in evaluating and selecting sites for new defence training areas, bases and facilities and other defence infrastructure development.

- Assessment of the environmental and socio-economic impact of terrorist attacks on defence installations or of catastrophes such as explosions of ammunition dumps and ignition of fuel depots.

- Informing the development of strategic plans for the defence of Australia, including the location and characteristics of major port and airfield facilities and major terrain features such as escarpments, rivers and vegetation.

- Informing the design or selection of defence equipment (e.g., the use of terrain analysis to determine the design of the Army's replacement for the MII3 light armoured fighting vehicles, as in Project Waler).

- Operational intelligence relating to movement (e.g., information on road surfaces, bridge construction and capacity, and cross-country trafficability); siting of communication, radar and electronic warfare systems; placement of weapons such as artillery, mortars and surface-to-air missiles; and battlefield operations (e.g., information on cover and concealment, fields of fire, and terrain and vegetation features suitable for ambush and envelopment).

- Support for coastal surveillance operations.

- Support for naval operations in Australian waters and possible areas of engagement.

Numerous other applications are identified elsewhere throughout this volume, and it is likely that many more will be identified as GIS models, techniques and capabilities progress.

It would obviously be useful for the Department of Defence and the Australian Defence Force (ADF) to participate directly in the identification, clarification and explication of potential applications.

Secondly, the development of GIS is extremely dynamic. Although the discipline dates back to the mid-1970s, important methodological advances are still occurring at a rapid pace. Moreover, widespread application of GIS principles in relevant government departments and agencies is only now under way. Governmental implementation of GIS will provide additional impetus to its further development.

The rapidity of this development means that the Defence establishment must create some machinery for continuously monitoring it and ensuring that Defence interests are taken into consideration. Already, important software developments have occurred without Defence interest. The ARC/INFO software package, for example, has a specialised format and is difficult to interface with other software packages, including many others useful to Defence.

Third, it is readily apparent that there is too little dialogue and coordination between the numerous government departments, research organisations, computer companies and university centres involved in the development and intensive use of GIS capabilities. There is a need for some national machinery for coordinating or at least monitoring GIS developments throughout Australia — and Defence must of course be included in this.

Fourth, we have been impressed by the fact that although the potential of GIS for defence planning and the conduct of ADF exercises and operations is immense, there is a general lack of appreciation of its relevance and potential within the Defence establishment. There are, of course, exceptions, but these are the specialised support organisations such as the Royal Australian Survey Corps, the Navy's Hydrographic Office, and the Defence Research Centre Salisbury (DRCS) in the Defence Science and Technology Organisation (DSTO). However, if full advantage is to be taken of GIS, then the defence policy and planning areas must also become more cognisant of its relevance.

It is important to be aware of the limitations of GIS. The visual outputs (VDU displays or paper plots) can conceal critical data vagaries and model idiosyncrasies. Data acquired through interface with unfamiliar software packages and inventories can be outdated (and forests since converted to pasture!) or might only apply in certain specific times of the year (such as the monsoon season). It is very rare that all data are collected at the same time for a given project. As P.A. Burrough has noted, 'carefully drawn boundaries and contour lines on maps are elegant misrepresentations of changes that are often gradual, vague, or fuzzy'.[6] Data confidence levels are rarely apparent. In the case of geotechnical data, contractual disputes have become increasingly common with respect to 'latent conditions', that is, data which was unknown at the time information was provided, but which turns out to be critical to the effective use of the information.[7] It would be prudent to assume that issues pertaining to latent conditions will increasingly be encountered with GIS databases.

GIS also has particular limitations in some military environments. The dependence upon keyboards and terminals, displays or print-outs, and digital data links to the data storage and processing centres, poses obvious vulnerability. Conventional maps can be taken anywhere. GIS can never be a substitute for personal reconnaissance of the battlefield or for a good first-hand knowledge of Australia's northern environments.

The purposes of this volume are to discuss, first, the current state of the art and the potential of GIS in Australia; second, the requirements of the Department of Defence and the Australian Defence Force (ADF) for GIS; and, third, the ways in which the Department of Defence and the ADF might make optimum use of GIS.

The current state of GIS developments in Australia is described comprehensively in Chapter 2 by Professor Ken Lyons, Captain Owen Moss and Paul Perrett of the Australian Key Centre in Land Information Studies at the University of Queensland. Chapter 2 describes the basic concepts involved in GIS, the functions and objectives of GIS, and current GIS activities throughout Australia. It notes that although there has been great progress with the development of GIS by state governments and many local government authorities, it remains the case that 'the most necessary and difficult stage', that is, the integration of these various developments into a workable GIS accessible by all relevant users, has 'yet to be achieved in Australia'.

Other contributions to the volume describe the current state of particular GIS developments. Chapter 3, also by Lyons, Moss and Perrett, describes the current state of the art with respect to remote sensing. In Chapter 8, the same team provide a detailed overview of LIS activities in Queensland — where the REGIS program is well developed, but where there has been some resistance to efforts to coordinate the State's activities with those of the other states and the Commonwealth. The Queensland program demonstrates clearly that 'a broad range of land-related data can be successfully integrated' over an enormous geographical area, but also that if the defence applications of GIS are to be realised then 'the early involvement of the Defence Forces in the current developmental activities [of the States] is vital'.

The current state of the art with respect to hydrographic information systems is described by Kenneth Burrows in Chapter 6. This chapter demonstrates that the Navy's Hydrographic Service has a well-established program for the automated acquisition of hydrographic and oceanographic data, which has been complemented by the development and installation of GIS for the manipulation and management of this data. On the other hand, however, much of the information remains in manuscript form; it varies widely in terms of quality, spatial density and date of acquisition (with some survey information dating back to the nineteenth century); and there remains 'no comprehensive or coherent information coverage for most' of the 40 million square kilometres of ocean for which the Service has charting responsibility.

More particular GIS models and their applications include the Australian Resources Information System (ARIS), described in Chapter 7 by Dr Doug Cocks and Paul Walker of the CSIRO Division of Wildlife and Ecology, which is a proven facility already used for policy analyses and decisional support; the Chrysalis project, undertaken by the Australian Survey Office (ASO) and described by Michael Phillips and John Blackburn in Chapter 10, which is a pilot GIS concerning the Jervis Bay region of NSW and which is unique in bringing together interests at all levels of government as well as in the academic and private sectors; and the model of cross-country trafficability in Cape York Peninsula, described by Dr Peter Laut and Dr Richard Davis of the CSIRO Division of Water Resources, which illustrates the current state of applicability of 'expert systems' to GIS.

The requirements of the Australian Defence Force (ADF) for land-related information are described comprehensively by Colonel Alex Laing, the Director of Survey (Army) and Head of the Royal Australian Survey Corps (RASvy), and Major Dennis Puniard (RASvy) in Chapter 4. This chapter describes the responsibilities of each of the individual Services with respect to GIS data collection; the sorts of terrain and other land information, and infrastructure intelligence necessary for defence planning and operations; and the current state of GIS activities within the Department of Defence and the ADF. It demonstrates not only the potential which GIS offers for military planning and operations, but also that liaison between Defence and the various civil authorities concerned with the development of GIS has been poor and that realisation of the full potential of GIS for defence 'is far from reality'.

Chapter 5 by Moss, Lyons and Perrett describes the components of military geographic information (MGI) and the current policies and procedures for MGI collection; it notes that 'the current methods of [MGI] acquisition and presentation are far from ideal', and offers a solution for integrating specialised MGI requirements with relevant civilian GIS databases which would greatly enhance ADF planning and operational effectiveness.

Further exemplification of the utility of GIS for Australian defence planning is contained in Chapters 6, 7, 9 and 10. In Chapter 6, Kenneth Burrows describes how information on sea-floor terrain and the physical properties of particular sea areas can be used to improve sonar capabilities, while information on sea-floor terrain, beach gradients, gravity and magnetic anomalies, and physical oceanography has obvious applications with respect to, for example, anti-submarine warfare and mine countermeasure operations. In Chapter 7, Doug Cocks and Paul Walker describe how ARIS was used to identify alternative areas throughout Australia which were similar to the proposed Army training area near Cobar, NSW, in terms of soils, vegetation, climate and topography.[8] They also describe a range of other potential applications of ARIS, including the design of coastal surveillance strategies, the routing of long-distance cross-country vehicular movements, the preparation of on-line regional defence land information handbooks, and the servicing of civil defence and counter disaster activities. In Chapter 9, Peter Laut and Richard Davis provide a superb case study of the concept and methodology involved in using GIS for the evaluation of landscapes for cross-country trafficability. And in Chapter 10, Michael Phillips and John Blackburn use the Chrysalis project to demonstrate how GIS can be used to support strategic decision-making with respect to the acquisition of land for defence basing and management.

In his Foreword to this volume, the Minister for Defence, Mr Kim Beazley, states that while the importance of geographic information has been recognised within the Defence Department, 'the question now is how are we to establish and maintain a system which will meet the comprehensive needs of defence planners'. Chapter 11, by Dr Ross Babbage, explicitly addresses this question.

Dr Babbage's chapter, which serves as the conclusion to the volume, is designed to summarise the key issues concerning GIS and the defence of Australia and to outline how the Defence Department might best proceed to establish and maintain a GIS activity. It notes that Australian defence planners face a major challenge in preparing an effective defence of Australian territory and the relevant offshore areas, but that 'one very important and potentially decisive advantage that Australia can work to exploit is knowledge and understanding of the local environment'. It reviews the vast range of potential defence applications of GIS, and argues that GIS 'provides the only practical means of exploiting to the full the natural advantage possessed by the Defence Force in preparing to operate on and from Australian territory'.

On the other hand, Dr Babbage also observes that 'the Defence organisation has experienced difficulty in coming to grips with the management of its geographic information requirements during the last 15 years', and that without clearer policy direction and more effective coordination, the Defence GIS activities will be characterised by 'great inefficiency and waste' rather than by the full realisation of the potential of GIS for defence planning and operations. As Dr Babbage concludes,

> The potential [of GIS] for Defence is substantial. The benefits will not, however, flow automatically into the Defence organisation. The corporate development of Defence GIS is deserving of early high-level attention.

# NOTES

1 See Robert O'Neill (ed.), *The Defence of Australia — Fundamental New Aspects* (Australian National University, Canberra, 1977); and Ross Babbage, *Rethinking Australia's Defence* (University of Queensland Press, St Lucia, Queensland, 1980).

2 Department of Defence, *The Defence of Australia 1987*, White Paper presented to Parliament by the Minister for Defence, the Hon. Kim C. Beazley, March 1987 (Australian Government Publishing Service, Canberra, 1987), p. 1.

3 See J.O. Langtry and Desmond Ball (eds), *A Vulnerable Country? Civil Resources in the Defence of Australia* (Australian National University Press, Canberra, 1986).

4 See P.A. Burrough, *Principles of Geographical Information Systems for Land Resources Assessment* (Clarendon Press, Oxford, 1986), pp. 1–12.

5 Australian Survey Office, *A Pilot Geographic Information System (GIS) for Jervis Bay* (Brochure prepared by the Australian Survey Office, Department of Local Government and Administrative Services, Canberra, 1986).

6 P.A. Burrough, *Principles of Geographical Information Systems for Land Resources Assessment*, p. 103.

7 Institution of Engineers, Australia, Construction Industry Committee, Guidelines for the Provision of Geotechnical Information in Construction Contracts, Mimeo, 3 December 1986; and correspondence from M. Cole, Acting Director of Construction and Don de Vries, Regional Engineering Geoscientist, Construction Group, Department of Administrative Services, Canberra, 27 August 1987.

8 See also K.D. Cocks, Representativeness of the Proposed Army Training Area at Cobar. CSIRO Division of Water and Land Resources. Land Use Planning Group Working Document No. 86/3, Canberra, 1986.

# CHAPTER TWO

# Geographic Information Systems

## K.J. Lyons   O.F. Moss
## P. Perrett

The need to collect, store, analyse and output land-related information has existed for many centuries.

Information pertaining to the ownership, use and characteristics of land is today used in a broad range of disciplines (e.g., land administration, engineering, town planning, agricultural science, community service planning, conservation, demography, criminology, traffic planning and the military). These disciplines have many data requirements in common.

Historically, however, different organisations within such disciplines have collected and maintained their own data sets in support of their own functions. This has resulted in much duplicated effort, data redundancy, data inaccuracy, inconsistency and incompatability between similar data sets held by different organisations.

Improved efficiency through the use of information system technology may well lead to high financial rewards. The value of land-related Australian exports in 1985–86 was estimated at over $31 000M out of total exports of over $32 000M.[1] If systems such as Geographic Information Systems (GIS) can increase efficiency by just 0.1 per cent, the 'value added' contribution of GIS would be $31M.

In recent times there has been an increased need for more timely responses to promote effective administration, planning, decision-making and development processes. Coupled with the complexity and volume of today's data requirements traditional paper-based data handling, spatial analysis and display methods have proved inadequate.

The introduction of computer technology has offered a solution to these deficiencies and is now being more widely used. The application of 'database' and 'information system' technology has led to the development of computerised geographic information systems. The concept of a GIS includes the collection, storage, analysis and dissemination of integrated land-related information.

In many cases the development of GIS involved automation of an organisation's existing procedures in response to the growth in the number of routine inquiries being made of these records.

However, automation of individual systems alone does not overcome the serious problems of data duplication, inaccuracy and incompatability which had

8

arisen from the separate agencies having to collect and maintain their own data in support of their given functions. Development of GIS enables the sharing of data between independent and separate computer systems. The advantages of this integrated approach are:

- Eventual elimination of all redundant data through the creation of a readily accessible database.
- Accessibility and availability of data through on-line sharing of the data via remote terminals.
- Consistency and compatibility of data through the use of the same data by all users of that data.
- Reliability and currency of data through less data duplication and through data revision by the 'owner'.

As well, advances in computer graphics hardware and software have meant that the spatial position component of the land-related information can be readily captured and stored in the form of points, lines and polygons.

The linking of attribute textual data files with spatial data files enables a GIS to perform a range of highly specialised inquiries. Examples of possible civilian and military applications are detailed later, together with the concept of GIS database integration.

## BASIC CONCEPTS

The concept of an information system was defined by Martin as:

> . . . a system in which the data stored will be used in spontaneous ways which are not fully predictable in advance for obtaining information.[2]

In a broad sense, it is a means of acquiring, storing, retrieving and analysing data to produce information and later disseminating the information to users.

This modern technology has found great application in dealing with land-related information and has given rise to the concept of geographic information systems. A conceptual scheme is shown at Figure 2.1.

### Data Types and Linkages

The concept of GIS includes land-related data in the form of graphical representation, showing spatial relationships (graphical data), and in the form of attributes of the land itself (attribute data).

#### Attribute Data

Attribute data consists of textual descriptions or properties which may be associated with graphical entities, for example:

- Owner's name, address
- Valuation
- Land-use category
- Electricity voltage
- Vegetation characteristics
- Storage capacity of fuel tanks
- Lifting capacity of dock facilities

Many of the attribute data files can be linked together through the use of a common *identifier* or *key*. A number of these keys might exist, with one usually being designated the primary key. In Queensland, for example, the *lot on plan* number of a land parcel is used as a primary key. Secondary keys may also be used.

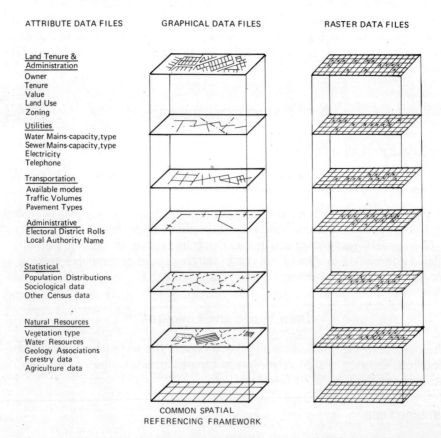

ATTRIBUTE DATA FILES

Land Tenure &
Administration
Owner
Tenure
Value
Land Use
Zoning

Utilities
Water Mains-capacity,type
Sewer Mains-capacity,type
Electricity
Telephone

Transportation
Available modes
Traffic Volumes
Pavement Types

Administrative
Electoral District Rolls
Local Authority Name

Statistical
Population Distributions
Sociological data
Other Census data

Natural Resources
Vegetation type
Water Resources
Geology Associations
Forestry data
Agriculture data

GRAPHICAL DATA FILES

RASTER DATA FILES

COMMON SPATIAL
REFERENCING FRAMEWORK

*Figure 2.1  Concept of a Geographic Information System, based on the Western Australian Concept for a Land Information System.*

## Graphical Data

Graphical data files are digital representations of spatial entities. Traditionally such graphical records were kept in the form of maps. Computer graphics hardware and software have meant that the graphical component of land-related data can be readily captured and stored in graphical data files in the form of:

- *Points* which represent the location of a feature, that is, a bore hole sample, water point, bridge, etc.

- *Lines* which represent linear features, that is, road networks, water pipes, powerlines, etc.

- *Polygons* which represent area features, that is, land parcels, census collector districts, land subject to flooding, etc.

These graphical components are referenced and stored in terms of a spatial referencing network which enables different types of graphical data to be linked together. There are many different types of spatial referencing system (e.g., grid squares, geographical coordinates — latitude and longitude — grid coordinates — x and y or Easting and Northing), which can be used as geographical locatives of graphical entities or points.

The integration of graphical data requires that the various types of spatial references can themselves be integrated. In this manner the graphical data can all be related to a common spatial reference as seen in Figure 2.1. This allows the graphical data files to be overlayed and aligned in the same way as a pack of cards. This further allows any or all desired combinations of the graphical data to be displayed.

## Raster and Vector Data Representation

There are two fundamentally different ways in which graphical data can be represented in the computer. These are raster representation (the explicit means) and vector representation (the implicit means).

Figure 2.2 simplistically illustrates these concepts by showing how a drainage pattern and lake would be portrayed using both forms of graphic representation. Figure 2.2(a) shows the explicit form of representation whereby the drainage is built up from a set of points on a grid or 'raster'. Each grid cell of the array can be referenced by a row and column number and contains a value for the type of attribute being represented. In this case the cells corresponding to the representation of the drainage pattern are labelled 'o'. Alternatively, the values in the cells may be represented by a number or a colour or a grey scale value.

In a raster data structure a point is represented by a single grid cell, a line by a number of neighbouring cells strung out in a given direction, and an area by an agglomeration of neighbouring cells.

In the field of GIS, raster data is commonly obtained from scanning devices.

Some of these devices are used to convert line data from paper-based source maps and plans into raster representations of that linework. The selection of grid size dictates the precision with which the raster image reproduces the original scanned linework. Smaller grids represent more exactly; however, they also increase the data storage requirement. Larger grids generalise original data with a resulting loss of detail and decreased storage requirement.

One of the most common forms of raster data is from remote sensing devices. Many of these sensors use scanning devices to record their images as small grid cell elements, each with an assigned grey scale value. These are described in more detail in Chapter 3.

Figure 2.2(b) shows the implicit form of representation which makes use of a set of lines defined by start and end points, and some form of connectivity. The start and end points of lines define vectors that represent the form of the drainage pattern. Pointers between the lines indicate to the computer how the lines link together to form the chain.

Vectors can represent an object exactly. The coordinate space is assumed to be continuous, not quantised as it is with the raster space. This allows all positions, lengths, and dimensions to be defined precisely.

## Linkage Mechanisms

The concept of a GIS as discussed here is based on storing both graphical and attribute land-related data in a computerised information system. The computer files thus created are linked together relating specific attributes to their graphical representation.

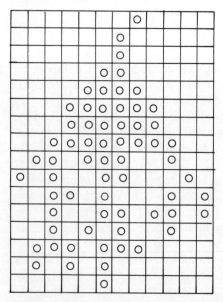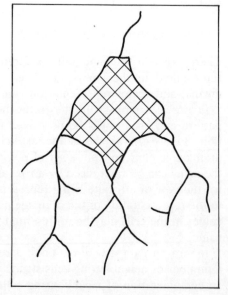

*Figures 2.2a and b   Raster and Vector Representations.*

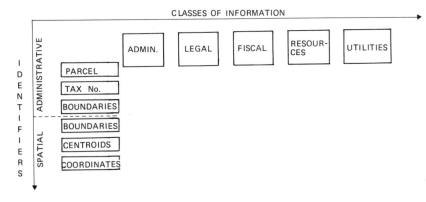

*Figure 2.3   Information Systems for Land.*

Source: R.J. Eden, Modelling for Land Information Systems Development in Australia and particularly Queensland. Draft PhD Thesis, Department of Geographical Sciences. University of Queensland, 1987.

The concept of a GIS as shown in Figure 2.1 illustrates two types of data linking. Horizontal linking is that which takes place between corresponding attributes and graphical data files. Vertical linking is that which links either or both of these two files to the other combinations of graphical and attribute data files.

Without the computerised integration and linking mechanisms between the data types there is no GIS. The original systems of data storage and retrieval do not constitute a true GIS because they can not be integrated to provide information without great effort on the part of the user/inquirer.

## Data and Information

The terms 'data' and 'information' are often (incorrectly) used interchangeably. It is therefore important to distinguish between the two. Data should be considered as independent or isolated facts. Information is the accumulation of data records which are organised to provide knowledge or intelligence. Consequently there is a difference between a 'database' and an 'information system'. The database stores and recalls for later use, whereas an information system transforms data into meaningful information for decision-making processes.

## Special Purpose Sub-Systems

GIS is a technique involving data integration and processing. The operation of a GIS does not usually involve having either all data available at one time or holding data over an extensive area. It includes having access to many classes of data (such as those shown in Figure 2.1) and various types of spatial identifier, some of which are shown in Figure 2.3.

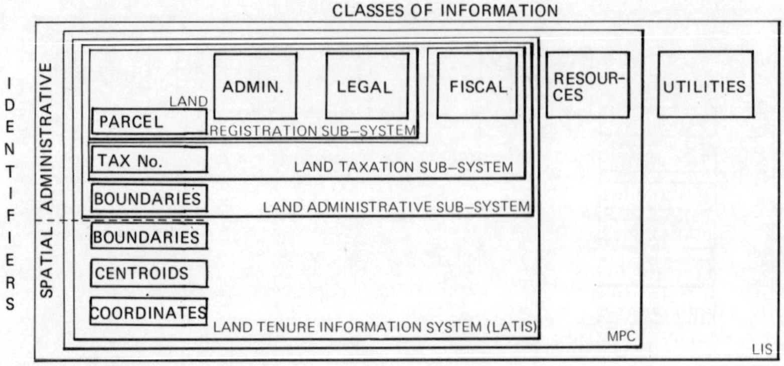

CLASSES OF INFORMATION

Figure 2.4   *Generalised Representations of Sub-systems.*

Source: R.J. Eden, Modelling for Land Information Systems Development in Australia and particularly Queensland.

A number of classes of data can be grouped together to form specific-purpose sub-systems. These sub-systems group data using one or more of the spatial identifiers. One example of the many possible interpretations of sub-system grouping to form user-defined information systems is provided by Eden[3] in Figure 2.4, an extension of Figure 2.3.

It is important at this stage to point out the difference between some of the terms used. The terms Spatial Information System (SIS) is an information system which simply relates all features and attributes of the earth by their location. LIS and GIS should therefore be considered as types of SIS.

LIS is a generic term used frequently to refer loosely to many specific or combination information systems. In this chapter, however, a LIS is used to describe the group of information systems such as land administration and land tenure. They are designed primarily for data collection and inquiry answering concerned with individual land parcels, and thus they tend to be focused on detailed data.

Geographic information systems are not necessarily parcel based and tend to rely more upon coordinate systems as a means of spatial referencing. GIS are more likely to contain a wide variety of polygon data sets over large areas for the purpose of management and planning of that area. Functional components of GIS are similar to those of LIS. There is often less importance attached to high positional accuracy when compared to the land-parcel oriented LIS.

## GIS Sub-Systems

For the purpose of discussion here, a GIS is defined to be the total of the special-purpose sub-systems listed below, as in practice it is likely that data will be available from these sub-systems using geographical spatial identifiers as the linking mechanism. The GIS can therefore be considered as consisting of separate system components such as:

- A land tenure information system
- A facility information system
- A socioeconomic information system
- A natural resources information system.

Specific applications draw their data from any of these sub-systems as required. The classes of data associated with these sub-systems are discussed briefly below.

### Land Tenure Information System (LATIS)

This is the most widely developed GIS sub-system and has two main functions: land registration and land administration. It has developed due to a perceived requirement to make these functions more efficient by the application of computer technology. The type of data compiled is primarily 'parcel based', that is, data concerning individual land parcels, including the legal owner, tenure, fiscal data, land use and zoning.

### Facility Information System

This concerns the location and technical details of water, sewerage, electricity, telephone and gas services. As utilities are responsible for the survey, design, installation and management of these services, they generate and maintain a great deal of information useful for other authorities. Many utilities have already undertaken the introduction of computerised information system technology within their respective organisations. These have been termed Facility Information Systems (FIS) or Facility Management Systems (FMS). They will provide a valuable source for GIS in the future.

### Socio-Economic Information System

This concerns the widely ranging fields of transportation, general administration and statistical census data. The sources of this type of data are also wide ranging, but are generally government departments concerned with specific attributes; for example, the departments of main roads, local government, railways, aviation, and harbours could all contribute transportation data to a GIS. The Australian Bureau of Statistics publishes useful census data on a regular basis in map, tabular and digital format. Census data is also recently available on a Read-Only Memory (ROM) disk.

### Natural Resources Information System

Natural resources are those aspects of the earth's natural and agricultural vegetation, its water and mineral resources. Data of this type is produced by several agencies, including CSIRO, Departments of Primary Industry, Forestry, Environment, Energy, and Water Resources Boards, etc. This data generally covers large areas in accordance with the responsibilities of the listed departments. For this reason it too will become an especially valuable form of data input to planners requiring data at regional, state or national level.

It is envisaged that all of the above data sets will be available in a GIS. Figure 2.1 referred to earlier illustrates the integration of these data sets.

## Uses of GIS

The combination of a diverse range of data sets in the manner described above provides a powerful tool for analysis and output of land-related information for a broad range of applications. As more and more data sets are incorporated in a GIS, the total worth of the integrated data is far greater than that of the individual data sets used in isolation. The linking of the separate data files enables the GIS to perform a number of highly specialised inquiries.

### Civilian uses

There are many applications of GIS for civilian authorities (both government and non-government) concerned with land administration, roads, utilities and resources, etc. Examples of these could include:

● Listing the details of the properties 500 metres either side of a proposed freeway and calculating the value of the land to be resumed for the freeway.

● Giving a list of specific land attributes, such as slope, soil, stock capacity and agricultural potential, preparing a map that has these qualities within certain values, then showing the present use and value of that land with its ownership or lease boundaries.

### Military uses

Information requirements for the military are extensive and are detailed in Chapters 4 and 5. GIS can provide facilities for inquiries and presentation of information to satisfy the following:

● Peace time
— List and depict at a scale of 1:5 000 000, the training areas within Queensland which are subject to restrictions of use, and list these restrictions.
— Given a proposed exercise area list the owners and addresses of properties within the exercise area and depict the property boundaries on a map at a scale of 1:100 000.

● Operational
— Given the site of a possible enemy landing, list and depict at a scale of 1:250 000
1. the three nearest landing zones capable of supporting C130 aircraft;
2. the road network (showing the classification and capacity) into and within the Area of Operations (AO);

3. all townships which have the following facilities: hospital (with a surgical facility), POL storage greater than 100 000 litres, and populations greater than 500 in the AO.

Numerous other applications are discussed in Chapter 5.

Traditional methods of answering such inquiries are cumbersome and time-consuming. The development of a GIS is the most suitable way in which they may be handled efficiently and effectively.

## GIS Functions

A GIS or any of its sub-systems may carry out a number of general functions (i.e., collection, merging, analysis and dissemination). Figure 2.5 illustrates the general layout of GIS components. The total GIS can be considered as three main components namely:

- Input
- Geographic database management
- Output.

Each of these has both hardware and software to carry out its role. The components are described individually below.

### Data Input

All information systems require some form of data gathering. In GIS the sources and formats of the data are quite varied. The formats of data for inclusion into a GIS would include:

- Maps in graphical or digital form.
- Field observations in notebook form.

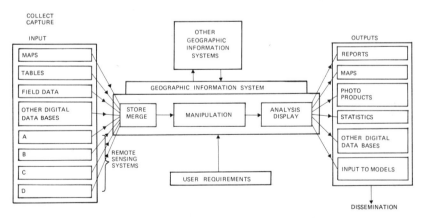

*Figure 2.5   GIS Components.*

- Tabular data in paper or digital form.
- Remote sensor data in digital form. This can be a major source of data and is discussed in Chapter 3.

Some source data requires conversion into a digital format that is compatible to the GIS. This is done by using one of several input system methods. In general this stage requires a computer operation with some degree of manual intervention (interactive procedure). Digitisers and scanners take a graphic image and convert it to a series of coordinate points. Raster scanners capture linework quickly; however the manual process of coding the coordinate feature strings is a time-consuming process. Whilst a great deal of data is held in previously published map form, only some of these are digitally recorded. This leaves a large task ahead of GIS input systems to incorporate this important data source.

## Geographic Database Management System (GDBMS)

Whilst this system functions in a similar manner to normal database management systems, the single most distinguishing feature is that the data to be managed in a GIS is spatially referenced data. GDBMS is responsible for a number of functions within the GIS. It could well be considered the heart of the GIS, as it carries out functions such as:

- Pre-storage Data Manipulations. The type of functions carried out here include:
  — error detection within input data;
  — merging and transformation of the data to the common spatial referencing systems used by the GIS;
  — building the topological (spatial) relationships for the data.
- Data Storage. Data is stored on magnetic media such as disks or tapes. These constitute the geographic database files. The data is stored in a form that later allows very rapid access.
- Query or Requirement Interpretation, Analysis and Formatting. Where a user has a query or requirement for the GIS, it must be interpreted into a form which can be analysed by the system before an output format can be produced.
- Output Presentation. The data which is produced as a result of a request must be formatted for the particular output device according to user requirements, prior to the data being dispatched.

## Output System

The output system is particularly important as it is here that the results of the previous systems can be assessed. It is only at the output stage that it can be determined if any further input of data or manipulation is required to obtain information useful for decision-making.

The output system can be considered as both the output device and the product it creates. The type of output devices which a user may choose include the following:

- Visual Display Unit (VDU). These can be used for both line drawings and characters, and have the additional advantage that the scale and display can be changed rapidly. These are most commonly used by interactive GIS. These terminals can be subdivided into the two functional components, namely high-resolution graphic terminals and text screens. In general, the higher the price, the better the ability of the terminal to provide the detailed graphics required of a GIS.
- Line Printer. These produce alphabet characters only and are therefore used for text reports.
- Plotter. These can produce line drawings and some lettering in limited colours. These instruments are the same as those used for computer cartography. The emphasis in GIS tends towards speed of plotting as opposed to extremely high precision.
- Magnetic Media. Digital recorders such as disk and tape are integral components of GIS, but can be used as output devices to allow data transfer to other computers or systems. This allows organisations using GIS to decentralise using this data transportability feature. Thus any element of an organisation can be supplied with data computed at a central location.

The range of products available from a GIS includes:

- Maps
- Overlays
- Tabular data
- Reports
- Disks and tapes
- Any combination of the above.

This function demonstrates that GIS is far superior to normal methods of gathered data output, especially where complex data sets are concerned. The important advantage is that the attribute and graphical data compiled into any user combination, as earlier discussed, can be delivered in any or all of the forms listed above. This removes the requirement of users to combine, mentally or physically, the attributes into a form that can be interpreted. The result is that users gain a greater amount of useful and relevant information in a far reduced time frame.

## GIS OBJECTIVES

GIS are oriented towards multiple participants who each have specific objectives. These aims will influence the direction of the system as a whole. The objective of the overall GIS will nevertheless normally be set as a broad statement of the total participant aims. In addition to these two levels there may be other aims, such as the testing of technical components of the system.

Because of the multi-user nature of GIS, system objectives may be defined at a series of levels. At the broader level, for example, the general objectives for the overall GIS may be:

- Maximise the efficiency of planning and decision making to optimise land use.
- Cut government costs.
- Provide an efficient means of data distribution.
- Meet the objectives of users.

At the next level are examples of objectives for specific users, such as the Australian Defence Force (ADF). These could include:

- Outlining available concealment within an area.
- Showing areas of difficult cross-country movement including obstacles, surface materials, drainage, and surface configuration.
- Providing details of available transportation routes.

## SYSTEM INTEGRATION

Integration of information system data sets from several authorities requires a high degree of cooperation and coordination between the possible users. Among other requirements, it is imperative that data gathered is sufficiently detailed to meet the user expectations. Conversely, redundant data must not be maintained as it will lead to an inefficient and perhaps overloaded system. Solving these types of problems will take time.

The problems of data set integration are reflected in the current emphasis towards development of smaller, and hence simpler, information systems such as LATIS. Various methods already exist for the collection, storage and delivery of limited data sets within individual organisations because the requirements have been well established over many years of operation. The integration of these data sets into GIS will proceed as the future benefits are perceived by individuals or groups.

Characteristically, the number of land attributes or data sets in a LATIS is generally less than that of a GIS, and therefore it could be anticipated that GIS development will, to some extent, follow LATIS. The current trend appears to be that LATIS development will proceed to completion, with GIS being developed to incorporate the LATIS data at a later stage.

A GIS may be viewed as the final step in land data integration. Benefits of a GIS are not always so readily apparent, as they concern larger areas and longer term planning, and hence are more complex. As Martin stated, realisation of the comprehensive benefits of GIS will therefore only be made upon completion of the integration process.[4]

Some integration of land data has already occurred at various levels of sophistication. The actual achievements of various organisations at all levels in Australia, and in general for overseas, are detailed in the following sections.

# THE TECHNOLOGICAL ENVIRONMENT

Computer technology is continuing to advance at a rapid pace. The development of GIS is a highly dynamic and constantly evolving process because of the availability of new hardware, software and modelling techniques.

## Data Quality

An aspect of GIS technology commonly overlooked is data quality. Data quality can be assessed in terms of the following important factors:

- Accuracy. This is a measure of the absolute (i.e., closeness to 'correct') position and classificaton.
- Precision. This refers to the degree of exactness or similarity of the measurements.
- Resolution. This is the minimum detectable spatial separation.
- Currency. How up-to-date the data is (i.e., collection date).
- Completeness. The availability of consistent data over the whole area.

In many GIS developments these factors are not conveyed to the system users. This can lead to data utilisation for questionable or unsuitable purposes. To overcome such problems it is essential to attach statements pertaining to each of the factors described above with all data in a GIS.

## Data Analysis and Modelling

For a computerised system to successfully input, store, analyse, manipulate and output land-related data, it is necessary to fully understand the relationship of the data to the real world. To do this, data intricacies and perceptions must be analysed in terms of nature, content and applications. This is part of the extensive and very necessary process commonly called data analysis.

From data analysis a data model can be developed. Data models are powerful conceptual tools allowing the representation and organisation of information in a manner translatable into data structures. These data structures describe the data in terms of computer concepts and machine representations, and thus allow final incorporation into the computer system.

## Software

The main software requirements for GIS concern aspects of:

- Databases and the tools used to manipulate them;
- Data access and interchange;
- Data capture and maintenance; and
- Specific applications.

Specific software packages should be assessed in terms of their ability to manage the integration of attribute and graphical data.

Commercially available GIS software packages have characteristics which reflect the origin of their design. These origins are primarily:

- Computer Aided Drafting/Design (CAD); and
- Packages developed specifically for GIS.

The CAD-based data systems grew out of automated design for engineers and draftsmen. Their application was later widened to include Computer Assisted Mapping (CAM). CAD/CAM systems brought to mapping the increased ability of rapid data capture, high speed and high quality graphical interaction, and were therefore readily included into the mapping process. In general, however, the volume of data generated by mapping led to some database management problems. An example of this is that database inquiries of CAD/CAM systems are generally performed using pre-defined procedures and menus. Ad hoc inquiries are more difficult to handle without additional programming.

The inclusion of attribute data was considered following the initial development of CAD/CAM systems. This resulted in a limited integration functionality. Specialised GIS applications (such as extensive polygon analysis, natural resource management and socioeconomic studies), are in general not well supported.

Overall, CAD/CAM-based software is not totally suitable as a base for large-scale GIS, as it is difficult to build applications, and does not generally support future trends in hardware.

Recently developed software designed specifically for GIS applications enables a more comprehensive approach to be taken. In some cases the graphic and attribute components are held in the same database, making the integration of these two types of data a simple task. If separate databases are used their structure is designed to facilitate integration. This allows access to attribute data through graphics and, conversely, access to graphic data through attributes.

Specific GIS software is designed to allow the management of large amounts of mapped environmental and natural resource data. Whilst the data capture for both systems is similar, the database management capabilities of specific GIS exceed those of CAD/CAM-based systems as their design is more structured, and therefore more sophisticated in operation. General and specific applications are more easily developed on specialised GIS packages. This type of software is therefore the most suitable for large-scale GIS development.

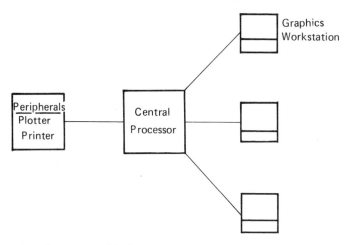

Figure 2.6   The Centralised Model.

## Hardware and Networking

GIS processing models can take one of two forms:

- Centralised model
- Distributed model.

The centralised model is representative of many existing systems whereby all database operations are centrally located and controlled (see Figure 2.6). Hardware utilised by a centralised model includes mainframe or minicomputer graphics terminals and workstations.

The distributed model is shown in Figure 2.7. It consists of a number of network nodes and graphics workstations. This model functions by extracting the required data from the file server for processing locally on a workstation. The database may be distributed over several nodes and workstations.

In such a model the file server may be a microcomputer, minicomputer or mainframe. The workstations can consist of graphics workstations or personal computers.

This model has many advantages over the centralised model. Processing at the workstation reduces the processing load on the file server. As a consequence, lower volume data transmission is required throughout the network. This generally allows a more flexible user/system interface and method of data presentation.

Networking within the distributed model is typically via high speed Local Area Networks (LANs). To facilitate the linking of multiple LANs there is considerable effort being directed towards communication standards.

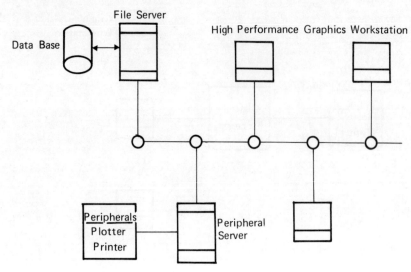

*Figure 2.7   The Distributed Model.*

## Data Storage

Recent developments in computer data storage techniques have meant that a much larger volume of data can now be stored with greater accessibility and less expense. This is increasing data availability options tremendously.

Optical disks offer a cheap form of mass storage, for example CD-ROM (Compact Disk Read Only Memory) and WORM (Write Once, Read Many (times)). Typical storage capacities for these storage media are:

CD-ROM — 4.7 inch with 540 MByte ($540 \times 10^6$)
WORM — 5.5 to 12 inches with up to 2 Gbytes ($2 \times 10^9$)

# CURRENT GIS DEVELOPMENT

To gain an up-to-date appreciation of the development of GIS we now look briefly at the overseas experience, followed by the movement within Australia to develop GIS at various levels of government.

## Overseas Development

Overseas development of geographical data collection has occurred mainly in Western Europe and North America. During the last 20 years, modern automated systems have been developed for organising and planning urban and regional land use. Limited cadastral and large-scale mapping experience led North America towards a more idealistic approach in the development of land data systems.

European development of GIS features strong links to the importance of title registration. In a somewhat similar way, Australian systems of land registration, surveying and mapping developed independently prior to Federation.

## Activity Within Australia

### General

Land administration has traditionally been a state role, and the states have therefore taken the lead in automation and coordination of these activities within their respective boundaries. A great deal of activity is also under way developing information systems at local government and public utility level.

### Commonwealth Government

1983 — Commonwealth Inter-Departmental Steering Committee established to investigate coordination of land-related information within the Commonwealth government.

1984 — National Conference held. National Coordination Committee on Land Information Exchange established, comprising the chairmen of existing Commonwealth, state and territory LIS steering committees to develop national strategy.

1985 — Commonwealth Land Information Support Group was established in the Australian Survey Office. This group was tasked with preparing the LANDSEARCH Directory, the first of which was published in late 1985. A second edition has since been produced.

### State Government

Each state in Australia has established an administrative structure to guide LIS development and strategy. While they have different structures, responsibilities and levels of authority, all have a primary role of coordination and advice.

In each of the states, the major thrust to date has been to establish textual and spatial databases of land parcels. In 1986, Williamson described the situation as follows:

> To some extent the development of the textual data is undertaken separately from the development of the spatial component in the form of a Digital Cadastral Database (DCDB). In general this is the approach taken by South Australia, Queensland, Victoria and Tasmania. Western Australia (and the planned initiatives in New South Wales) are placing more or at least equal emphasis on the spatial component (cadastral survey and mapping). The Northern Territory and Australian Capital Territory are also planning equal emphasis on the textual and spatial side, however, in these cases the basic cadastral mapping is in general complete, the result being that the creation of a DCDB is not as critical.[5]

The Australian Urban and Regional Information Systems Association (AURISA) working group on statewide parcel-based land information systems in Australasia indicated that although many states have developed or are developing LIS, this does not mean that the systems are complete in the sense of a modern cadastre.[6] The development of LIS in South Australia is cited as not yet providing for a spatial component, other than by reference to existing charts or cadastral maps which themselves do not give complete coverage. Nevertheless, a DCDB is being developed.

The provision of a unique identifier for every parcel of land is necessary for a LIS to operate efficiently. In most states this has not yet been achieved. However, in Queensland a 'lot on plan' identifier number will soon be available.

While all states have taken slightly different approaches, there is a trend towards the centralisation of the administration of land-based departments. The states of New South Wales, South Australia, Victoria and Western Australia are examples of this.

In the case of Victoria the Department of Property and Services includes:

- LANDATA (the Victorian LIS Unit)
- Division of Survey and Mapping
- Titles Office
- Valuer-General's Office
- Government Computing Service.

This structure combines all major parcel-based systems within the one government department. To complement this structure the natural resource based systems are all combined into the Department of Conservation, Forests and Lands.

In South Australia, the Department of Lands combines the offices of the Registrar-General, Surveyor-General and Valuer-General. Also included is the Land Operations Division, responsible for all crown land management, and the Land Information Unit, responsible for overseeing all LIS development in the state.

The alternative approach to centralising the administration of land-based departments is to maintain a non-centralised or distributed structure. Such is the case in Queensland where the land-based departments remain as individual entities. An overview of LIS activities in Queensland is given in Chapter 8.

All states in Australia have recognised the need for the integration of resource/environmental/socioeconomic data into a broad GIS, but few major developments have been achieved in this direction. Western Australia and Queensland, however, have undertaken some interesting pilot studies integrating such data using complex polygon processing packages. South Australia, on the other hand, is the only state that has developed a model to incorporate environmental/resource/socioeconomic data. This is all compatible with the South Australian land information system.

## Local Government

Local governments are the originators and users of many forms of data. For this reason they have been involved in the development of information systems for many years. Whilst the state authorities may be made responsible for system coordination through, for example, the maintenance of ownership parcel data, local government may be made responsible for maintaining other important data elements.

In Australia there are over 800 local government organisations, of which 30 are committed to a LIS strategy. In general these organisations manage up to 100 000 parcels with populations of up to 500 000 persons.

The systems vary greatly in sophistication and design. Some have a strong emphasis on land information management, financial management, corporate planning and land administration, while others emphasise graphics and CAD. Some systems are only textual or graphic, while others are a combination.

Wide use is made of commercially available graphic and database management software packages, which are, in many cases, based on microcomputers. The current trend towards the use of microcomputers by local government has developed strongly with the availability of greatly improved graphics. An important trend appears to be the integration of their systems with state-based systems, which provide a wider database.

## Utility Authorities

Facility information systems have developed rapidly in Australia. Williamson cites autonomy and thus more access to funding as the reason.[7] The Sydney Water Board and the Melbourne Metropolitan Board of Works are good examples of extensive FIS using large commercially available information systems.

## Coordination of LIS Activities

Different approaches to administration and information system structure have been adopted by each of the states. However, the development of or negotiations for development of state-coordinated GIS are at an advanced stage in all states. The Commonwealth is expected to continue a background coordinating role.

Summaries of the various individual state-LIS status (as at September 1987) have been obtained from the organisations within each of the states. These are contained in the Annex to this chapter.

# NEW TECHNIQUES AND METHODS

The description of the earth's surface features using current digital formats creates voluminous data files. This is partially due to the complexity of the surface, but could also be considered as due to the means of modelling employed. Burrough believes that future research

> ... should be looking for better ways in which to describe the vagaries of the world, and new methods for dealing with the imprecision of qualitative judgements that

are an integral part of human thought processes. These directions suggest that we should be looking seriously at the new ideas afforded by fractals, fuzzy logic and methods of artificial intelligence, if only to attempt to cope with the technical problems that have arisen as a result of our present conceptual shortcomings.[8]

The arrival of computer technology enabled the development of GIS. Systems have subsequently developed in many local and regional applications. Increased computer storage and data access technology has provided the opportunity for larger area and perhaps nationwide data storage capacity.

The most necessary and most difficult stage in the development of GIS is yet to be reached in Australia. This is the integration of numerous data sets from as many sources into a workable GIS. At present many organisations which have some particular interest in land maintain their own information system. The trend has been towards modernisation or computerisation of their once manual systems. In many cases this has led to specific-purpose information systems developed according to user requirements. The identification of common and specific data types, and their integration into a system accessible by numerous land data users, will see a great advancement towards the achievement of a complete GIS.

# ANNEX

# State LIS Summary*

## AUSTRALIAN CAPITAL TERRITORY

### 1986 Activities

1986 saw considerable progress being made towards a cooperative and coordinated approach to Land Information Management (LIM) in the ACT.

### Integrated Land Information System (LIS) for the ACT

In June 1986, an initiative was made to form a high-level steering committee responsible for establishing an integrated land information system for the ACT. A working group, comprising two senior officers each from the major land agencies — the Australian Survey Office (ASO), the National Capital

*    Acknowledgements: The assistance of the following people was greatly appreciated in preparing the summaries of LIS/GIS activity in the states and territories of Australia: Mr K. Bell (ACT); Mr K. Bullock (NSW); Mr V. Stephens (NT); Mr M. Sedunary (SA); Mr G. Roberts (Tasmania); Mr R. Eddington (Victoria); and Mr I. Hyde (WA).

Development Commission (NCDC) and the Department of Territories (DoT) — was formed. The group undertook a feasibility study into the development of an integrated LIS for the ACT. The first report was submitted to the steering committee. Reorganisation within ACT land agencies has resulted in some delays to further action.

## ACT Digital Cadastral Database

The ACT Digital Cadastral Database (DCDB) is called the Subdivision Database (SDB) and is a responsibility of the Surveying and Land Information Group. Currently, the SDB holds 85 000 land parcels, or 90 per cent of the total ACT parcels. The SDB has primarily been used to provide the cadastral control base for land development.

New SDB services include:

- The production of valuation maps.
- The sale of SDB digital data to private engineering consultants for input to their CAD/CAM systems.
- The provision of SDB as the control base for development of utility infrastructure systems.

## Administration

The Register of Titles has completed a preliminary study for automation of the ACT Land Titles Office. The introduction involves two phases. Phase 1, the Tenure Disposal System, is to be complete by March 1988. Phase 2 is the development of the automated Titles Register Indexing System, to be complete by the end of 1988. The system will allow users full access to all registered material, access to specific current information relating to title and the capacity to issue computerised titles.

## Facilities Information Systems

The ACT Electricity Authority (ACTEA) is to introduce a computer-based, design, drafting, costing, mapping and plant data information system. Tenders closed in September 1987.

A cooperative FIS pilot project between the ACT Water Administration Branch and the Surveying and Land Information Group is being undertaken in the Woden Valley.

## Geographic Information Systems

The Surveying and Land Information Group has developed a GIS over the Jervis Bay region, utilising 'ARC/INFO' software (See Chapter 10). The GIS is a pilot project and has objectives such as the investigation of integration through technology and staff education. The GIS comprises data sets for soils, vegetation, remote sensing imagery, aquatic/marine studies, topography, cadastral boundaries and engineering/utility services.

The ACT Parks and Conservation Service is developing a GIS over the territory, for parks and reserves. This GIS is to be part of a national co-operative effort, instigated by the Australian National Parks and Wildlife Service, to create a national database, using 'PREPLAN' software. The ACT GIS will have an AMG grid-cell control base. Resolutions of between 100 metres to 1000 metres are proposed. The GIS will be operated on IBM compatible microcomputers. It is proposed to utilise both 'PREPLAN' and 'ARC/INFO' for the ACT.

## Future Development

As the Commonwealth Government is pursuing a 'user pays' approach, land administration and management must become more efficient. It is believed that an integrated ACT LIS will assist this. Minimal progress has been achieved following the working group in 1986 due to administrative changes to land management agencies.

# NEW SOUTH WALES

The State Land Information Council (SLIC) is responsible for setting up and managing the State's land information system. State Cabinet has given SLIC the following responsibilities:

(a) To develop and control a New South Wales land information system. This arose from the SLIC decision that a state land information system be established in the form of a linked network of individual systems introduced progressively.

(b) In establishing the SLIC, Cabinet charged the Council with the responsibility for development and control of the land information system, including the setting of principles, standards and priorities.

(c) To facilitate the coordinated development and control responsibility, Cabinet has directed that all proposals to modify an existing land information system, or to develop a new system, be referred to the State Land Information Council.

(d) The Council reports to a subcommittee of Cabinet, comprising the following ministers

- Lands (convenor)
- Housing
- Attorney General
- Planning and Environment
- Small Business and Technology

(e) It has been approved by the Minister for Lands that the part-time Council be involved in issues of policy and broad direction of LIS development, assisted and guided by its permanent full-time staff, which will in future be known as the State Land Information Council Directorate.

(f) The SLIC thus has an ongoing executive role with powers of direction conferred by Cabinet, via a subcommittee. For implementation of these powers SLIC is responsible to the Minister for Lands via the Secretary of the Department of Lands.

The New South Wales system has completed its planning stages, and implementation has begun. The implementation plan has been revised in the light of funding received.

The plan has been designed to ensure that implementation of the LIS HUB is based upon the needs of key applications of the LIS principles of data sharing and single point updating and access. These are Project RAPID, Project NORLIS, the Spatial Reference System, and a Government Property Register. The plan is designed to provide early implementation based upon already computerised non-graphic data.

The State Land Information Council (SLIC) Directorate already has parts of the 1987/88 implementation plan under way:

- A recommendation on hardware and software for the Spatial Reference System is due shortly, in conjunction with the graphic database system for which new tenders were issued in June 1987.

- Project RAPID is now almost at the end of its initial planning and investigation stage (i.e., Phase 1 of Spectrum project management methodology — system definition).

- Project NORLIS has been developing via a joint SLIC/Lands Department/ local councils' working party since April 1987; the project is now in two parts — a prototype system covering Lismore and Byron being developed by a small specialist team, and a full regional LIS being developed as a pilot LIS for which consultants will soon be engaged to conduct the system design phase.

- A market research study recently completed of the community's need for integrated land data and of the potential revenue base for such a service.

- The preparation of specifications for system design studies (Spectrum phase 1) for Project NORLIS, the Spatial Reference System, and the LIS HUB database.

## NORTHERN TERRITORY

Administrative changes created the Department of Lands and Housing, which is now the main agency involved in LIS development. All utility agencies were combined into a single Power and Water Authority.

Due to concern that development of the NT LIS is not being sufficiently coordinated a new management structure relating to all LIS components is being developed for implementation in 1988.

A joint government and private sector Land Information Systems Support Team (LISST) has been created to identify, develop and market new LIS products and to promote the LIS concept.

In response to the need for public access to land and legal information it is likely that the private sector will be invited to express interest in providing a service to distribute government information.

Broad policy on the sale of LIS products is in place and detailed guidelines are being developed.

The complex of integrated parcel-based systems controlling land administration known as 'LIS' has been in operation since 1981 and current activities relate primarily to maintenance, revision of applications, and integration with other applications. In order to avoid confusion with the total NT LIS the acronym LAIS (Land Administration Information System) will be used.

The NT geographic database (MAPNET) is being developed around the IBM product Geo-Facilities Information System (GFIS). Currently the program module GPG is used to capture and maintain a variety of administrative geographical data, including the NT cadastral database.

Cadastral data capture at September 1987 was 97 per cent complete in terms of parcels captured. A complete map of the NT can now be displayed on screen and the user can progressively zoom in to cadastral details at different scales. All cadastral mapping and associated products are now generated via MAPNET and data is maintained on a daily basis. Town plan zoning polygons are also being captured and maintained.

Rural data relating to such items as bores, yards and fences, is to be captured as a separate data layer and will form the basis of a 'rural' database of relevance to defence agencies.

Investigations are continuing into the feasibility of creating a survey information database.

The major limitation of providing remote access to MAPNET data has been overcome with the development of the SLISE (Selected Land Information System Extraction) program. This converts graphic data in GPG format to Autocad DXF format so that it can be used on any microcomputer workstation equipped with Autocad. Attribute data can be down-loaded with the graphics, and workstations using this facility are now in place.

Investigations will begin early in 1988 into the feasibility of providing update facilities to the MAPNET database via Autocad DXF.

## Resources/Environmental Data

All topographic data capture and mapping is based on a system using Geovision's RAMS software. Data can now be transferred into MAPNET via a routine that converts the data to GPG format and generalises features and contours to reduce data storage requirements. Digital topographic data from the Commonwealth agencies is also being transferred into the Geovision system or directly into MAPNET. Both systems are converting to AS2482 1984 prior to the creation of a topographic database within MAPNET.

The NT Conservation Commission currently uses a number of PC-based systems including Micro-Brian and Autocad for GIS applications, including bush fires planning and control, wildlife management, soil conservation and recreation planning. A recently completed information plan envisages the transfer of corporate data relating to environmental management to MAPNET from an in-house GIS.

The Department of Mines and Energy is proposing to pilot a mapping system for 12 months which will include consideration of transferring geological and resources data to MAPNET.

Major achievements during 1987 included:

- Distributed access to MAPNET data via the MAPVIEW workstation.

- Completion of the electronic titles feasibility study.

- Introduction of new systems for crown land/lease management.

- Development of clear policy on distribution of and charging for land information products.

- Virtual completion of cadastral data capture.

- Provision of facilities for recording unidentified land within cadastral management systems.

- Ability to create a topographic database within MAPNET.

## Key Issues and Problem Areas are:

- Direct public access to land information.

- The need for a revised management structure and a long-term management and development plan for the NT LIS.

## Future Developments

The main projects planned for 1988 included:

- Reorganisation of cadastral entities in MAPNET to conform to AS2482 1984.

- Rural data capture and creation of a rural database.

- Continuing capture of plumbing and drainage data.

- Develop the facility for Autocad DXF format to GPG format data transfer.

- Specification and creation of a survey information database.

- Integration of selected LAIS and MAPNET processes.

- Selected development relating to electronic land titles.

- Completion of LAIS revision.

# QUEENSLAND

Separate computer system developments are under way for:

- Titles Office (initially index and unregistered dealings leading to on-line searching).
- Lands Department (initially lease index and location of Crown reserves leading to computerised leasehold register and land rent accounting).
- Valuer-General (well established batch computer system for virtually all land in the State. On-line inquiry 'front-end' being implemented. Valuation and sales information available. Database system being planned).
- Mapping and Surveying (towards a DCEB for Queensland enabling computerised mapping and linkage of LIS components).
- Mines Department (mining tenures database system, with the first phase covering Authorities to Prospect).
- Land Tax (towards on-line access to details of land holdings leading to automatic production of assessment notices).

These separate developments are being coordinated by the LISC through its Departmental Project Leaders Group. The objective is to achieve compatibility of systems and of the data held, particularly of access keys. Data compatibility, even standardisation where appropriate, is being pursued via the compilation and maintenance of a data dictionary. The latter is the concern of the Standards Sub Committee.

The State Government Computer Centre, with the support of the Departmental Project Leaders Group, is working on the development of the HUB, the computer system which will enable access to and linking between the various separate computer systems which will make up the total LIS.

System design and programming are well advanced in many of these areas and partial production status has been achieved or is imminent in many cases. The pattern of development is that parts of the separate component systems are being implemented progressively.

Further LIS activities will be discussed in Chapter 8, which describes activities in Queensland in some detail.

# SOUTH AUSTRALIA

## Land Ownership and Tenure System (LOTS)

South Australia has adopted an incremental approach to the development of its LIS, and LOTS was implemented as the first logical step in that approach.

Whilst parcel ownership was initially the primary basis of the system, the data content of LOTS has since been considerably enlarged. Its general characteristics can now be viewed as being that of a multi-purpose database gathering information from a variety of sources, centralising it in one comprehensive recording system and making it available on-line to numerous inquiry locations.

When examined in detail, the LOTS database can be viewed as an integration of a number of separate component systems, each with characteristics dictated by the type of data stored, their data collection unit, the method and manner of update, and the agency under which and whose administration the system falls.

Primary files on the LOTS database include the title file of the Registrar-General, the valuation file of the Valuer-General, and the land tax file of the Commissioner of State Taxes, in addition to a number of subsidiary files and comprehensive indices. LOTS has been incrementally enhanced to the stage where it is now a major legal/fiscal database responsible for the collection of some $600 million annually of state and local government revenues and for answering some 8000 on-line inquiries per day.

## Land Information System

The successful introduction and operation of LOTS has led the South Australian Government to further pursue the concept of a 'total' LIS. It is characterised by the establishment of major databases as primary nodes within the LIS framework, centralising systems with a strong interrelationship. These primary nodes act as communication hubs to secondary, dependent systems serving relatively individual applications and located on comparatively minor, peripheral databases.

The characteristic of each primary node is that of a 'functional database', centralising systems relating to similar functions and/or with strong interdependencies or affinities. Systems capable of integration, and requiring it for reasons of efficiency, are located on the same functional database.

Primary databases have now been developed in accordance with this concept in the following functional areas:

- *Legal/Fiscal.* LOTS has now been established as the major legal/fiscal database for the State.
- *Geographic.* A Digital Cadastral Database (DCDB), holding the land parcel framework of the State in digital form, has been developed as the essential spatial underlay of the LIS. The DCDB is the first step in the creation of the major geographic database holding all positional data relating to the State's survey and mapping functions.
- *Environment.* The environmental database has been introduced as the primary LIS node responsible for the integration, processing and analysis of the environmental and natural resource data of the State.
- *Socio-Economic.* A feasibility study has recently been completed into the development of a major database to provide a comprehensive source of socioeconomic and demographic information of the State.

Secondary databases are also being developed in a number of functional areas. Perhaps the most significant of these is the Digital Facilities Information System being implemented by the Engineering and Water Supply Department. Portraying extensive details of the water and sewerage networks of the State, it accesses the DCDB for its depiction of the current cadastral framework.

# TASMANIA

## Management

The Land Information Directorate has been in operation for more than a year. The Directorate consists of a single officer responsible to Cabinet through an Inter-departmental Land Information Committee.

In the rapidly developing field of information science, and where there are few precedents to plan strategies, it has become apparent that the functions of the Land Information Directorate cannot be properly carried out by the Director only.

## Achievements for 1986

The Valuation and Taxation (Valtax) System Management Committee was established, with the Director of Land Information as Convenor, to oversee the implementation recommendations from an internal review, and to maintain a management overview of the system.

A survey of the State's agencies for land data sources has been completed. The data is being analysed before entry into a MAPPER database. This task should be completed by the end of February 1987. The data will be structured so that it forms a subset of the data structure being implemented by the Australian Survey Office but will have a separate index file of data items for searching. The categories adopted will agree to the second level with those being used in the Australian Survey Office (ASO).

Due to the multiplicity of indexing systems for parcels and properties it has been decided that a Cross Reference System (LICRS) should be set up for at least eight of the major indexes currently in use. The indexes will include the certificate of title number, deeds registry number, Crown land reference, parcel centroid, survey plan and lot number, unique parcel identifier (map), property identifier (valuation), municipality and original grant number.

In an attempt to provide guiding principles for land information systems within the Tasmanian Public Service the following have been agreed upon:

- Land information is a community resource which should be readily available throughout the State.
- The State land information should be stored in a number of separate but interlinked databases.

- One data source — many users.
- Stored data to conform to agreed standards of quality, integrity, reliability and format.
- There is to be one spatial reference system — AMG66.
- Each data item to have a 'Custodian', which will be the agency best able to provide the item.

## Future Activities

- An industrial land information system is being investigated for long-term industrial planning.
- A possible GIS for the Coal River Catchment area is being investigated.
- A possible GIS for national park management is being studied.
- The needs of local government for digitised map information are being investigated by the University of Tasmania in conjunction with state and local government agencies and private industry.
- The need to place the existing 70000 card index in Titles Office records of completed cadastral surveys by licensed surveyors onto computer format has been investigated.

# VICTORIA

In July 1982, Cabinet approved as a government priority the establishment of a computer-based land information system known as LANDATA. The purpose of LANDATA is to develop a textual and graphical land information system for Victoria which will facilitate ready access to information relating to individual blocks of land and will encompass all government, public and freehold land in the State.

The nucleus of LANDATA is contained in two core components, one in which all land in the State is properly identified and its ownership correctly recorded, and the other in which the property map of the State is held in computer form.

LANDATA together with the Division of Survey and Mapping, the Land Titles Office and the Valuer-General's Office form the Land Information Group of the Department of Property and Services.

In conjunction with other key agencies, including the Land Tax Office and the Melbourne and Metropolitan Board of Works, substantial progress has been made towards the integration of procedures and systems related to land.

Major achievements to date have included:

- Resolution of tenders for computing facilities to run the integrated land information systems. A Unisys A15 computer was installed early in 1987 and is now operating the legal/fiscal components of LANDATA, the Land

Tax Office and the Valuer-General's Office. Intergraph equipment is due for installation in September 1987 to supply the facilities for the digital mapping component of LANDATA.

- The development of a computerised master index for the metropolitan municipalities allows for the efficient interchange of data contained on the property files of the Land Tax Office, Melbourne and Metropolitan Board of Works, and individual councils.

- Significant progress has been made in the capture of volume/folio numbers, proprietorship, and lot/plan details from the registration system at the Land Titles Office. It is anticipated that this exercise will be completed by the end of 1987, and as a consequences of this capture, progress towards the automation of the title register will be possible.

Digital cadastral mapping is now being undertaken jointly by LANDATA and the Division of Survey and Mapping which will result in a continuous digital property map of the State. This map will be used initially by the public utilities for service delivery but in the longer term will provide a continuous spatial reference system for the State's parcel-based information network. In January 1987, the Melbourne and Metropolitan Board of Works, under the authority of the Surveyor-General, began a program of digitising maps in the metropolitan area.

The major thrust of LANDATA is currently towards the restructuring of the conveyancing services and the implementation of an initial inquiry service based on the Land Titles Office and incorporating data from other systems. Remote access will be available to these property records and the service will introduce new economies and simplify many of the procedures relating to the conveyancing process. The system is planned to be implemented by the end of 1987.

# WESTERN AUSTRALIA

## Management and Administration

The Department of Land Administration (DOLA) was formed in 1987 encompassing the 'old' Departments of Land and Surveys and the Office of Titles. The operational components of the Western Australian Land Information System Support Centre (LISSC) have been assimilated into the new Department.

To facilitate, coordinate, and promote the effective development of the WALIS, a WALIS Secretariat has been established. A small group consisting of a WALIS coordinator and three administrative and research support staff, the Secretariat represents a return to the original concept of LISSC, that of a small catalytic body.

The WALIS Council is the focus of representation of the WALIS community. The council conveys the views of users and submits plans on behalf of the WALIS community to the WALIS Executive Policy Committee.

Special interest groups have been replaced with project teams, with specified objectives and a short life span. Current project teams include those working on data exchange and dissemination and the custodianship of selected corporate data items.

A system called the Land Tenure Information — Customer Remote Searching and Customer Accounting System will be operational from October 1987. The system allows clients to perform searching functions from their own offices using computer dial-up facilities.

The Spatial Cadastral Database (SCDB) will replace the existing Graphics Database (GDB) and LIS reporting system. It will provide not only a complete data management system but also on-line textual inquiry and a 'tracking' mechanism for the land development process.

Land valuation has been updated from a batch system to a fully interactive on-line system, linked to the land tax system and to water and local authorities.

## Resource and Environmental Systems

Conservation and Land Management Information System (CALMIS) is a grid based, map storage, and overlay system developed by the Department of Conservation and Land Management. In a later developmental stage the system will utilise data from sectors such as:

- Department of Agriculture — vegetation data, soils, land systems.
- Mining tenement information.
- Remote sensing data.

## Facilities Information Systems

Distributed Facilities Mapping and Information System (DFIS) has been developed by the State Energy Commission to satisfy the need for current map and network information. Using the cadastral base maintained by the Department of Land Administration, the system will record details of electricity and gas distribution networks down to consumer level, providing on-line graphics and inquiry.

The Western Australian Index to Land Information data gazetteer has been compiled of the available land-related data held within government departments in Western Australia. The index is available primarily in microfiche or hard copy, and on-line enquiry has been developed, available via the government shared network.

## Key Issues and Problem Areas

*Custodianship*. To ensure that one organisation is responsible for the capture, maintenance and integrity of each corporate data item within WALIS, even though several organisations may have a proprietary interest. Working groups have been established to rationalise the data items under question and the custodians are being determined. Inherent difficulties remain within the custodians role, in that to service the WALIS community's data requirements the organisation may have to capture and maintain data beyond its own requirements.

*Data Exchange/Dissemination.* Several issues are associated with the dissemination of land-related data — Initially those regarding compatibility criteria, custodianship responsibilities and data exchange framework.

Issues such as compatibility and data exchange framework, plus those concerning data exchange policy, crown copyright and royalty issues, are currently being addressed by an interdepartmental project team.

*Use of Technology.* To facilitate the transmission and 'across the board' use of WALIS data, the development of the necessary hardware and software infrastructure must be encouraged and coordinated. This requires the promotion of resourcing in the areas of research and development education and technology transfer.

*Role of the Private Sector.* Though intrinsically linked with the issues of data exchange and dissemination, the role of the private sector in relation to utilisation of land-related data is being examined. In particular, consideration needs to be given to the copyright and exchange aspects of value-added data. Currently, data is being provided to two private bureaus which are 'value enhancing' the data and creating new products.

## LIS/GIS Policy and Program Support

With the aid of management consultants to facilitate communication, representatives of the WALIS community and WALIS Secretariat have completed the initial stages of corporate planning of WALIS. This has led to the identification of 10 priority areas which are being developed to form working strategies. It is intended that even when complete, the corporate plan will not be viewed as finite, but as a working document to be reviewed annually.

## New Programs

Three major facets of activity can be identified within the WALIS arena. Within the LIS environment, operational systems are now being modified and enhanced to improve aspects of data integrity, access and exchange, and overall system efficiency.

The GIS area is characterised by an escalation of activity with the emphasis on data capture and project orientated databases.

Legislative activity in progress is heralding major modifications to the Western Australian Land Act, Transfer of Land Act and Surveyors Licensing Act. These changes will have far-reaching implications on the management of land within Western Australia.

# . NOTES

1 Australian Bureau of Statistics (ABS), *Exports, Australia — Annual Summary Figures 1985–86*, Cat. No. 5424.0 (ABS, Canberra, 1987), p. 31.

2 James Martin, *Principles of Data-base Management* (Prentice Hall, Englewood Cliffs, New Jersey, 1976), p. 332.

3 R.J. Eden, Modelling for Land Information Systems Development in Australia and Particularly Queensland. Draft Ph.D. Thesis, Department of Geographical Sciences, University of Queensland, 1987, pp. 63, 66.

4 James Martin, *Principles of Data-base Management*, pp. 71–72.

5 Ian P. Williamson, 'Trends in Land Information System Administration in Australia', in *Proceedings*, Auto-Carto Conference, London, September 1986, pp. 149–161.

6 Australian Urban and Regional Information Systems Association (AURISA), *Report of the Working Group on Statewide Parcel-based Land Information Systems in Australasia*, Technical Monograph No. 1 (AURISA, Sydney, 1985).

7 Ian P. Williamson, 'Trends in Land Information System Administration in Australia'.

8 P.A. Burrough, *Principles of Geographical Information Systems for Land Resources Assessment* (Clarendon Press, Oxford, 1986), p. 11.

# CHAPTER THREE
# Remote Sensing

## O.F. Moss   K.J. Lyons
## P. Perrett

Remote sensing is an important source of data for Geographic Information Systems (GIS). Remote sensing is defined as the acquisition of data about a target without physical contact with that target. The data is collected by aircraft and satellite mounted instruments which receive reflected energy from a target in some frequency of the electromagnetic spectrum. The processes involved in remote sensing are illustrated in Figure 3.1 below.

Part of the spectrum relevant to remote sensing is shown in Figure 3.2. Until the mid-1960s the most common form of remote sensing was aerial photography, which used the visible light section of the electromagnetic spectrum. Newer sensors can acquire data in this and other sections of the electromagnetic spectrum, such as the non-visible infrared and near infrared wavelengths, as well as the microwaves used for radar. Many of these sensors can

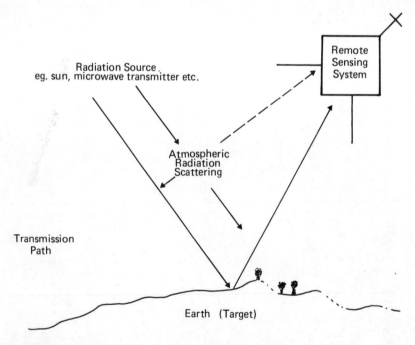

Figure 3.1   The Remote Sensing Process.

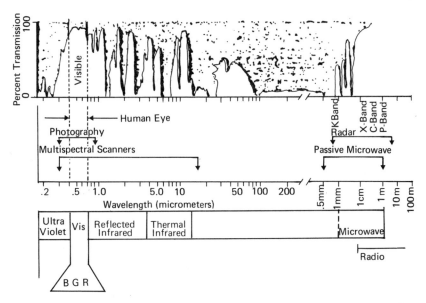

*Figure 3.2   The Electromagnetic Spectrum and its Relationship to Remote Sensing Systems.*

acquire several sections of the spectrum concurrently, and may be termed multi-spectral scanners. Some general characteristics of remote sensor systems are listed as an Annex to this chapter.

Aerial photography is a relatively slow form of data acquisition because it relies upon analogue data and manual interpretation of the photographs to extract data. In contrast, new forms of remote sensing use digital acquisition techniques which allow rapid computer assisted processing. This is substantially different to the current procedure as all data is digitally corrected, enhanced, recombined and presented using any of several methods, depending on the desired result. The output of digital scanners present completely new data sets to those of traditional remote sensing, and for this reason are considered sufficiently important to be described in detail in this chapter.

## RELATIVE MERITS — AERIAL PHOTOGRAPHY VS NEWER REMOTE SENSING SYSTEMS

Aerial photography has been used for mapping and monitoring since demonstrating its potential for interpretation and information conveyance. From the 1930s when the Zeiss Multiplex mapping system came into use, stereo photogrammetry became the foundation of mapping throughout the world. Colwell cites World War II as the main impetus for the development of photo-interpretation skills.[1]

Remote sensing is a comparatively recent addition to the means of data acquisition available to potential users. Since the introduction of data-acquiring satellites in the late-1960s and 1970s, remote sensing has undergone considerable research. It has already developed into a tool suitable for a wide range of applications. It is important to consider the rapid progress made already when predicting that remote sensing technology will undoubtably improve given further development time. Disadvantages of today's remote sensors may well be reversed in the future.

As the most common present form of data acquisition is aerial photography, it makes sense to draw a comparison with newer state-of-the-art remote sensing data sources. Where a system feature is cited as an advantage, it necessarily follows that the equivalent component or feature of the alternate system is at a comparative disadvantage for a specific purpose.

## Aerial Photography Advantages

- It is in common use, well documented and understood. Introduction of newer remote sensing systems is usually accompanied by additional staff training and equipment purchases.

- Aerial photography for mapping is usually acquired at altitudes (therefore scales) which allow resolution (the ability to distinguish between two ground objects) of the order less than 1m. Picture elements (pixels) of the order 10m × 10m to 30m × 30m are currently the best available for civil satellite remote sensors, whilst aircraft scanners have pixels of approximately 2m × 2m. Resolution is *not* equivalent to pixel size. Scanner resolution equates to approximately 2.5 times the pixel size. Higher resolution means:
  - Much higher accuracy measurements can be obtained from aerial photography.
  - High complexity ground features can be identified more successfully. The pixel size limits the size of objects that can be distinguished and identified, thus larger pixels detrimentally affect the reliability of remote sensing for some tasks.
  - There are fewer 'identification clues' for interpretation in remote sensing, hence a feature may be discriminated but may not be identified.

- The date of acquisition can be planned according to requirements. Satellite remote sensing is only acquired on a revisit cycle, varying according to the satellite.

## Newer Remote Sensing System Advantages

- The data is available in photographic (analogue) or in digital form. This allows:
  - Manual and/or computer image processing for highlighting important features, compared to only manual for aerial photography.

— User-required digital analysis, whereas only analogue analysis is available for aerial photography.
— Consistent and systematic interpretation.
— Multiple colour-coded overlay display which is not possible without extensive additional cartography with aerial photography.
— Integration into other forms of data storage, for example, geographic information systems or any purpose-specific information system, for example, the Australian Army Command and Control System (AUSTACCS). Aerial photography needs to be manually digitised as a separate function.
— Stereo images to be synthesised. This is already available from aerial photography in analogue form.

• Data is sensed in several sections of the electromagnetic spectrum; aerial photography is only one small portion of the spectrum. This dramatically improves data interpretation, and increases the range of useful applications.

• Each remote sensing scene covers a very large area. This is useful for extensive area studies where an overview of the area is required, or where excessive detail of a photograph mosaic can detract from the important features. Space photography (when available) can also cover a large area.

Table 3.1  AERIAL PHOTOGRAPHY VS REMOTE SENSING (SCANNERS)

| Aerial Photography | Remote Sensing |
| --- | --- |
| Widely used and documented | Many techniques and sensors still under development |
| High resolution (<1m):<br>— high accuracy<br>— determination of complex ground features<br>— high information content | Best available pixel size 10m<br><br>Suits regional studies |
| Acquisition as required | Some sensors as required, others available as acquired |
| Analogue data:<br>— manual or semi-automated orientations<br>— manual plotting | Digital data:<br>— rapid digital processing, analysis and overlays<br>— integration with other systems and data types<br>— multi-date and change detection |
| Small coverage per scene | Large areal coverage |
| Visible to near infra-red wavelengths only | Wide acquisition spectrum and multi-spectral ability |
| 3 to 500 times the data cost of other remote sensors | |

- Accurate satellite acquisition position, stable platforms and high internal image accuracy allow pre-programmed-correction processing. This allows easier multi-date analysis of data, for detection of change over time. Aerial photography requires manual or semi-automatic orientations to correct for aircraft movement prior to use.

- Low cost per unit area for data acquisition and analysis. $0.01 to $1.60 per sq km as against $5.00 plus for aerial photography.

- Pixel count gives immediate ground coverage. No similar facility is available for aerial photography.

Table 3.1 summarises these relevant advantages and disadvantages.

## SENSOR CHARACTERISTICS

Having introduced the broad differences between aerial photography as a form of data acquisition and state-of-the-art remote sensing it is necessary to present the general and specific characteristics of some remote sensing systems. These sections illustrate how different the data and its acquisition is from traditional data sources.

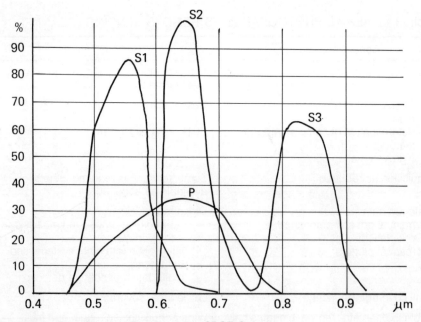

*Figure 3.3   Four Spectral Bands of the SPOT Scanner.*

Source: Centre National d'Etudes Spatiales (CNES) diagram reproduced by Groupement pour le Développement de la Télédétection Aérospatiale (GTDA), for SPOT Technical Course, April 1986.

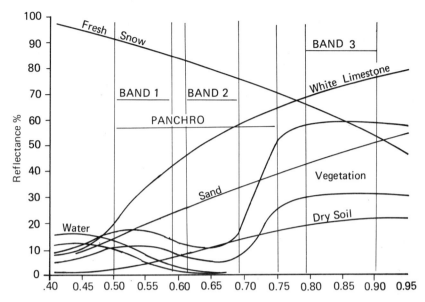

*Figure 3.4   Spectral Reflectance Signatures of Typical Ground Cover, superimposed with SPOT Spectral Bands.*

Source: Centre National d'Etudes Spatiales (CNES) diagram reproduced by Groupement pour le Développement de la Télédétection Aérospatiale (GDTA), for SPOT Technical Course, April 1986.

## Multi-Spectral Scanners

As indicated above, a major proportion of remote sensing data is obtained using multi-spectral scanners. Most scanners are able to sense and record received energy simultaneously in several specific wavelengths (called frequency *bands*). These bands can extend both above and below the visible wavelengths of $0.4 - 0.7 \times 10^{-6}$m. Scanners with this ability are referred to as *multi-spectral scanners*.

Figure 3.3 shows the three narrow bands (S1 — S3) and one panchromatic band (P) of the French Satellite Probatoire de l'Observation de la Terre (SPOT) system and their relationship within the electromagnetic spectrum.

The multi-spectral nature of the data is particularly useful when trying to distinguish between different types of vegetation or land cover. Each cover type absorbs and reflects energy in a different, but characteristic manner (see Figure 3.4 below). These are referred to as the *spectral signatures* of cover types. An entire scene can be classified as belonging to a particular land cover category by comparing the digital value for the pixel, in one or more bands, with that of previously determined spectral signature values. Usually, individual remote sensing systems acquire data in only one, or sometimes two, closely related ranges. For example, LANDSAT sensors acquire data in the visible and the nearby near-infrared wavelengths.

Scanners record their data by various means. Some, like LANDSAT Multi-Spectral Scanner (MSS), record one pixel at a time by using mechanically activated mirrors to reflect the incident energy onto the receiving sensor (see Figure 3.5) one row at a time as the satellite passes from south-west to north-east.

Systems such as the SPOT satellite use a 'push-broom' scanner where a linear array of 6000 detectors acquires data directly through a lens system as the satellite tracks around the earth (see Figure 3.6).

## Radar

Unlike the remote sensors described so far, radar is an active sensor, that is, it emits energy and records the reflections from its target. The principle of operation is that the measurement of the time interval between the emitted and reflected pulse gives the object distance from the antenna. As the aircraft or satellite travels over an area a complete coverage is built up by acquiring strips at right angles to the flight path.

Radar uses the microwave section of the electromagnetic spectrum from about 8 to 300mm wavelength. Resolution limits are a problem as resolution is

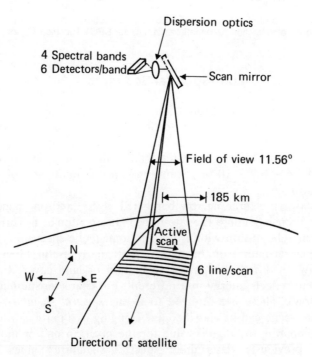

*Figure 3.5  Landsat MSS Data Recording.*

Source: J.T.M. Kennie and M.C. Matthews, *Romote Sensing in Civil Engineering* (John Wiley and Sons, New York, 1985).

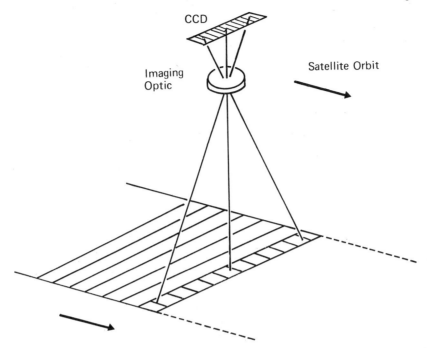

CCD

Imaging
Optic

Satellite Orbit

*Figure 3.6   SPOT's Push-broom Scanner.*

Source: Centre National d'Etudes Spatiales (CNES) diagram reproduced by Groupement pour le Développement de la Télédétection Aérospatiale (GDTA), for SPOT Technical Course, April 1986.

related to the antenna length and the wavelength. That is, a longer antenna gives better resolution. Side-Looking Airborne Radar (SLAR) resolution is limited by the length of the antenna that can practically be carried by an aircraft. Synthetic Aperture Radar (SAR) overcomes this problem by synthesising a very long antenna using the distance the aircraft travels during the emission/reflection time interval. This is an extremely complex operation and requires lengthy processing to produce an image.

The images produced by radar are very different to those of earlier scanning instruments. Generally produced in black and white, the appearance of the object will depend on its surface texture, conductivity, and, of course, its aspect to the antenna.

## Sensor Platforms

Sensing instruments can be carried by aircraft and by satellites. Those mounted in aircraft are subject to the same problems of weather and planning requirements as those which apply to aerial photography. Satellite-mounted sensors are placed in specific earth orbits. *Geo-stationary* orbits like those of the weather satellites remain at a fixed altitude above one specific point on the earth. *Sun-Synchronous Near-Polar* (SSNP) orbits are those in which the satellite orbits the earth around or near the poles, acquiring data at approximately local noon, that is, in synchronisation with the overhead sun. Satellites such as the LANDSAT series and SPOT use this type of orbit as it allows:

— receiving energy from the sun reflected from the earth in the visible and near-infrared wavelengths, and

— the satellites to provide as near to worldwide coverage as possible.

Advanced Very High Resolution Radiometer (AVHRR) is an active sensor and hence can acquire data day or night. It need not be sun synchronous, but should provide wide coverage.

Figure 3.7 is a diagram of the SPOT satellite, which has a typical SSNP orbit.

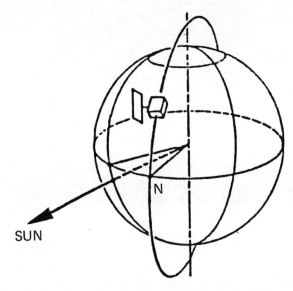

SUN

N

*Figure 3.7   SPOT Example of a Sun-synchronous Near-polar Orbit.*

Source: Centre National d'Etudes Spatiales (CNES) diagram reproduced by Groupement pour le Développement de la Télédétection Aérospatiale (GDTA), for SPOT Technical Course, April 1986.

## Data

### Pixel Data

Many remote sensing instruments contain electro-optical devices called scanners. These devices do not use photographic emulsions on which to record the scene as in normal photography, but instead process the received signal into digital format. To do this the scene is divided into small grid-like picture elements called *pixels*. This rectangular pixel format is similar to the grid-based raster format data of geographic information systems referred to in Chapter 2.

The size of the pixels of a scanner determines the size of an object that can be distinguished on the ground. The smaller the pixel, the better the image approximates the real scene and hence the greater the amount of available data and possible applications for the data. Individual pixels can be resampled to form a new grid at any desired size (with a resulting loss of data). This resampled grid could correspond to an established GIS grid to provide for simple data integration.

A digital numeric 'brightness' value, which is, in practice, an average of the received energy from that pixel element on the ground, is recorded for each pixel in a particular wavelength band until the scene is fully complete.

Figure 3.8 below shows the use of pixels and their averaging effect on surface features for one representative band.

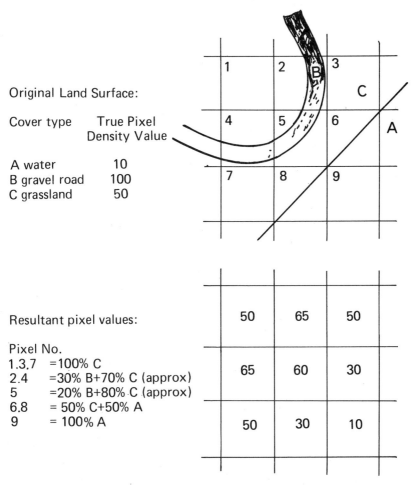

Original Land Surface:

| Cover type | True Pixel Density Value |
|---|---|
| A water | 10 |
| B gravel road | 100 |
| C grassland | 50 |

Resultant pixel values:

Pixel No.
1.3.7  =100% C
2.4    =30% B+70% C (approx)
5      =20% B+80% C (approx)
6.8    = 50% C+50% A
9      = 100% A

*Figure 3.8   Pixel Data Recording of Typical Land Surface.*

pixel values result from the reflectance of each surface type and the
percentage of each surface type contained in each pixel. Although the
itself cannot be seen, its effects on the pixel values will result in values
where between those of the real land surface and the real road surface
value. (Real in this context means the pixel value if one cover type filled one
complete pixel.) Similarly, the true position of the land–water boundary cannot
be correctly determined in this example, as the pixels covering the boundary
will have recorded values which contain percentages of both surface types. For
reasons such as these, remote sensing accuracy is limited by the very important
parameter of pixel size.

The pixel size is the result of the type of scanner and the flying height of the
sensor system. Whilst some scanners acquire pixels individually (LANDSAT
MSS), others scan using a linear array (SPOT), giving more acquisition time
per pixel, thus allowing acquisition of smaller pixels. The instantaneous field of
view (IFOV) of one scanning element is a measure of the angular aperture
from which the pixel is acquired. Figure 3.9 illustrates this relationship.

Pixel sizes are chosen according to the intended purpose of the sensor.
Advanced Very High Resolution Radiometer (AVHRR) is used for purposes
such as monitoring weather, sea surface and studies which require a large areal
extent, and thus it has a pixel size of 1km × 1km. LANDSAT's Multi-Spectral
Scanner (MSS) had a pixel size of 79m × 79m, whereas the later LANDSAT
Thematic Mapper (TM) has a pixel size of 30m × 30m.

The SPOT sensor has two pixel sizes, 10m × 10m for panchromatic mode
and 20m × 20m for multi-spectral mode. Both LANDSAT and SPOT are used
for similar purposes of land use, soil, geological, marine, and other similar
surveys; however the greater resolution of SPOT may allow it to be used in a

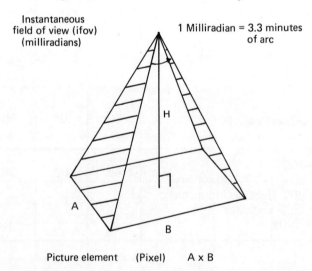

Figure 3.9   *Instantaneous Field of View (IFOV) Related to Flying Height. Dimension A is proportional to Flying Height (H).*

far wider range of applications, such as updating of medium and smaller scale topographic maps.

Aircraft-mounted versions of the satellite scanners are now available and can provide the user with pixel data with much improved resolutions in the order of 0.2m–20m. These may prove useful for rapid, high resolution data acquisition, suitable for mapping at larger scales, given appropriate and accurate rectification procedures.

With scanner data beginning to rival aerial photography for image quality it may not be long before aircraft scanners may be used in place of normal aerial photography as they are in digital format and hence are easily computer processed. This would be useful given the introduction of digital image correlators for image processing. In addition, the ability to acquire data quickly in an emergency or for a specific task is an important feature. Recently developed airborne scanners have more bands than those of current satellites and may therefore provide more conclusive evidence of the existence and locations of ground features.

## Acquisition Frequency

Due to the scan width of the sensors and the requirement for sun-synchronous orbits it is only possible for satellite mounted sensors to acquire data of an area on a regular revisit-cycle basis. For example, LANDSAT's revisit frequency is once per 16 days. The SPOT satellite has a revisit capability of between one to five days, due to its ability to acquire data off its orbital path by programming adjustments to its sensor lens/mirror combination.

The systems presently available acquire data in one of several wavelengths, including ultraviolet, visible, infrared and microwave (radar). Depending on the requirement, this allows some data to be acquired at times when other wavelengths cannot. Two examples of this are: thermal infrared which can be received by night as well as by day and radar reception which can be received through cloud.

Data availability is important, as the sooner the data can be used the greater its potential benefit, particularly in a rapidly changing situation. Aerial photography, like aircraft scanner data, is acquired by special aircraft tasking. This can have a distinct advantage, as rapid response to special tasks can be achieved by aircraft-borne remote sensors, whilst satellites may not be able to acquire data within the required time-frame.

Satellites generally acquire data on a fixed schedule, and this is often satisfactory for many remote sensing tasks. It is necessary only to request the data from the relevant distributor as acquired by the sensor rather than arrange special acquisition tasks. (SPOT data can be requested in advance for a specific period and location.) The data is available soon after it is received and processed by the relevant distributor. The potential exists for real-time viewing of satellite images as they are received by the Australian Landsat Station (ALS) at Alice Springs.

## Precision

Many sensors are mounted on satellite platforms. As the satellites are in high orbits (LANDSAT is 705km), and the areal coverage per image is small by comparison, the resulting data is acquired in an almost orthogonal direction to the surface. The result of this, in combination with the above scanning systems, is that the data exhibits high internal precision and little or no relief displacement. Following correction for earth curvature only, measurements can be taken directly from the images for low accuracy work. For greater accuracy and to correct for more oblique images, rectification can be made by mathematical transformations using identifiable ground control points.

## Format

Remote sensing systems can provide a number of products for users including computer-produced images and computer-compatible magnetic tapes (CCT). CCTs are basically lists of digital values for the image pixels. These can be manipulated using many digital image processing techniques to highlight user-required features, and thus assist identification of areas of interest. As the data is digital, the processing is computer-assisted to a high degree. This leads to higher levels of objectivity, consistency and increased processing speed.

# AVAILABLE REMOTE SENSING SYSTEMS

A table showing the current systems and their characteristics is attached as an annex to this chapter. However, it is useful to identify some of the more commonly used sensors and list their characteristics. (In order of decreasing pixel size.)

- Advanced Very High Resolution Radiometer (AVHRR).
  - Pixels 1km.
  - Five-band scanning radiometer on board the National Oceanic Atmospheric and Administration (NOAA) series of weather satellites.
  - Digital data received in visible, near infrared, and infrared water vapour bands.
  - Scene coverage 1600km × 1800km.
  - Acquired every eight hrs.
  - Cost $100 per scene, or $0.01 per sq km.
  - Used for measuring temperature of clouds, sea surface and land.
- Coastal Zone Colour Scanner (CZCS).
  - Pixels 825m.
  - Six-band multi-spectral scanning radiometer on board the NIMBUS-7 satellite.
  - Digital data received in the visible, near infrared and thermal infrared.

— Cost $100 per scene.
— Used for estimating near surface concentrations of marine phyto-plankton pigments by measuring the ocean colour.
— Available through CSIRO.

● LANDSAT Multi-Spectral Scanner (MSS).
— Pixels 80m.
— Digital data received and available in four bands, in the visible and near infrared.
— Photograph-like image products also available.
— Scene coverage 185km × 185km.
— Acquired every 16 days.
— Cost $720, or $0.02 per sq km.
— Used for 1:250 000 mapping of land use/cover and shallow water mapping.
— Available through the Australian Landsat Station (ALS).

● Thematic Mapper.
— Pixels 30m.
— Digital data received and available in seven bands in the visible, near infrared, reflected infrared, and thermal infrared.
— Photograph-like image products also available.
— Scene coverage 185km × 185km.
— Acquired every 16 days.
— Cost $5000, or $0.18 per sq km.
— Used for 1:100 000 mapping of land use/cover and shallow water mapping.
— Currently data not widely available in Australia due to ALS incapable of accepting data (although some data has been acquired). ALS upgrade is expected in the near future.

● SPOT.
— Pixels 10m panchromatic and 20m multi-spectral.
— Digital data received and available in four bands, three in the visible and near infrared, and one wide-band visible panchromatic band.
— Products also include photograph-like images, both colour and black and white at various scales. Processing is available according to a user selection of one of four levels of corrections. (This also applies to digital tapes.)
— Scene coverage 60km × 60km.
— Acquired as specially requested prior to the orbit, with possible available orbit intervals between one to five days.
— Ability to view off-nadir by pointing the imaging instrument allows stereo capability.

— Cost $2500, or $1.60 per sq km.

— Used for revision mapping at scale of 1:50 000 mapping, possible cartographic work at 1:100 000.

— Available through Australian distributor of French company SPOT IMAGE.

(Plate 1 shows SPOT imagery over the city of Adelaide. Plate 2 demonstrates the resolution of this imagery by showing imagery acquired over the Adelaide airport zoomed by a factor of 2×.)

## IMPORTANCE OF REMOTE SENSING TO AUSTRALIA

The importance of remote sensing must be judged by considering how it can make a contribution towards fulfilling the requirements of data acquisition and analysis for Australia. In these tasks there are several problems which are specific to Australia. The following paragraphs identify some of these problems and suggest how remote sensing may overcome some of them, hence proving it a worthwhile data source.

The vast size of the Australian landmass creates many problems, one of which is the enormous effort required to locate and record surface features adequately. Compounding this is the fact that Australia has only a small population in respect to its size. This has led to less information gathering activity per unit area than is common in other technologically comparable nations. A small population also means that there are less funds to allocate for locational and recording tasks. Due to the above, much of the continent remains unexplored or unmapped at useful scales.

For large area regional studies, remote sensing systems such as LANDSAT MSS, TM or SPOT may provide sufficient data to satisfy specific inquiries such as the location of surface water in the north of Australia. On the negative side, however, these systems use the visible light band wavelengths, and thus cloud cover and nightfall may preclude data acquisition by these sensors. In this event, radar may be used to penetrate cloud and darkness to provide the required data. This example illustrates the extreme importance of selecting the correct sensor for each specific task. Thus to employ remote sensing to its full capacity, personnel must be fully conversant with all types of sensor systems and their characteristics, and have access to a wide range of sensor data.

Australia's map-producing authorities are already burdened with the formidable task of completing a topographic coverage of the continent. Whilst this is not finished, it would be ideal if a systematic means of identifying those areas of rapid change which require initial or revision mapping was available. It is extremely likely that monitoring using remote sensor scanners will provide this service. This could help prioritise, and hence increase the efficiency of the available mapping effort. Remote sensing's relatively low acquisition and analysis costs, together with its ability to compare multi-date imagery, therefore has major implications for Australia.

Revision mapping is the process of updating the most recently produced maps in an area. In much of Australia maps are 20 to 30 years out of date. Using the original map as a base, up-to-date remote sensing imagery could be used to assist this revision process. Revision mapping has already been attempted at small scale (i.e., 1:1 000 000) by the Division of National Mapping.[2] Whilst not completely successful using LANDSAT MSS data, the same exercise using higher resolution LANDSAT TM or SPOT data may well prove fruitful.

Welch concluded that SPOT data may permit the compilation of 1:50 000 to 1:250 000 scale maps for areas with limited map coverage.[3] This is yet to be demonstrated in an Australian context but may well prove to be one of remote sensing's great advantages. Mapping using newer remote sensing data integrated with current map data is worthy of further investigation.

The quality of SPOT imagery has been compared to high altitude aerial photography.[4] Added to this is the ability to sense in the visible and near infrared regions of the spectrum. Given these features, SPOT could prove useful for monitoring land development in peacetime and enemy troop movement and activity in the event of war.

The development of remote sensing to full potential capability is a long and involved process, and must therefore be developed and tested in times of peace if it is later to prove useful in conflict.

Current remote sensing provides, at the very least, a partial solution to Australia's data acquisition problems. The situation will only improve as technology upgrades specifications like pixel size, spectral bands, frequency, cost and analysis software. Due to the large coverage of each scene, and the relative speed with which image processing could be undertaken, remote sensing is well-suited to providing an alternative to aerial photography. The comparatively low cost of data acquisition and analysis over extensive areas is also very important. Whilst the scale of analysis may presently be limited to what is generally referred to as medium to small scale, this will improve, and in any case it is better to have some rather than no information over many parts of the continent.

## IMPORTANCE OF REMOTE SENSING TO THE MILITARY

Many of the points made above are relevant generally to the military. There are some features of remote sensing, however, which point to it being extremely useful for specific military requirements. The areas where present military capability may be enhanced as a result of the employment of newer remote sensing systems are listed below.

- Vegetation mapping and classification must be up-to-date as important command decisions of deployment locations may depend upon the availability of camouflage using the natural vegetation cover. Certain types of vegetation may inhibit the progress of vehicles due to their size, density or structure, thus their location must be known. Remote sensing has demonstrated an ability to differentiate many types of vegetation. This should be further investigated with a view to providing the capability to update vegetation cover data rapidly.

- Identificaton of resource locations such as water, timber and other construction materials like stone and gravel in an area of operations is important to the military because it minimises the logistic support required. Remote sensing can be used to assist the delineation of suitable areas in support of this task.

- Identification and location of soil types which inhibit vehicle and troop movement can be assisted using remote sensing.

- Monitoring patterns and seasonal variation and locations of other modifications (both natural and man-made such as flooding, bushfires and the development of roads, tracks and clearings) in the north of Australia, can be assisted greatly using newer remote sensing systems. The ability to assess very quickly the digital difference between one image and another acquired at a later date is a feature which has great potential for this application.

- Identification of enemy troop movements could be achieved using higher resolution remote sensors such as LANDSAT TM or SPOT and aircraft sensors, on a regular or special task basis. These sensors acquire data in the visible and infrared wavelengths, which reduces the amount of cover provided by vegetation, and hence assists in the location of men and equipment.

## CONCLUSION

Remote sensing has been shown to possess many desirable features from both the civilian and military viewpoint. The development and integration of these features into operational systems must be undertaken to provide new and comprehensive data sources. Because of many shared data characteristics it is important that remote sensing and GIS are developed concurrently, as together they form a powerful information acquisition and dissemination tool for decision-makers.

## Table 3.2  CHARACTERISTICS OF REMOTE SENSING SYSTEMS

| Spectral Region and Sensor | Wavelength (micrometres) | Approximate Spatial Resolution (milliradians) | Atmospheric Penetration Capability[*] | Acquisition Capability | Geometric Quality (for planimetric mapping) | System/ Sensor examples |
|---|---|---|---|---|---|---|
| Ultraviolet<br>Scanners, image orthicons, and cameras w/IR film | 0.01–0.4 | 0.01–0.1 | | Day only | Good | |
| Visible<br>Scanners, and conventional cameras | 0.4–0.7 | 0.001–0.01 | H | Day only | Good | A/P, A/S MSS, TM, SPOT |
| Reflected IR<br>Scanners, and conventional cameras w/IR sensitive film | 0.7–3.5 | 0.01–0.1 | H,Sg | Day only | Good | A/P, A/S MSS, TM, SPOT |
| Thermal IR<br>Scanners and radiometers | 3.5–14 | 1.0 | H,S | Day/Night | Good/Fair | TM, A/S, AVHRR |
| Microwave<br>Scanners, radiometers | $10^3$–$10^6$ | 10 | H,S,F | Day/Night | Fair | |
| Radar[**]<br>Scanners and scatterometers | $8.3 \times 10^3$<br>$1.3 \times 10^6$ | 10 | H,S,F,R[a] | Day/Night | Fair | SAR, SIR Seasat, ERS-1, SLAR |

[*]  Denotes atmospheric conditions penetrated. H= haze, S=smoke, Sg=smog, F=cloud or fog, R=rain.
[**]  While radar operates in the microwave region, its utility is significantly different to that of radiometers.
[a]  Penetration capability increases with increasing wavelength.

*Source*: Adapted from J.E. Estes and L.W. Senger, *Remote Sensing: Techniques for Environmental Analysis* (Hamilton Publishing Company, California, 1974), pp. 22, 23.

# NOTES

1   R.N. Colwell. 'The Remote Sensing Picture in 1984', Keynote Address, in *Technical Papers*, American Society of Photogrammetry and Remote Sensing, Fall Convention, San Antonio, Texas, 1984 (American Society of Photogrammetry and Remote Sensing, Falls Church, Virginia, 1984), pp. 5-6.

2   See J.K. Payne and P.G. Lawler, 'Revision of 1:1 Million Scale Topographic Maps Using Satellite Imagery', in International Cartographic Association (ICA), *Technical Papers*, 2 vols, 12th International Conference of the International Cartographic Association (12th ICA Conference Committee, Perth, 1984), Vol. 2, pp. 13-21.

3   R. Welch, 'Cartographic Potential of SPOT Image Data', *Photogrammetric Engineering and Remote Sensing*, Vol. 51, No. 8, August 1985, pp. 1085-1091.

4   Robert N. Colwell and Charles E. Poulton, 'SPOT Simulation Imagery for Urban Monitoring: A Comparison with Landsat TM and MSS Imagery and with High Altitude Colour Infrared Photography', *Photogrammetric Engineering and Remote Sensing*, Vol. 51, No. 8, August 1985, pp. 1093-1101.

CHAPTER FOUR

# The Australian Defence Force Requirements for Land Related Information

## A.W. Laing
## D.J. Puniard*

The defence of Australia against infiltration or attack by a foreign adversary is a daunting task. With our small population and vast expanse of territory we cannot hope to defend every part of our shores from foreign invasion, nor is it possible for us to build defence installations and support facilities at all possible strategic target areas. Thus to deter an enemy from attacking us we must have well equipped, mobile forces ready to counter any pending attack immediately, or to dislodge quickly an enemy who may have already landed some of his forces.

To achieve economy of effort in the deployment of military forces, the Defence Force must have ready access to information on the terrain and factors associated with it. Details of the existing civilian infrastructure are also needed to allow effective use to be made of civilian resources and to ensure that military resources are used to their best effect.

The need for land-related data by the military is not new, as the land and its resources has vitally affected battles since before the days of the Roman legions. The requirement has been met in the past by personal observation (or, in military terms, reconnaissance), and through the use of various kinds of maps. The advent of instantly accessible computer databases and associated graphics hardware and software could drastically alter the way battles are fought. Personal reconnaissance of a proposed battlefield may never be entirely superseded; however, the use of digital terrain models, associated graphic displays and purpose-designed information databases will allow many important strategic and tactical decisions to be made before even seeing the proposed area of operations.

The introduction of computerised Land Information Systems (LIS) on a broad scale throughout Australia, together with the introduction of military digital mapping systems and automated command and control systems, should be able to provide the basis for much more reliable, timely and accessible land-related data than is currently the case.

---

\* The views expressed by the authors do not necessarily reflect the views of the Department of Defence or the Australian Defence Force.

# INDIVIDUAL SERVICE RESPONSIBILITIES

Within the Australian Defence Force (ADF), the Headquarters Australian Defence Force (HQ ADF) is responsible for policy and coordination of the three Services — Navy, Army and Air Force. Each service has specific and joint roles according to their various charters. The Navy and Air Force share the responsibility for surveillance of our shores to detect and deter any possible unfriendly movements towards our coast. They also have a role to support the Army in its land-based operations. This support may be logistic, such as the transportation of supplies, equipment and troops, or offensive support such as naval weapon support from offshore, or the RAAF's aerial firepower in support of ground troops.

The Army's primary role is land warfare. Incursions onto our shores are likely to require land forces to expel them. The Army is thus vitally concerned with the land and its characteristics, both natural and man-made, and will be the prime user and beneficiary of a defence computerised LIS.

# LEVELS OF INFORMATION

The amount and detail of land-related information required depends on the level at which operations are being considered. Strategic requirements are for general information on which to develop strategic plans over wide areas. The location and characteristics of major port and airfield facilities are the types of information needed for high level planning. By comparison, the tactical requirement is for very detailed information to plan battles at formation (e.g., division) or unit (e.g., battalion) level. An infantry battalion commander will want the best contour map available, and the most accurate road and track information. The engineer squadron commander will want to know details of road surfaces, bridge construction and capacity, and the location of resources for construction tasks.

The current debate on the development of threat scenarios in the wake of the Dibb Report[1] and the Defence White Paper of March 1987[2] makes it difficult to relate the need for land information to threat levels. Recent defence philosophy has been to concentrate on the areas of northern Australia identified as likely enemy approaches. The large-scale mapping program and other data collection program, such as the 1st Division efforts in their Divisional Deployment Area Studies (DDAS), have concentrated on these areas.

A more reasoned approach is necessary and should include the use of existing national databases such as ARIS (see Chapter 7) for strategic assessment and the development of suitable interfaces with civilian Land Information Systems (LIS) and a detailed appraisal of the contribution of such systems to the military requirement.

# GEOGRAPHIC INFORMATION CATEGORIES

Geographic information is but a part of the overall requirement for intelligence by the military, along with strategic and economic intelligence to assess the intentions of potential enemies and intelligence about an enemy's capabilities and equipment. The geographic information requirement can broadly be divided into three areas, namely:

- Infrastructure information, primarily about man-made features but with a geographic location.
- Terrain intelligence, primarily concerned with the natural features of the terrain.
- Environmental data, such as climate and weather.

There is also an area of overlap in certain topographic features such as roads, railways, and bridges which are part of the terrain but also have infrastructure elements such as load classifications.

# INFRASTRUCTURE INFORMATION

Several recent studies within the Defence Department have examined the requirement for infrastructure information.[3] Not all infrastructure information is land related (e.g., the allocation of radio frequencies, loading facilities at ports and railheads), however most of it has a geographic location as its key element with other attributes as the secondary level of information.

In 1983 a prime policy document on infrastructure information requirements for defence was issued — JSP(AS)205(A), entitled 'The Directory of Service Responsibilities for Australian Infrastructure Information'.[4] It gives a very detailed list of information required and allocates responsibilities for collection of the data needed. The following section headings and detail taken from this document give an idea of the scope of requirements:

- *Ports and Harbours.* Both Navy and Army require detailed information on the size of ship able to be handled, the availability of tugs, wharfage facilities, anchorages, storage space, loading and unloading facilities, fuel availability, and ship repair.
- *Beaches.* Again both Navy and Army need detail on beach surface and subsurface, access to and from the beach, tidal and weather effects, nearby anchorages, and back of beach terrain. A combined Army/Navy program called BEACHCOMBER has acquired a great deal of this data for strategic areas, although it has all been recorded manually.
- *Airfields.* Air Force and Army require a great deal of detail about airfields for both tactical and logistic support operations. Information needed includes runway dimensions and surface, navigation aids, hard standing, fuel availability, and access to and from the airfield.

- *Resources and Utilities*. All three Services, but primarily Army, need information on such things as water supply, sewerage, power supply, fire services, fuel storage, road building materials, and food and medical services.

- *Transportation*. This information is mostly needed by Army but some elements such as civilian shipping and aircraft data are primarily Navy and Air Force concerns. Army needs information on railways, roads, bridges, pipelines, and details of civilian transport facilities and capabilities.

- *Communications*. All three Services need detailed data on national and international telecommunication facilities, including line, radio and satellite systems. Civilian maritime and aeronautical communication capabilities could also be useful for defence purposes.

- *Civilian Stores Support, Repair and Maintenance*. Detail on warehouse and other specialised storage, such as fuel, are needed by defence planners, as is also detail on civilian repair and maintenance facilities for a wide range of equipments from road vehicles to aircraft.

- *Terrain*. In addition to standard topographic maps at various scales a great deal of other terrain information is needed for military purposes. This includes vegetation, soils, geology, climate, water features, and detail on urban areas.

The concept of JSP (AS) 205 is quite sound, but due mainly to a lack of resources available the collection of the data has been rather tardy.

## INFORMATION VS INTELLIGENCE

Land-related information, to be of use to the military commander in the field, often needs to be edited and restructured into a format immediately digestible and of direct relevance to the task in hand. This is the process of the conversion of information into intelligence. Intelligence is often presented in the form of map overlays or as a concise listing or report specific to current operations. Intelligence staffs are deployed at all levels to carry out this task. One specific form of intelligence is 'terrain intelligence', which is, in reality, a military geographic information system which draws together information on natural terrain features to produce such things as cross-country movement maps or camouflage and concealment maps.

The process of integrating geographic information into products useful for specific strategic or operational circumstances is often referred to as terrain analysis. The NATO armies, particularly those of the USA and UK, have developed detailed procedures for such analysis by manual techniques and more recently have begun to consider computer-assisted techniques using digital map data and related attribute databases.

## EXERCISES VS OPERATIONS

In peacetime the military is restricted in practising what may be required of it in time of conflict. Major exercises involving the deployment of troops and major equipments such as tanks and artillery are expensive and are usually confined to closed military training areas with virtually no civilian infrastructure, or to thinly populated outback areas. This naturally precludes making real use of LIS-type data derived from civilian sources. This shortcoming is, however, recognised and many exercises are conducted without the real deployment of troops and weapons. The Army Tactical Exercises Without Troops (TEWTs) or at the higher level Chief of General Staff (CGS) exercises are conducted in areas of strategic importance and offer the opportunity to interact with civilian information sources. Sometimes, as in 1983, when the Kangaroo 83 exercise was conducted in the Pilbara region of Western Australia, the opportunity does arise to interact with civilian agencies in a realistic scenario with the real deployment of troops and weapons.

Kangaroo 86 was an exercise conducted in Central Queensland, west of Rockhampton. The scenario revolved around enemy incursions into the coalfields of the area. The existing mapping of the area was over ten years old and considerable manual effort was needed to upgrade these to show the present extent of mine development and associated cultural development. The township of Blackwater had almost doubled in size. An associated increase in the civilian infrastructure in the area had also occurred, again requiring considerable manual effort to upgrade information available to the Defence Force.

Had a digital map database of the area existed and techniques developed for its rapid updating (e.g., high resolution satellite imagery) the information would have been available to the commander far more rapidly and in highly appropriate forms. Similarly, if links had been developed between Army databases and those of the mine authorities other data would have been more readily available.

## TYPICAL EXAMPLES OF DATA REQUIRED

In addition to the Defence policy outlined in JSP(AS)205(A), the Army has considered the problems of data acquisition in some depth over the past year or two. As a result, the Army has prepared a draft Army Office Staff Instruction (AOSI) to specify policy, responsibility, and precedence within the Army for the collection, storage and dissemination of Defence Land Information (DLI)[5]. One of the requirements identified in this document is the need for regional handbooks to assist at the planning level. The 'Guide to Content' reproduced in Table 4.1 gives an indication of the scope of such handbooks.

Table 4.1  REGIONAL DEFENCE LAND INFORMATION
HANDBOOKS — A GUIDE TO CONTENT

---

Authority for issue and directions for use. Security classification where necessary (normally RESTRICTED).

Region Definition.

- Historical background of military significance
- Geographical data (terrain, vegetation, climate, seasonal variations)
- Time zone and unique public holidays (e.g., Canberra Day)
- Population composition and distribution
- Land use and economy.

Communications Facilities.

- Road
- Rail
- Air
- Shipping
- Telecommunications.

Resources and Facilities.

- Water supply
- Fuel storage and resupply arrangement
- Electricity.

Defence Force Facilities.

State Government Facilities.

Significant Commercial Facilities.

List of published information, including special studies and reports held by Military District Headquarters.

Reference to Maps and Charts

---

The requirement for transportation information is illustrated by Table 4.2, which is an extract from the Army Logistic Infrastructure Data System (LIDS) concept of requirements.

Table 4.2   TRANSPORT INFORMATION IN LIDS

| Subject | Information | Required for |
|---|---|---|
| Transport Railways | General description of the system | Planning and general policy formulation. (Level 1) |
| | Description of rail system including controlling authority; track gauge; sidings-locations, length and cargo handling facilities; branch lines-length and purpose; distances to commercial centres/ reference points; loading and structure gauges for section; local weather patterns and effects on rail operations. | Planning and decision-making on deployment and logistic concepts. (Level 2) |
| | As above, plus: Size and nature of hardstands adjacent to sidings, main track; availability of MHE; road access details. | Army detailed planning of force structure and logistics. (Level 3) |
| Roads | General description of major highways and trunk roads. | Level 1 |
| | Location of section, length, pavement width, load classification, critical points if all-weather, time-frame sections are inundated due to weather, bypass routes and alternatives, capacity. | Level 2 |
| | As above, plus: Pavement type, sub-grade classification, gap crossing details. | Level 3 |

Another example of data requirements is shown in Table 4.3 which is an extract of JSP(AS)205(A) under the general Ports and Harbour section. The table lists the detail needed on wharfage facilities and shows the division between the Navy and the Army responsibilities.

Table 4.3   EXTRACT OF JSP(AS)205(A)

| Wharfage (for each wharf) | Service Responsibility |
| --- | --- |
| Name and location | Navy |
| Construction and pile spacing | |
| Length and width | |
| Number of berths | |
| Length of bearing surface | |
| Depth alongside with least charted depth | |
| Nature of bottom | |
| Capacity to continue discharge if bottomed at low water | |
| Height of wharf above chart datum | |
| Nature of lighting and power supplies | |
| Availability of telephone and telex outlets | |
| Distance of supply points from berths | |
| Rate of supply in tonnes per hour | |
| Number of catamarans and sizes | |
| Nature of fire-fighting equipment | |
| Number of supply points for fresh, distilled, and salt water | |
| Number and capacity of FFO and DIESO points | |
| Nature of discharge facilities at each berth | Army |
| Roll-on/roll-off facilities | |
| Maximum weight-bearing factor | |
| Whether connected to railway | |
| Number of tracks on wharf | |
| Gauge of tracks | |
| Whether rails raised or flush | |
| Details of rail access and suitability of wharf approaches for tracked/wheeled vehicles | |
| Engineer data on construction and repair | |

A third example is Table 4.4 which details the Army's logistic requirements for airfield data (taken from LIDS). It should be recognised that the RAAF's needs for airfield information would be much more extensive than the Army's and would include detail on:

- Runway dimensions and construction
- Fuel storage facilities
- Repair facilities
- Fire services
- Communications and radio navigation aids.

Table 4.4   AIRFIELD INFORMATION IN LIDS

| Subject | Information | Required for |
|---|---|---|
| Airfields | Name and location of DOT registered and RAAF airfields and capability for strategic/tactical aircraft. | Level 1 |
| | As above, plus: | Level 2 |
| | Nearest commercial centre for reference point and general description of road/rail links thereto; name and location of other airfields/airstrips and capability for strategic/tactical aircraft; controlling authorities; nearest commercial centre or reference point and general description of road/rail links thereto; operating limitations (weather etc); civilian operators for passenger/freight handling at airfield; terminal facilities available; details of power/water supply. | |
| | As above, plus: | Level 3 |
| | Details of hard standings. Adjacent storage areas, dimensions and capacity, location; open space availability and dimensions. | |

# RESPONSIBILITY FOR DATA GATHERING AT THE TOP LEVEL

Defence Central, Air Force Office and Navy Office are responsible for the collection of some LIS/infrastructure information. However, the bulk of the information is required by and is gathered by the Army. Policy and coordination responsibilities are vested in Army Office in Canberra. Responsibilities for data collection are delegated through Headquarters Field Force Command for operational formations and units and through Headquarters Logistic Command for logistic units. Superimposed on this system are the geographically based Military Districts organisation. Figure 4.1 illustrates this structure.

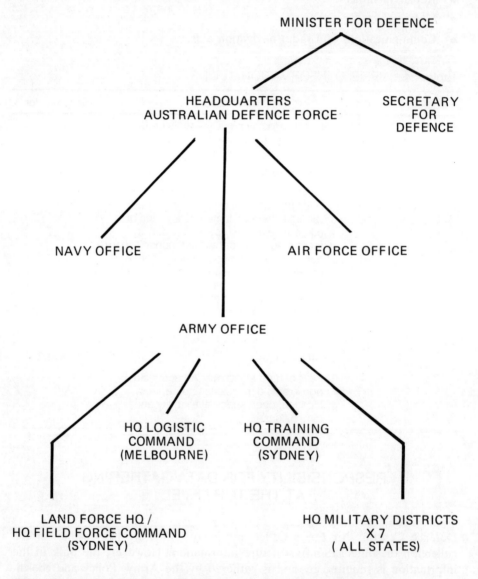

*Figure 4.1    Top-level Defence Organisation, as at October 1987.*

# ARMY OFFICE RESPONSIBILITIES

Army Office is divided into four branches — Operations, Logistics, Personnel and Material. The responsibility for LIS data falls chiefly to Operations Branch with some responsibility for logistics-related data falling within Logistic Branch through the Director of Logistic Plans (DLP). Within Operations Branch the coordinator and policy-maker is the Director General of Operations and Plans. He is assisted with technical advice and resources from the Director of Command and Control Systems (DCCS) for computer applications, from the Director of Intelligence in intelligence matters, and from the Director of Engineers for engineering requirements. Other arms directorates also have policy input. The organisation is illustrated in Figure 4.2.

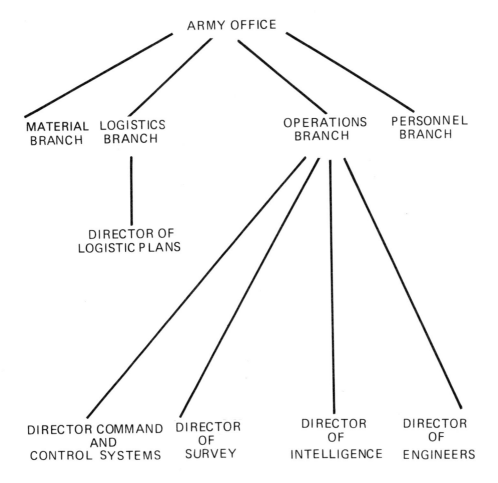

*Figure 4.2 Army Office LIS Responsibilities.*

## THE MILITARY DISTRICTS AND THEIR ROLE IN LIS

In the gathering of infrastructure/LIS information the Military Districts have, under the current concept of AOSI 22/86, been given an important role. The Military Districts organisation is broadly based on state boundaries and their headquarters are located in the state capitals as shown in Figure 4.3. This places the Military Districts in a good position to liaise with state government organisations for the collection of Australian Infrastructure Data, part of which the state LIS should be able to provide. This responsibility would normally fall to the Staff Officer Grade 1 (SO1) Operations of the Headquarters. He would, in turn, task Army units within the state to collect information. Computerised data management systems are presently being introduced to both Army Office and to the Military District Headquarters and may in the future be able to assist in accessing computerised state land information systems. Current activity, however, has been restricted to compiling manual directories, with no development of computer databases of directory information or of links to existing state or Commonwealth digital databases.

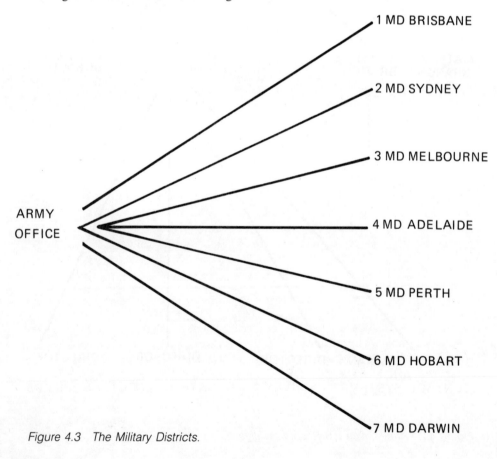

Figure 4.3   The Military Districts.

# ARMY COMPUTER DATABASES

In respect to land information, the Army has two computerised database systems which will play an important role in LIS development. These are AUTOMAP and AUSTACCS.

## AUTOMAP

AUTOMAP is the computerised mapping system run by the Royal Australian Survey Corps at its Army Survey Regiment at Bendigo in Victoria. AUTO-MAP 1 was installed by Systems House Limited of Canada in 1977 and has been gathering digital topographic data since that time. AUTOMAP 2 was installed by the US Intergraph Corporation in 1984 and has increased and improved digital data production.

Digital map data is captured either directly from aerial photography or by the digitisation of existing maps. The database is held in 1:25 000 map areas in four separate files, namely vegetation, drainage, relief and cultural information. The prime current use of the system is the production of 1:50 000 scale topographic maps of areas of defence significance with derived products at small scales produced for both the Army and the Air Force. Figure 4.4 illustrates progress achieved to date in the capture of digital topographic data.

The system also has the capability to produce digital terrain models (DTMs) and to assist in orthophotomap production. AUTOMAP also has the capability to hold and manipulate other geographically based data should a specific need be identified by the Army or Defence. AUTOMAP 3 is planned to expand the data capture facilities to survey units located in Perth, Brisbane, Sydney, Adelaide and Albury/Wodonga, and to improve data structures for uses other than topographic map production. AUTOMAP digital data is at present being used by the Army War Games Centre for terrain modelling. It has been used in the development of a terrain matching navigation system called TACTERM developed by the Defence Aeronautical Research Laboratories and its use is being investigated for other applications including communications planning, mortar locating radar and terrain analysis.

## AUSTACCS

AUSTACCS is an acronym for Australian Army Automated Command and Control System. It is designed to provide computer support in the field for the Army. It will have database and graphics capabilities. The system is still under development. However, a test bed system is installed adjacent to Headquarters 1st Division at Enoggera in Brisbane and includes mobile sub-systems mounted in portable shelters. Development of the operations and intelligence sub-systems is well progressed with an operational capability planned for the late 1980s. AUSTACCS has the potential to provide GIS data to commanders in

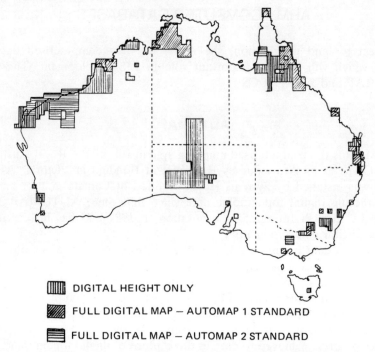

DIGITAL HEIGHT ONLY

FULL DIGITAL MAP – AUTOMAP 1 STANDARD

FULL DIGITAL MAP – AUTOMAP 2 STANDARD

*Figure 4.4    The Royal Australian Survey Corps Digital Map Database, as at August 1987.*

the field. The project team is now investigating possible uses of digital map data and digital terrain models in an operational environment. The overlaying of tactical information and troop dispositions onto the digital map has already been demonstrated successfully.

## OTHER MILITARY GEOGRAPHIC DATABASES

### Maps and Charts

Apart from the digital maps produced on the AUTOMAP system, the Army also produces maps in the scales ranging from 1:10 000 through to 1:2 000 000. These range from orthophotomaps of military installations through to the jet navigation charts used by long-range RAAF aircraft. The Navy has an equivalent system to AUTOMAP called AUTOCHART based in Sydney and is capturing hydrographic data digitally. The Navy Hydrographer also maintains several hydrographic ships and has an active charting program.

## Aerial Photography

Both the Army and the Air Force acquire aerial photography for mapping purposes. They maintain their own aircraft and cameras for this task. Access to this data is normally available to government departments and civilian organisations. The Air Force also has a capability to acquire reconnaissance photography.

## LIDS

The Logistic Infrastructure Data System (LIDS) is operated by the Director of Logistic Plans to provide a database for logistic planning purposes in specific areas of defence significance. It is presently a manual system usually resulting in the production of regional reports covering specific items including:

- Transport systems
- Topography and terrain weather
- Existing resources (medical, repair and supply)
- Natural resources
- Disease surveys
- Existing communications.

Some detail of the transport data and airfield data needed is given in Tables 4.2 and 4.4 respectively.

One report that LIDS has produced is on the Pilbara region and includes town surveys of Port Hedland, Whim Creek, Karratha, Marble Bar, and Newman.[6]

## Headquarters Field Force Command Handbooks

Several regional handbooks have been produced under the direction of HQ Field Force Command to meet strategic planning requirements and provide basic regional information for commanders. Content is generally as outlined previously in Table 4.1. Some areas covered and the dates of publication are:

- North West Western Australia (1976)
- Northern Queensland (1977)
- South West Western Australia (1978)
- Northern New South Wales (1979)
- Kimberley Division and Northern Territory (1983).

# DDAS

Headquarters 1st Division has identified a need for extensive databases on areas of likely deployment for the Division and its units. It has thus instigated a range of studies and information gathering operations in four main areas of interest, namely the Pilbara, the Kimberleys, Arnhem Land, and North Queensland. The study is called the Divisional Deployment Area Study (DDAS) and is actively carried out under the direction of the HQ 1st Division Intelligence Unit. It is, at present, a manual system but involves a much greater depth of information than either LIDS or the HQ Field Force Command handbooks.

A recent product (April 1985) of the DDAS team is a publication called the *Far North Queensland Area Information Handbook* which includes textual information and map overlays on the following:

- Points of Entry (ports and airfields)
- Population
- Shire Boundaries
- Land Use
- Communication
- Vegetation
- Police Boundaries
- Natural Water Resources
- Roads and Railways.

It also includes town surveys on Bamaga, Coen, Cooktown, Laura, and Weipa.

# CSE Studies

The former Central Studies Establishment (CSE) of the Defence Science and Technology Organisation (DSTO), that was based at Campbell Park Offices in Canberra (until its disbandment in late 1987), became involved in modelling the major transportation links for the whole of Australia. It developed an extensive computer database to support these studies.

# The Queensland Model

In Queensland a concept is being developed which involves State government departments continuing in their present role collecting land information and maintaining their own data banks. Whilst departments will also continue to introduce advanced computer technology to assist in this task, they will be linked together in a computer network through a central HUB, probably located at the State Government Computer Centre (SGCC) in Brisbane.

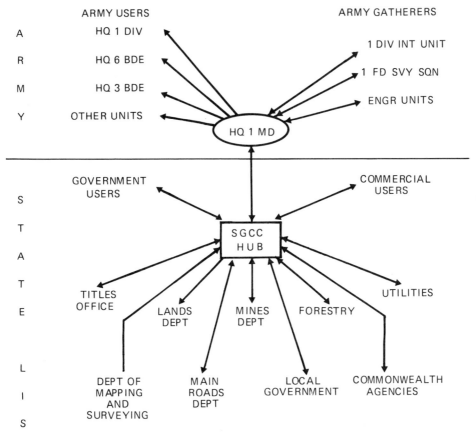

*Figure 4.5 The Queensland Model.*

Future remote terminals throughout Brisbane and the State will provide access for outlying users. Commercial and government users will gain access to LIS data held in state (and some Commonwealth) departments through the HUB. The Army through its computer facilities at HQ 1st Military District, located only one kilometre from the SGCC, could easily become another user of the State LIS. It could extract information through the HUB and then manipulate and reformat the data to its own requirements before dissemination to user formations and units such as HQ 1st Division and HQ 6 Brigade in Brisbane and HQ 3 Brigade (the Operational Deployment Force) at Townsville. Computer links could be established to facilitate data interchange to user units and Army data collectors. The Army would still need to collect some specialist or classified information through its own sources such as HQ 1st Division Intelligence Unit, 1st Field Survey Squadron or Engineer Units. However, the bulk of required data could be obtained through the HUB, ensuring the most up-to-date and accurate data is used for military purposes. The concept is illustrated in Figure 4.5.

## OTHER STATE LIS/GIS

All Australian states now have programs in place for the development and implementation of land information systems. The initial phases of these developments have concentrated on land tenure and land administration requirements. Such systems are now in place in South Australia (LOTS), Western Australia (WALIS) and Queensland (Digital Cadastal Data Base (DCDB)). Some environmental databases have also been developed on a state basis such as those in South Australia and the Northern Territory. Larger local government organisations, such as Sutherland Shire in NSW, and Townsville City and Logan Shire in Queensland, have sophisticated LIS/GIS in place.

All states now have LIS steering committees which coordinate efforts within their states and, at the Commonwealth level, a Commonwealth Land Information Support Group has been established and has produced the first edition of the LANDSEARCH directory of Commonwealth agencies which are involved with land-related data.

To date Defence, and the Army in particular, has not participated in the development of these systems, and little liaison has occurred. Swift action is now needed to remedy this situation.

## CONCLUSION

The Department of Defence, and particularly the Army, has not been idle in gathering LIS data for the defence of this country. A great deal of digital topographic data is available whose potential for uses other than topographic map production is now beginning to be recognised. Very detailed information has been gathered and is maintained on areas of defence significance. The ideal of all needed land-related data being instantly accessible is, however, far from reality, and probably will never be possible. Nevertheless, the introduction of computerised command and control systems and data management systems within Defence at the same time as the states are developing computerised LIS presents a unique opportunity for cooperation in the important task of defence preparedness.

# NOTES

1  Paul Dibb, *Review of Australia's Defence Capabilities*, Report to the Minister for Defence (Australian Government Publishing Service, Canberra, 1986).

2  Department of Defence, *The Defence of Australia 1987*, White Paper presented to Parliament by the Minister for Defence, the Hon. Kim C. Beazley, March 1987 (Australian Government Publishing Service, Canberra, 1987).

3  See Department of Defence, Army Office, *Defence Land Information*, Staff Instruction No. 22/86 (Department of Defence, Canberra, 1986); and Department of Defence, Army Office, The Army Logistic Infrastructure Data System, Departmental Working Paper, Canberra, February 1983.

4  Australian Defence Force, Joint Services Administration, *The Directory of Service Responsibilities for Australian Infrastructure Information*, JSP(AS)205(A) (Department of Defence, Canberra, 1983).

5  Department of Defence, Army Office, *Defence Land Information*.

6  Attachment to Department of Defence, Army Office, The Army Logistic Infrastructure Data System.

# CHAPTER FIVE

# Military Geographic Information

### O.F. Moss   K.J. Lyons
### P. Perrett

The belief that a sound knowledge of natural and man-made features of a battlefield constitutes one of the most important factors in the process of 'military appreciation' has long been recognised. Puniard has cited several examples of the importance of information referred to as 'geographic information', including the following:[1]

> ...geography and the character of the ground bear a close and ever present relation to warfare. They have a decisive influence on the engagement, both to its course and to its planning and exploitation.[2]

> The characteristics of the areas...of operations influence the organisation, equipment, training and logistic requirements of forces...and thus they influence the feasibility of different military strategies.

> The specific battlefield conditions influence the tactics that are used. The relative chance of occurrence of different battlefield conditions in a theatre of operations influences the organisation, equipment and training of military forces.

> ...technological changes impose changes in the military evaluation of geographical conditions.[3]

Reinforcement of the importance of geographic information can be found elsewhere. Field Marshall Montgomery once attributed victory in battle to transportation, administration, and geography, with emphasis on the latter.[4]

If geographic information is accepted as being important, then what is Australia's current situation in relation to acquisition, storage, and use of it? From the comments made by Greville below, it would appear that we face quite a task to achieve the real advantage of knowing the terrain better than any possible enemy:

> Defending one's own territory should give the defender many advantages — spiritual and material — not the least factor being familiarity. Unfortunately, central and northern Australia is as foreign to most Australians as it is to any prospective enemy.[5]

This aspect of lack of familiarity with the terrain in some parts of Australia has to some extent been reduced by the staging of recent exercises in the general regions considered most likely to come under attack. The requirement for current geographic information remains a high priority within these areas, and to a lesser extent in all areas of Australia. This is due to the fact that no amount of exercises can adequately give any commander or troops the 'geographic knowledge-base' required to operate effectively in any area, without consultation with other sources of information.

Whilst geographic information is important, it is but a part of the information gathered by the process known as 'military intelligence'. The relevance of geographic information to the complete military intelligence process is put into context by O'Sullivan and Miller:

> The decision whether to fight or not ought to be informed by a keen sense of geopolitical realities. Although the question of how to fight is governed by technological and economic capabilities, it is essentially a response to environmental possibilities and limitations. Once if and how to fight have been determined, the problems of war become much more specifically geographical and the principal matter for decision is where to commit forces to battle.[6]

Given acceptance of the above, that is, geographic information is important, there are several questions posed:

- What exactly is geographic information, and what elements constitute Military Geographic Information (MGI)?
- What is the importance of each element
  - in general?
  - for specific purposes?
  - in relation to the emphasis of the Dibb Review?[7]
- What are the current policies and adopted procedures for gathering MGI, and can these be improved through the use of civil geographic information systems?

It is intended to approach the topic through a general examination of these questions.

## WHAT IS MILITARY GEOGRAPHIC INFORMATION?

### Military Intelligence

There are many types of geographic and other information required by the military user, as Puniard notes:

> Geographic information is but a part of the overall requirement for intelligence by the military, along with strategic and economic intelligence to assess the intentions of potential enemies and intelligence about an enemy's capabilities and equipment.[8]

When considering information five aspects can be considered:
- Data gathering
- Data collation
- Data synthesis

- Information presentation
- Information dissemination.

Gathering information on objectives, likely approaches to and of the enemy, the location of obstacles and movement channels, all require consideration. These must also be viewed from a possible enemy's point of view. In addition, information must be provided concerning the logistic situation of one's own forces, such as manpower and material.

Once this data has been collected it must be collated into *military intelligence*. Decisions can be made on where and what force to commit, as well as movement and deployment plans. Locations for attack and defence depend heavily on the input of position-related information.

The process of converting geographic information into military intelligence is explained by Puniard:

> Land related information, to be of use to the military commander in the field often needs to be edited and restructured into a format immediately digestible and of direct relevance to the task in hand. This is the process of the conversion of 'Information' into 'Intelligence'. Intelligence is often presented in the form of map overlays or as a concise listing or report specific to current operations.[9]

Military intelligence can be considered as containing four separate components, as illustrated in Figure 5.1 below.

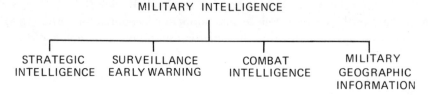

Figure 5.1   *The Components of Military Intelligence.*

## Military Geographic Information

Puniard divides geographic information into two main areas, namely:

> *Infrastructure* information, primarily about man made features but with a geographical location, and *Terrain* information, primarily concerned with the natural features of the terrain.
>
> There is also an area of overlap in certain topographic features such as roads, railways and bridges which are part of the terrain but also have infrastructure elements.[10]

It could be argued that environmental elements, such as climatic and weather conditions, contribute to the conduct of military operations, and therefore must be known prior to the planning of any operation. Environmental characteristics information can be added as a third element of MGI. Figure 5.2 illustrates the three components of MGI.

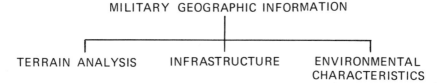

Figure 5.2   *The Components of Military Geographic Information.*

# ELEMENTS OF MILITARY GEOGRAPHIC INFORMATION

The three components of MGI illustrated above are examined individually in the following sections. Included in the examination is a definition of the terms, the importance, functions, information content, and the current accessibility of data produced for each element.

## Terrain Analysis

### Definition

Some of the definitions for terrain analysis include:

> Terrain analysis — The process of interpreting natural and man-made features of a geographic area, and the influence of weather and climate, to determine effects on Military Operations.[11]

> Terrain analysis is the process of collecting, analysing and storing geographic information on the natural and man-made features of the terrain and its interpretation in combination with other relevant factors to provide information and advice about the effects of the terrain on military operations.[12]

Terrain analysis is therefore a heading under which many functions, specific activities, and procedures are grouped. In this chapter terrain analysis is equated with terrain evaluation.

Terrain analysis is essentially an examination of the properties also referred to as *factors* of the earth's surface. Some factors used by the US Corps of Engineers, Engineering Topographic Laboratory (ETL) are:

- Natural construction materials
- Surface drainage
- Surface material
- Vegetation.

The analysis task(s) to be performed dictates the type of information and level of detail to be acquired and stored for that property or factor. These details are referred to as *data elements*. Over 5000 individual data elements have been identified. The case of vegetation, for example, is divided into the following element headings by ETL:[13]

- Vegetation area boundaries
- Area identification
- Vegetation type

These elements are 'dynamic', that is, they need periodic revision.

- Height to top of canopy
- Canopy closure
- Stems per hectare
- Stem spacing
- Stem diameter
- Species
- Ground cover
- Litter
- Height to lowest branches
- Representative transect
- Seasonality

These elements only change slowly, if at all. Once they are defined for an area, minimal revision is required.

This examination is undertaken for the purpose of making predicted statements about terrain character and its effect on military operations at a locality without the necessity of visiting the site.

Attributes are spatially related to each other by some system of linking the attribute to its position on the earth, usually by some form of coordinate or map reference system. The referencing systems employed are similar to those described in Chapter 2. Similarly, the creation of databases for terrain analysis bears a strong resemblance to those assembled for a GIS. A terrain analysis database could even be considered as a subset of that for a GIS.

Figure 5.3 shows diagrammatically how these properties and attributes are linked. Any number of properties and attributes may be linked according to the requirements of users and the extent or level of analysis to be performed.

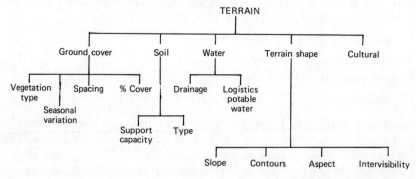

Figure 5.3   Terrain Analysis, Part 1: Establishing the Properties and Attributes.

Terrain analysis is not just listing or detailing these properties and attributes, however. Terrain analysis attempts to group together user-specified properties or attribute types in graphical representations for the purposes of planning and estimation of activities that rely upon these terrain properties.

There are several forms of this process of 'recombination' of data, due to the many perceived needs. Topographic maps in a sense represent a basic form of terrain analysis in that they display one combination of attributes (albeit a widely useable combination) with which many types of users plan and estimate. Another recognised form of terrain analysis is the so called 'going map'. This shows the likelihood of cross-country overland transport by bringing together a specific combination of the properties and attributes.

Figure 5.4 illustrates the USA Defense Mapping Agency (DMA) example of the second part of the terrain analysis, that is, the recombination of the data to form useable products. It is only one of the many methods of employing terrain analysis and will be examined in more detail below.

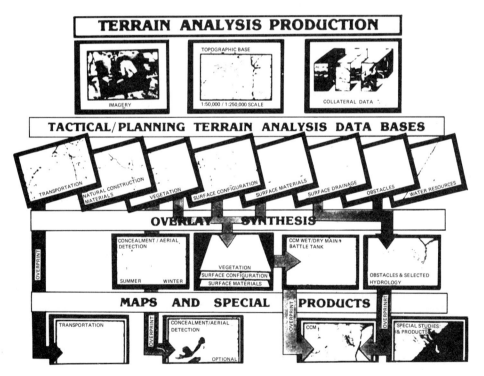

Figure 5.4   Terrain Analysis, Part 2: Recombination of Data.

Source: US Defense Mapping Agency (DMA), slide in possession of authors.

## Importance of Terrain Analysis

Each of the above examples is useful. However, is terrain analysis beneficial to the military in general? Lyons provides some reasons for it being considered so:

> To make the best use of terrain, commanders and planners must know how to recognise the different types of terrain in their theatre and what they are good for. There is a need to know more precisely what information we need about the terrain so as to make judgements about the terrain effect on operations.[14]

O'Connor adds to this by providing a general idea of the use of terrain evaluation when he states:

> The purpose of terrain evaluation is to provide military commanders with reliable estimates of the effect of the terrain on their activities and machines. The requirements of detail vary from the generality required by the strategist to the detail of the tactician.[15]

## Uses of Terrain Analysis

Lyons notes the following points in relation to the uses of terrain evaluation:

> If we define terrain evaluation as the evaluation (judging the worth) of environmental factors that effect defence operations on the landmass and the production of likely effects on operations, then it is possible to state some broad general uses of terrain evaluation, and then expand them into various areas. Defence operations vary from those purely of a military nature, i.e., offensive and defensive operations, to those closely related to civil tasks, i.e., road building and base construction. The uses below relate to military activities only.[16]

The paper then lists general and specific military functional areas served by terrain evaluation. The complete list is summarised in the following paragraphs, which provide a fairly comprehensive list of uses for terrain analysis.

*Strategic*

- Ascertain according to terrain the size, type, and location of forces to be deployed, and the suitability of existing lines of communication to support the force.

*Operations*

- Determine terrain factors which maximise our own use of equipment and tactics and minimise an enemy's.
- Predict an enemy's advance rates by the terrain to be covered and his transport. In addition this may allow us to predict the location and sequence of enemy objectives.
- Plan rapid deployment routes.
- Select aircraft drop zones and landing grounds.

- Increase the effectiveness of small force groups by selecting terrain most suited to their travel and weapons.
- Increase the effectiveness of weapon systems.

### Training

- Select training areas with similar characteristics to those over which we expect to fight. Exercise men and equipment in these conditions to determine the effect of terrain and the most suitable tactics.

### Design

Use known terrain factors in which the equipment is to operate as input data for the design of equipment and vehicles.
(An important study using terrain analysis was Project Waler which used a computer-assisted information and analysis system over North West Australia to determine the most important factors for the design of the Army's replacement for the armoured personnel carrier, using an Environmental Systems Research Institute (ESRI) system.)

### Engineer Tasks

- Selection of suitable sites for airfields, bridges and route location of roads, according to construction materials and surface terrain.
- Provide more accurate estimates of time and materials required for the tasks prior to visiting the site.

## Current Information Accessibility

With limited resources (until recently, mostly manual) with which to undertake terrain analysis, few products have been forthcoming. Additionally, manual terrain analysis techniques do not lend themselves to aggregating and comparing large areas, a feature which is required for Australian conditions. Therefore, other than the production of the normal topographic maps, little is available which can be considered as valuable terrain analysis.

Although several forms of terrain analysis are used in other parts of the world there has been little proper terrain analysis undertaken in Australia. Possibly due to a lack of perceived benefit, few resources have been devoted to terrain analysis. Only basic terrain analysis has been attempted using labour-intensive manual techniques or basic cartography to create special-purpose maps and overprints in limited areas.

Two examples of the very few terrain analysis studies to date include the Shoalwater Bay Training Area[17] and a newly undertaken task in the Pucka-punyal Range, for management functions of the range area (e.g., soil conservation).

Some work has begun towards the creation of a database, in the form of digital topographic map data, from which later stages of terrain analysis may eventuate. Although the old adage that a map's information is outdated as soon as it is printed must be considered somewhat of a drawback to the accuracy of any information held, it is nevertheless a valuable data store, as much of this type of data only changes slowly.

## Overseas Terrain Evaluation

The most extensive published information on terrain analysis comes from the Engineering Topographic Laboratory (ETL) and the Defense Mapping Agency (DMA) in the United States. DMA provides as one of its services a series of overlays for tactical and strategic planning. This requires a topographic database together with additional imagery and other collateral data. From this source data 'neutral factor overlays', such as transportation, vegetation and surface configuration, are produced. These are synthesised in specific combinations to produce overprints which are applied to the topographic base maps to disseminate the terrain information.

A great amount of detailed work has already been carried out by ETL. Whilst similar to the above-mentioned process, the work of ETL is of a more detailed nature. ETL uses analytical modelling to compute the relevance of individual factors. This results in variations of output products. For example, the transportation model can be varied to incorporate characteristics and limitations of each vehicle used by the military, resulting in several specific vehicle overprints. Examples of ETL products are as follows:

- Intelligence Presentation of the Battlefield (IPB) graphics
- Built-up area maps
- Cross-Country Movement (CCM) graphics
- Cover and concealment maps
- Fields of fire.

Puniard makes the observation that whilst US and Australian maps contain a similar amount of vegetation elements, those of the USSR present far greater detail.[18] Moreover, while the US maintains a commitment to terrain analysis, Australia does not. The fact that the two main world powers maintain additional terrain-relevant information should lead us to consider one of two alternatives:

(1)   Increase the amount of information on our maps, or
(2)   Undertake terrain analysis.

As map sheets already contain an amount of data which could be considered cluttered (and notwithstanding other influencing factors), the second of the alternatives is to be preferred.

The principle of the United States method of terrain analysis (i.e., combination of neutral factor overlays) would appear to be applicable to the Australian situation, as Australia already has partially created databases which could be used. However, whilst the principle may be applicable, the method of operation may not. DMA and ETL use mostly manual systems for data recombination. This system is labour intensive and could be improved dramatically through the employment of computer techniques. This is currently under development. Australia should be aware of the problems faced in a manual system and develop a terrain analysis strategy accordingly.

## Infrastructure Information

### Definition

As stated previously, infrastructure is concerned with man-made structures and facilities. Each individual structure or facility has some descriptive attribute data to define its capacity and availability. These attributes are essential to determine its ability to be employed or used in given circumstances. The important requirements are that this data is kept up-to-date and is fully available to meet any possible contingency. If either of these requirements is not met, then the data is unreliable and is probably useless. In contrast to terrain data there is a tendency for infrastructure data to change rapidly, thus there is a higher maintenance commitment.

### Importance of Infrastructure Information

The importance of infrastructure information is demonstrated by examining how it can be used. A comprehensive and available study of infrastructure information allows a commander to plan effectively. It affects the military appreciation process by influencing the course of action to be undertaken in many ways. The presence or absence of a structure or facility initiates a sequence of alternate courses which require decisions.

If a particular facility or structure is not present in an Area of Operations (AO), then the first decision is whether or not it is important to the circumstances? If the answer is yes, then can it be constructed in the time frame? If no, then there is no action. If the answer to the second question is again yes, then where is the most suitable location for it and what is the manpower required? The process is obviously an iterative one as there are many alternatives to be considered.

Where a structure or facility is available, is it the only one available, and what are the alternatives? This, in turn, leads to the selection of a location, and indeed the plan for, and the conduct of, a specific action. For example, if a suitable aircraft landing area is available in an AO, then air transport may well be used for troop deployment. If, however, there are no roads suitable for ongoing transport and/or there are no civilian support facilities, then this course of action may be considered unsuitable.

### Information Content

Infrastructure information concerns man-made features of the earth and their relative positions. An indication of the scope of information required for the military was given in the first document to be produced by the Army on infrastructure, *The Directory of Service Responsibilities for Australian Infrastructure Information* (JSP(AS)205)(A).[19] As described in Chapter 4, this document details the collection procedures and responsibilities for the following types of information:

- Ports and harbours
- Beaches
- Airfields
- Resources and utilities
- Communications
- Transport
- Civilian stores support/repair and maintenance facilities
- Terrain and general.

## Current Data Accessibility

Much of the infrastructure information listed above concerns civilian organisations and facilities. Army Office Staff Instruction (AOSI) 22/86 provides the following list (by no means comprehensive) of the sources of strategic information for all three elements of MGI noted in this chapter[20]:

- Maps and charts
- Gazetteers
- Resource atlases
- Published books
- Reports by statutory authorities
- Telephone directories
- Commercial directories
- Resource studies.

AOSI 22/86 goes on to say that tactical information is usually obtained from a more detailed study of sources such as:

- Special-purpose maps and surveys
- Technical publications
- Military reports
- Consultation with appropriate authorities
- Construction plans and specifications
- Electoral rolls
- Special-to-purpose surveys.

This information is generally held by one or more of the responsible government or semi-government organisations. Information is usually not in the form required by the user, and hence some collation is required. Additional data collation may be necessary to piece together segments of data obtained from similar inquiries to several organisations, and to process this into information useful for decision-making.

The current methods of obtaining data range from requests to private industry and government organisations, to actual ground reconnaissance and data gathering operations in the area. This procedure is necessary due to the widely varying methods of data storage and its subsequent availability from within each of the data holding agencies. In addition, some types of data required by the military are not maintained by any other organisations on a regular basis, for example, lists and characteristics of fuel suppliers. Other types of information would require such extensive data searches that it is frequently more effective and accurate to undertake an autonomous collection program.

## Environmental Characteristics

### Definition

Environmental characteristics are those such as temperature and rainfall which contribute to the regional climate of an area. Each has some effect on the conduct of military operations. In general, the greater the climatic extreme, the greater the effect on military operations. This occurs because troops are trained and equipment built according to commonly occurring conditions.

### Importance of Environmental Information

Environmental information can affect both the timing and location of any military action. Examples illustrate the affect of environment on military operations. Recent experience in northern Australia has demonstrated the detrimental effect of heat and humidity on human and mechanical performance. When planning for operations in such climates, commanders are now aware that it may be necessary for troops to undergo acclimatisation, thus extending response times. Alternatively, military operations should be planned to coincide with the period normally associated with the most favourable conditions, if the stategic and tactical situation allows.

Rainfall has a marked affect on the mobility of vehicles in particular, however its effect is best studied in conjunction with terrain to determine overland mobility. Up-to-date information goes a long way towards the prediction of suitable methods of operation.

The north is subject to great seasonal variation, and it is desirable to study and thus understand the effects of the seasons. In this way it may be possible to predict the feasibility of movement via several routes to an objective given the recorded temperature and rainfall during the preceding period. This would reduce the necessity to gain the information through patrolling the area.

## Current Data Accessibility

The current agencies responsible for gathering environment information are the regional meteorology departments. The information collected is generally that of a graphical historical nature. Current meteorological data is gathered by some artillery units.

# CURRENT PROCEDURES

## Policies for MGI Collection

Whilst the policies for the general collection of MGI have been promulgated, with some minor exceptions there is little 'hard data' actually gathered as a result of the direction given by JSP(AS)205(A) and AOSI 22/86. In practice the documents serve only as 'wish lists' of the types of data that should be collected. Due to factors such as manpower shortages, it is unlikely that a high percentage of the data will ever be collected for large areas. The instructions therefore serve only to formalise the creation of a 'telephone directory' or data proprietor network, from which specific data can be acquired. The undertaking of Logistic Infrastructure Directory Studies (LIDS) exemplifies the belief that additional action was necessary.

To date most policy has been directed towards infrastructure information, with little aimed at terrain analysis or environmental information.

### Terrain Analysis

As the only step towards terrain analysis has been the assembly of databases of terrain information through topographic mapping, only policy for this task has been formed. This policy is given as a tasking directive each year following agreement between the National Mapping Council and the Army.

JSP(AS)205(A) details the category of information relevant to Australian Infrastructure Information (AII), for example:

- Physiography
- Vegetation
- Soils
- Geology
- Land rise
- Hydrology
- Drainage
- Special physical phenomena.

It nominates the responsibility for assembling this terrain data to the Army, specifically the Royal Australian Survey Corps (RA Svy) and Royal Australian Engineers (RAE).

JSP(AS)205(A) also allocates responsibilities for the entire mapping and charting program with the exception of nautical charts (Navy Hydrographer) to RA Svy.

## Infrastructure Information

JSP(AS)205(A) promulgates an index to the types of infrastructure information that are required for military planning purposes. The Directory also nominates:

- The *responsible military authority* for the collection of all types of infra-structure information required.
- The *procedures* to be adopted for obtaining and forwarding the informa-tion.
- The *response time* in which it is to be provided by that authority.

Specific-to-Army policy is issued by Army Office Staff Instructions (AOSI). In practice these instructions serve as planning guides for defence. AOSI 22/86 lists the available sources for data at strategic and tactical level.

## Environment Conditions

JSP(AS)205(A) refers to the collection of climatic and meteorological data under the 'Terrain and General' section. The Royal Australian Air Force is the nominated responsible authority for its collection.

## Current Situation

There are at least four corps within the Army that maintain information on terrain or infrastructure. These are: The Royal Australian Survey Corps, Australian Intelligence Corps, Royal Australian Engineers, and Royal Austra-lian Corps of Transport. Within the Army command structure each maintains a specific type of information relevant to its official corps and unit role.

In the military situation, two elements of MGI are currently provided by the above corps. These elements are information gathering for terrain analysis by mapping/charting and infrastructure information.

## Mapping/Charting

The situation stated by the Dibb Review in March 1986 was:

> . . at the current rate of progress, it will be more than 20 years before comprehensive up-to-date maps and charts of priority areas will be available.[21]

A similar 'warning' was made by Holden who stated:

> . . that if the present (1981) commitment is maintained, Australia will enter 1990 with:

   i) 53% of the land covered with contoured 1:100 000 maps, on average 15 years out of date,

   ii) 25% of the land covered with orthophotomaps based on photography up to 30 years out of date,

   iii) full coverage of new edition 1:250 000 maps,

   iv) 1:25 000 and 1:50 000 map coverage of limited areas as a requirement of the States and the defence forces.[22]

It would therefore appear that some method of hastening the pace of map production was a major requirement for the future. The Dibb Review and subsequent White Paper recommended some measures to combat precisely this problem, including personnel and financial assistance.

The current methods for presenting the limited amount of terrain data presently available are generally restricted to two-dimensional map-like products and printed reports. (The benefits of using other methods will be discussed below.) The present methods of transferring gathered data to other parts of the military include the following:

- Aerial photographs
- Topographic maps
- Orthophoto maps
- Thematic maps
- Overlays of specific nature
- Printed reports.

For each of these forms of data presentation, some procedure which extracts and collates the required command information or military intelligence is necessary. This requires personnel to be employed on this time-consuming and labour-intensive task, in turn reducing the manpower available for other important work.

## Infrastructure

Infrastructure information is gathered by all of the previously listed corps. Logistic Command has also undertaken several studies known as the Logistic Infrastructure Data System (LIDS). These were completed to assist the Chief of Logistics to determine a logistic concept of operations in locations of specific military interest. Their initiation was due to a perception that little work had been completed in accordance with JSP(AS)205(A), concerning infrastructure data gathering. Additionally it was believed that the response times given in the JSP(AS)205(A) were not consistent with the usual planning process. Several reports were completed in the northern regions of Australia.

Intelligence Corps maintains comprehensive studies of specific areas of strategic military importance. Extensive studies include the Divisional Deployment Area Study (DDAS), which is a manual system maintained by the 1st Division Intelligence Unit. Handbooks of the study areas are maintained for each area, and data is extracted for commander's briefings and exercises. The types of data recorded includes the following:

- Analysis of Area of Operations — including map references
- Local government and police
- Population and land use
- Telecommunications
- Health and medical
- Climate
- Towns — data and installations
- Airfields
- Beach landing sites
- Ports and harbours
- Road and rail systems
- Route reconnaissance reports.

Both infrastructure studies rely on a manual approach to data collection. It therefore follows that these systems will only be correct immediately following printing of the reports and maps etc. Additional revision on manually operated systems is extremely time-consuming and is often undertaken only in limited areas and as a result of a major exercise requirement.

A great deal of data is currently held by one or more large non-military organisations as a matter of daily operation. Some of these are already accessed manually by the military. Many already have or are in the process of developing computer-assisted systems to maintain their data. Creation and employment of a military-selective 'sieve and display' mechanism using computer communications linked to the civilian organisations would achieve efficient and up-to-date collection of data without the necessity to undertake data revision or storage of large databases.

## THE WHITE PAPER AND DIBB REVIEW

The *Review of Australia's Defence Capabilities* by Paul Dibb contained the most recent and in-depth analysis of defence policy as at March 1986. The White Paper on *The Defence of Australia 1987*, published in March 1987, represented the most detached public analysis of defence policy for many years! The White Paper

> 'sets the policy course for a decade of development towards self-reliance in the defence and security of Australia'.[23]

It is believed that these documents are of prime importance to the development of considerations for a systematic means of improving the capability of the ADF. Sections from either publication which are related to the development of a military GIS are listed in the following paragraphs, together with relevant conclusions which can be drawn from them.

# ADF Structure

Successive reviews of the strategic basis of Australian defence policy have noted the advantages an opponent might see in a campaign of sustained low level military pressure against Australia. The use of military force to harass remote settlements and other targets in northern Australia, our off-shore territories and resource assets, and shipping in proximate areas could be decided upon as an attempt to demonstrate Australia's vulnerability and thereby force political concessions over some disputed issue. In these circumstances, the attacker could hold the operational initiative. Attacks could be widely dispersed and unpredictable. Relatively modest military pressure could oblige Australia to respond with quite disproportionate effort.

The adversary could, if he wished, sustain low level activity virtually indefinitely. For Australia, there would be the cost of undertaking a wide variety of operations and of maintaining forces at a high state of readiness. Our operations would require highly effective intelligence and surveillance capabilities and forces with significant range, endurance and mobility.[24]

*Comment*: For intelligence to be effective requires access to and use of all available information sources to consider the most appropriate strategy and priority tasks.

The paucity of population and of transport and other infrastructure in northern Australia, and the nature of the land, would tend to focus military operations of substance on a few areas, for example, airfields, off-shore resource projects, shipping in coastal waters, port facilities, and communication and transport links.[25]

*Comment*: Therefore a major priority for ground forces is the protection and defence of:

● Military and infrastructure bases

● Defence of civil population

● Other key points.

Thus there is a need to know the locations and infrastructure attributes of these features, and to be able to plan for their defence requirements, that is, geographic information is of major importance.

Against the prospect that the adversary had been able to land and sustain more substantial forces, we need expansion base elements for conventional ground force conflict, but not at a high level of preparedness.[26]

*Comment*: The time taken to develop a MGI system suitable to support more substantial conflict is long, therefore development must begin at once to enable sufficient development time. Many civilian organisations already have GIS skills, therefore some time will be saved through cooperating with and studying these organisations.

These requirements indicate changes of emphasis rather than a significant departure from existing organisation. We need a force structure that includes a light air portable force, capable of rapid deployment; forces capable of following up an initial deployment; and the availability of greater combat power to reinforce deployed formations if necessary. In addition, elements capable of deploying to defend vital defence installations and national infrastructure, and a logistic organisation capable of supporting the deployment and subsequent operations of these forces, need to be given priority.[27]

*Comment*: Therefore a comprehensive and extensive area MGI database is required to support these forces.

## Civil Industry

Civil industry should contribute to the maintenance, adaption and through-life support of defence equipment.[28]

*Comment*: As a general principle, resources in civil infrastructure should only be duplicated by the ADF if:
- They are not readily available in peacetime, and
- Cannot be guaranteed in a combat situation.

This was referred to by Dibb.[29] Civilian GIS are already developing, therefore defence should attempt to link into these established databases.

The capacity to maintain, repair, modify and adapt defence equipment to the Australian environment, independently of overseas sources, is of fundamental importance for our combat effectiveness in all levels of conflict. This requires Australian involvement in design, development and production to acquire the necessary detailed knowledge, skills, and facilities.[30]

*Comment*: This may mean greater interaction and civilian access to ADF equipment. Civilians and military could work together to develop specific geographic information projects, as well as training individual military personnel in civilian agencies and vice versa.

It is important that Defence considerations influence civil infrastructure developments particularly in the north.[31]

*Comment*: Therefore it should also influence the types of data other government and local authorities collect and hold. This may be achieved through defence participation in the development of GIS to foster a cooperative spirit amongst participants, and hence establish and obtain its requirements.

## Technology

The effectiveness of the ADF depends to a significant extent on the maintenance of a high level of technology. Australia should favour advanced technology where it confers an operational advantage, reduces manpower or life-cycle cost, avoids early obsolescence or the need for additional equipment, simplifies operation and support, or where it is otherwise particularly suited to Australia's strategic circumstances.[32]

*Comment*: GIS is 'high tech' and certainly confers an operational advantage to its participants.

> This Government's policy of self-reliance in defence calls particularly for the enhancement of our own capabilities for technological support, modification and development. We cannot rely completely on imported technology and offshore technological support. Australia's strategic circumstances pose challenges that sometimes call for unique and therefore local solutions.
>
> While we procure major defence systems off the shelf from foreign suppliers, there are also some important Australian defence requirements not readily met by systems available overseas. In these cases there is a need for indigenous Australian development. This applies in particular to intelligence, surveillance and sensor equipment, together with associated command and control systems, which need to be tailored to Australia's specific environment. Such capabilities have priority when local technological development is under consideration.[33]

*Comment:* A great deal of expertise has already been developed in this field by civilian organisations involved directly in GIS evolution.

## Need for Geographic Information

> The availability of comprehensive and up-to-date military maps and charts, together with a detailed knowledge of the environment and its infrastructure, is fundamental to the effective conduct of military operations. The size of Australian sovereign territory and our area of direct military interest makes this an imposing task. Priority in this work is being given to operationally important geographic areas.[34]

*Comment*: The high priority given to speeding up this task can be assisted through the use of automated data gathering and through linking to established databases. Mapping and charting is but one aspect of geographic information.

> We need to be able to determine the performance in our own environment of equipment of both overseas and local origin and to modify and adapt overseas equipment as necessary to improve its performance in our likely theatres of military operations. For this we need a detailed knowledge of our physical environment (climate and meteorology, terrain characteristics, optical, infrared and radio propagation, oceanography, and ionospheric phenomena) so that we can understand its influence on the conduct and effectiveness of operations and the performance of equipment and systems.[35]

*Comment*: This is in essence terrain analysis. To undertake it requires that the data is both comprehensive and available in a readily accessible system. Much is held by civil authorities. A military system should draw from these rather than duplicate data gathering.

● Strategic intelligence is central to the adoption of future actions.[36]

*Comment*: A part of the intelligence required is geographic information, thus there is a need for a geographic information system capable of providing alternatives to assist decision-makers, or Decision Support Systems (DSS).

The Government has given a high priority to the development of an automated system to support the new command arrangements. This system will be capable of displaying, recalling and transmitting a wide variety of data,[37]
Computer based information systems are being developed to support the decision making of operational and higher level commanders.[38]

*Comment*: The network of all data sources and available data, including geographic, for systems such as these must be considered during their development to achieve the most efficient system.

# A POSSIBLE SOLUTION TO INFORMATION REQUIREMENTS

## Observation on the Current Situation

Whilst the current methods of MGI acquisition have undoubtedly proved valuable in use, they are now comparatively cumbersome as they are basically manual techniques adopted from before the advent of computer technology. The means of analysing and collating the data collected by these methods are inefficient compared to new techniques. Some method of improving the efficiency of Australian Defence Force (ADF) resources is therefore necessary.

The following summarises the observations which are important to the development of a solution:

- Manual MGI acquisition, analysis, and presentation techniques are cumbersome.
- Computerised geographic information system technology with highly refined capabilities in each of the above procedures is developing rapidly in all states of Australia.
- A great deal of geographic information useful for the military will be available to all system participants.
- The involvement of civil resources must be considered to increase ADF capability.

## A Possible Solution

From the preceding sections it should be recognised that the situation with respect to MGI is not ideal. The recent introduction of widespread computer databases and information systems have provided an opportunity for the military to improve an ageing manual information system.

Briefly, the solution is for computer-assisted MGI acquisition, analysis, and presentation which employs the integration of civil databases into a specialised military GIS. The operation of such a system is explained in the following sections.

## A Suggested Method of Operation

The Army policy for gathering MGI[39] specifies that while Army Office is responsible for the provision of a collection plan, the headquarters of each Military District (MD) is responsible for the operation of the AII System within their geographic boundary. This includes the collection, storage, and dissemination of data.

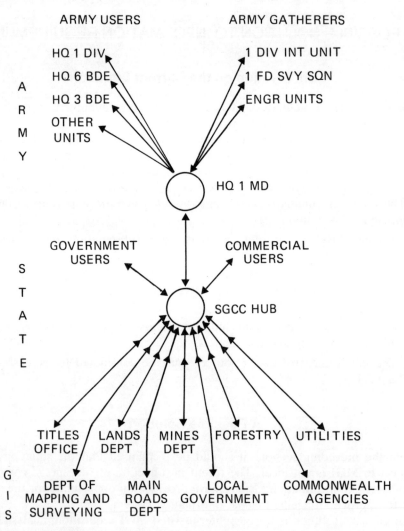

*Figure 5.5   The Military Link to a State GIS.*

Source: D.J. Puniard, The Vegetation Element in Military Terrain Intelligence.... Master's Project, Department of Surveying, University of Queensland, 1986.

As most of the GISs are state-based, MDs could establish access to the considerable databases of the respective GIS authorities. This would minimise the duplication of data collection and maintenance in many cases already undertaken as a state function. This access would be provided by data communications via satellite for remote and/or mobile operations, or Telecom land lines in more established facility locations. From these databases the staff could extract those data elements which were of relevance to the tasks currently under way and process them accordingly. Analysis for strategic operations would tend to be performed prior to exercises and operations, with the tactical analysis requirement being performed as demanded by the situation.

Figure 5.5 illustrates the possible digital data links between Military District Army users and the state-based Queensland GIS for an automated data acquisition system. This need not be the case, however. A national military system would see the replacement in the diagram of HQ 1 MD with a single analysis centre drawing from all states, with distribution of data to users accordingly.

Similar GIS networks could be envisaged for all states, thereby providing military access to an extremely wide database. Coordination of these data sources could be through either MDs or Army Office, depending on the scale and coverage of the data.

A generalised diagram of the sources and procedures to be adopted by Defence in the suggested system is shown at Figure 5.6. The diagram illustrates sources of data from all government and non-government organisations. Data is drawn from these organisations only as required. Initially it is sampled to confirm quality, availability, and suitability for planned purposes, and then tested and accessed as the requirement exists. Some data may not be available from civilian sources and may require defence collection and input.

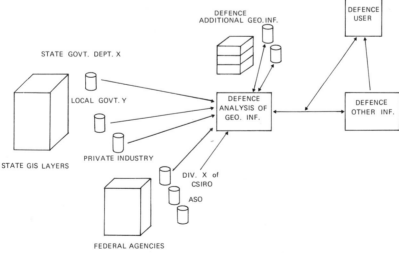

*Figure 5.6   Sources and Procedures for MGIS.*

Defence analysis involves several processes:

- Sieving for relevant data from all sources and creating an availability network.

- Storage of some low volatility data or complex processed information continuously used. 'Defence other information' refers to specific-to-defence infrastructure information, together with information which may be classified and held under security.

- Compiling and delivering to a user network, relevant data in a suitable information format, for example, reports, graphs, forecasts, maps.

The above process, firstly, requires analysis of the defence requirement. Secondly, the processes must be translated into data models. These models result in data movements which eventually achieve the three analysis processes. Data models need to be created specifically for defence purposes. The accuracy and flexibility of the data model design will later reflect in the capability of the system to fulfil its roles.

All geographical information is available to the defence users in a format tailored to meet their needs. The defence users, in turn, provide additional data and information, together with feedback concerning the information value.

No conclusive suggestion is made for either a state-based system or a national military system as both have advantages. The state-based system has the primary advantage of proximity to most database locations and development centres of GIS. The central system, on the other hand, has the advantages of expertise and hardware concentration.

### Terrain Analysis

The types of data elements or factor overlays required by the Australian military would most likely be similar (though certainly not the same) as those of DMA terrain analysis. The US system requires a vast amount of detailed data that Australia may never have. The size and population of Australia virtually precludes the availability of such data. Australian products therefore are not necessarily going to be the same as those of the US. The requirements of the ADF must therefore be examined in depth prior to commitment of resources to a terrain analysis system. The system should be developed using all available data resources and using Australian technology. This will ensure its application to Australian conditions and development of high technology within Australia.

Neutral factor overlays are similar to the basic form of data storage for GIS. As there will be links to many databases of this type, neutral factor overlays may be an excellent starting point for development of terrain analysis. With additional processing of the overlays according to an Australian military-defined process, final terrain analysis products such as cross-country movement or camouflage and concealment maps and graphics data may result.

Data models for terrain analysis will need to be created specifically. With suitable data models for additional processing of the input overlay data, they may prove to be successful for further terrain analysis.

### Infrastructure

Much of this data is held by state civil authorities. It would be expected that sources and hence data availability would be increased markedly by using an automated system drawing on the database network of civil authorities. Whilst most required data may well be available in some form, the determination of requirements satisfied by the existing databases would be time-consuming. Once complete, however, only monitoring of new data and its sources would be required.

Generation of infrastructure reports could be tested by large- and small-scale exercises. This would assist in directing the method of operation (i.e., hold no data and collect all as required; or hold some data and collect other data).

### Environment

Two types of data need to be available — historical records and forecasts/reports. As the former changes little it would be feasible either to request data as needed or to hold the data permanently if it is to be used regularly. Meteorological forecasts and regional condition reports are issued for a specific timeframe. For this reason they must be transferred to users with minimal delay. Digital data transfer provides an excellent means of achieving this.

## Advantages

### General

Some general advantages which may accrue to the military through the use of such a system are as follows:

- Provides access to more up-to-date data. The organisation charged by statute with responsibility for the data will maintain that data. Military users draw on current data as required.
- Quicker access to data.
- Provides access to a wider range of data, due to simplicity of access.
- Computer linking is quicker than a manual search and collation once the algorithms are established.
- Cost of data is less once 'up-front' expenses are met.
- Because of above points, the flow-on benefits include:
  - Quicker decision capability as the information is available at call.
  - Improved quality of decisions through greater variety and more timely information.
  - Availability to consider alternatives quickly. Several feasible alternatives can be compared using rapid and available digital data. Algorithms are possible to compare alternatives which may provide solutions.

*Specific*

- Access to a large number of government and non-government authority information databases. Operations to gather the information presently required by the Army would revolve around computer searches of civil databases. Operation MIDOP undertaken in 1983 by Royal Australian Engineers demonstrated that most of the information was available through civil authorities. The information not currently available from these sources may be sought through traditional, but reduced, ground reconnaissance operations.

- Searching of databases using one or more 'spatial keys' negates the need for constant referencing to maps of varying and inconsistent scales.

- Costs of data collation would be minimal as the cost of one computer workstation (or similar) would soon be justified by the reduction in field work required.

- Information gathering would be possible within a short timeframe of a requirement being identified. In addition, the information so found would be the most current available, as the authority responsible for constructing/ providing is the authority responsible for maintaining that segment of the database, thus changes are recorded as they are made.

- Report generation of infrastructure data would be virtually limited only by the imagination of the user.

- Unlimited combinations of map overlays would be possible to best demonstrate those aspects of greatest importance to any given situation. In addition, unlimited thematic maps may be generated, given a sufficiently broad database.

## Future Considerations

The identification of the elements required by the Australian military is an area that would require further study. The US ETL experience and listing of data elements could be used as a guide.

Following this, an extensive study would be required of the data types available from the currently proposed GIS. This would provide some basis for analysing the costs and benefits of an automated data acquisition system.

Some problems are still to be resolved in the various states as an earlier chapter has suggested. Included in these problems are the decisions of how and how much to store. For a MGIS to be effective, all data must be assured in all states. This may require some intervention by the Commonwealth to ensure it is an important contribution to MGI data gathering, as part of the preparations of the ADF.

## CONCLUSION

Military geographic information is an important part of military intelligence, as its uses demonstrate. Methods used for the collection, analysis, and presentation of intelligence have until recently been manual. This has led to the currently existing situation where collected and available data represents only a small percentage of the information requirement of the ADF for the defence of Australia.

The development of computerised geographic information systems in the civil sector has substantial benefits for the military. A GIS provides the military with the ability to collate data, analyse it, and present the information in a suitable manner. GIS will therefore assist terrain analysis, and infrastructure and environmental characteristics processes. Development of a GIS specifically for the ADF must be undertaken using overseas and civil experience as a guide only.

The suggested facility to link into civil authorities' databases provides the military with a huge extension in data-gathering capabilities. The implementation of automated military data acquisition will not only reduce the duplication that exists in the manual process, but will allow instantaneous military access to the most accurate and up-to-date information available. This will provide future benefits to the already approved computer information systems designed for the military.

# NOTES

1   See D.J. Puniard, The Vegetation Element in Military Intelligence: Its Acquisition and Integration into Military GIS. Master's Project, Department of Surveying, University of Queensland, 1986, ch. 2.

2   Carl von Clausewitz, *On War,* ed. and tr. Michael Howard and Peter Paret (Princeton University Press, Princeton, New Jersey, 1976), p. 348.

3   Louis C. Peltier and G. Etzel Pearcy, *Military Geography* (D. van Nostrand and Company, Princeton, New Jersey, 1966), pp. 16, 17.

4   Patrick O'Sullivan and Jesse W. Miller Jr, *The Geography of Warfare* (Croom Helm, London, 1983), p. 7.

5   P.J. Greville, 'National Defence and National Infrastructure', in Robert O'Neill and D.M. Horner (eds), *Australian Defence Policy for the 1980s* (University of Queensland Press, St Lucia, Queensland, 1982), p. 246.

6   Patrick O'Sullivan and Jesse W. Miller Jr, *The Geography of Warfare,* p. 7.

7   Paul Dibb, *Review of Australia's Defence Capabilities,* Report to the Minister for Defence (Australian Government Publishing Service, Canberra, 1986).

8   D.J. Puniard, The Vegetation Element in Military Terrain Intelligence, ch. 2, p. 3.

9   See D.J. Puniard, 'Australian Defence Force Requirements for Land Related Information', in P.J. Hocking (ed.), *Proceedings*, URPIS 13 Conference, Adelaide, 1985 (AURISA, Sydney, 1986), p. 177.

10  D.J. Puniard, The Vegetation Element in Military Terrain Intelligence, ch. 3, p. 2.

11  US Department of the Army, *Military Geographic Intelligence (Terrain)*, FM30-10 (US Department of the Army, Washington DC, March 1972).

12  Cited in Director of Military Survey, United Kingdom, *United Kingdom Five Nations Report*, North Atlantic Treaty Organisation Report, 1985, Appendix 1 to Annex A.

13  J.A. Messmore, T.C. Vogel and A.R. Alexander. *Terrain Analysis Procedural Guide for Vegetation*, ETL-0178 (US Army Corps of Engineers, Engineer Topographic Laboratories, Fort Belvoir, Virginia, March 1979).

14  Major K.J. Lyons, 'That Factor — Terrain', *Defence Force Journal*, No. 6, September–October 1977, p. 6.

15  Desmond O'Connor, *Problems of Research and Development Relating to the Defence of Northern Australia*, Working Paper No. 43 (Strategic and Defence Studies Centre, Research School of Pacific Studies, Australian National University, 1981), p. 7.

16  K.J. Lyons, 'Environmental Characteristics and Defence in Mapping the Environment: The Need for a Data Bank', in *Proceedings*, Symposium on Environmental Characteristics and Defence, Murdoch University, Perth, March 1978 (Australian Institute of Cartographers (WA) and School of Environmental and Life Sciences, Murdoch University, Perth, 1978).

17  K. Grant, A.A. Finlayson, A.P. Spate and T.G. Ferguson, *Terrain Analysis and Classification for Engineering and Conservation Purposes of the Port Clinton Area, Queensland*, Technical Paper No. 29 (CSIRO Division of Applied Geomechanics, Canberra, 1979).

18  D.J. Puniard, The Vegetation Element in Military Terrain Intelligence, ch. 2, p. 25.

19  Australian Defence Force, Joint Services Administration, *Directory of Service Responsibilities for Australian Infrastructure Information*, JSP(AS)205(A) (Department of Defence, Canberra, 1983).

20  Department of Defence, Army Office, *Defence Land Information*, Staff Instruction No. 22/86 (Department of Defence, Canberra, 1986).

21  Paul Dibb, *Review of Australia's Defence Capabilities*, p. 64.

22  G.J.F. Holden, 'Future Topographic Mapping Programme for Australia', in International Cartographic Association (ICA), *Technical Papers*, 2 vols, 12th International Conference of the International Cartographic Association (12th ICA Conference Committee, Perth, 1984), Vol. 2, p. 128.

23  Department of Defence, *The Defence of Australia 1987*, White Paper presented to Parliament by the Minister for Defence, the Hon. Kim C. Beazley, March 1987 (Australian Government Publishing Service, Canberra, 1987), p. vii.

24  ibid., p. 24.

25  ibid., p. 21.

26  ibid., p. 27.

27  ibid., p. 53.

28  Paul Dibb, *Review of Australia's Defence Capabilities*, p. 13.

29   ibid.

30   Department of Defence, *The Defence of Australia 1987*, p. 76.

31   Paul Dibb, *Review of Australia's Defence Capabilities*, p. 12.

32   Department of Defence, *The Defence of Australia 1987*, p. 69.

33   ibid., pp. 69–70.

34   ibid., p. 40.

35   ibid., p. 70.

36   Refer ibid., p. 34; and Paul Dibb, *Review of Australia's Defence Capabilities*, pp. 60–61.

37   Department of Defence, *The Defence of Australia 1987*, p. 61.

38   ibid., p. 62.

39   Refer Department of Defence, Army Office, *Defence Land Information*.

CHAPTER SIX

# Hydrography and the Management of Geographic Information for Defence

## Kenneth G. Burrows*

The management and coordination of geographic information is perhaps the most challenging problem facing the Australian defence community today. The performance capabilities and operation of defence equipment is becoming increasingly more dependent on our knowledge of the environment. It is of little value to have highly complex weapons systems capable, *inter alia*, of high positional accuracy, but unable to relate to essential geographic information from other sources. Command and control systems become useless if they cannot correlate real-time dynamic information against updated static data in a timely and coherent manner. The coordination of scientific intelligence on a geographic basis is a vital component of defence strategy for the planning and conduct of defence operations.

The development and deployment of defence technology is governed by limitations in our knowledge of the operational environment. The hostility of the marine environment poses significant technological barriers to the collection of geographic and environmental data. Special resources are necessary to acquire the appropriate information. Given the significance of maritime information and the immense area of the ocean interests, the coordination of the hydrographic science activities into a regional geographic information base is essential for the defence of Australia.

The Hydrographic Service of the Royal Australian Navy is the only organisation charged with hydrographic responsibility over the sea surrounding the Australian continent and its offshore territories. The traditional view of hydrography as providing navigation charts in a map-like format ignores the essence of the national information-gathering and management role performed by the Hydrographic Service. As was the case before the beginning of European settlement in Australia, the hydrographic function continues to provide a range of scientific activities within the marine environment. These activities comprise accurate scientific measurement, analysis, and intelligence-gathering which directly affects all operational deployments at sea.

To support safe navigation for both the national and defence roles, in addition to the defence oceanographic requirement, the hydrographic function requires the coordination of a diverse range of maritime information that

---

* The views expressed by the author do not necessarily reflect the views of the Department of Defence or the Australian Defence Force.

defines the structure and nature of the marine environment. The area of Australian hydrographic and oceanographic interest exceeds more than a quarter of the earth's surface, from 30° North to Antarctica and from 20° East (East African waters) to 120° West (Isle de Pascua) (see Figure 6.1). The area of international agreement for charting responsibility alone, covers some 40 million square kilometres of ocean from the Equator to Antarctica and from the mid-Indian Ocean to the South-West Pacific Ocean. The collection of information is significantly affected by the resources and technologies available to gather maritime scientific data and requires extensive coordination with the activities of other organisations. It also requires the appropriate professional information management practices to meet the existing and potential range of user demands for hydrographic information, held over such a vast geographic area. The information is derived from a wide range of public and private sector activities throughout the region and a high level of international coordination and cooperation is essential.

Figure 6.1   Area of Australian Hydrographic Interests for Oceanography, Surveying and Charting. The Internal Boundary Shows the Area of Charting Responsibility.

The international nature of hydrography and the unique character of the resources deployed for information gathering at sea, has seen the establishment of single hydrographic authorities within each maritime nation. Today, there is a high correlation in the functions performed by the 54 national hydrographic agencies throughout the world that comprise the International Hydrographic Organisation (IHO). Collectively, these agencies hold the entire world data-set of hydrographic information at the highest resolution available.

The hydrographic activity within the Navy provides the marine science force responsibility within the Australian Defence Force (ADF). The broad content of geographic information coordinated through hydrography for Naval and national purposes are:

- The measurement of seabed geology and geomorphology.
- The physical properties of the sea-water column.
- Water body and ocean dynamics.
- Environmental factors affecting the sea/air interface.
- Coastal topography and intelligence for maritime operations.

The hydrographic role provides the coordination and conduct of surveys and studies by the elements of the ADF Marine Science Force and interfaces with other agencies collecting marine survey and scientific data. The Hydrographic Service has an established information base of geographic maritime data.

## AUSTRALIAN HYDROGRAPHIC RESPONSIBILITIES

The single-service function of the Royal Australian Navy (RAN) is the conduct of operations at sea for the defence of Australia and Australian interests. In discharging this function, one role of the RAN is to:

> Conduct hydrographic and oceanographic surveys, and to act as the National Hydrographic Authority.

This role is performed by the RAN Hydrographic Service through the Hydrographer RAN who provides the policy, planning, data acquisition, analysis, and dissemination in respect to hydrography, to meet various maritime needs as described in DI(N) ADMIN 2–2.[1] The Hydrographer is also responsible for the development and coordination of oceanographic policies, priorities and practices within the RAN as outlined in DI(N)OPS45–1, entitled *Oceanography in the RAN-Policy, Responsibilities and Ship Programming*.[2] Within the Hydrographic Service, the Director of Oceanography and Meteorology is the Navy Office coordinating authority for all environmental matters affecting naval operations.

# BACKGROUND OF CURRENT HYDROGRAPHIC ACTIVITY

The Hydrographic Service is an integrated organisation of uniformed and civilian staff, providing comprehensive hydrographic surveying, charting, navigation and oceanographic services to the Department of Defence and to the maritime community. To assist in the discharge of hydrographic responsibilities the Navy has committed capital acquisition programs for sea-borne and air-borne survey platforms. The ship acquisition and replacement program has been supplemented by the development of the Laser Airborne Depth Sounder (LADS), applying modern laser sensor technology. There is an acquisition program for automated field data logging facilities which has been complemented by the development of geographic information systems for the manipulation and management of hydrographic and oceanographic data.

The primary factor affecting the functions and roles of hydrographic activity is the control and coordination of the national asset of hydrographic, oceanographic and marine operational intelligence information. The Hydrographer employs a range of facilities for the manipulation of geographic information and current activities are being directed towards the integration of the RAN Marine Science Force field activities with relevant data from other sources to provide a single information base for all maritime users.

The Hydrographer is continuing to develop computer systems technology to undertake the increasingly complex task of integrating the amassed geographic data to support modern defence requirements and to meet national and international civilian maritime responsibilities. These activities are highly specialised and aspects of development work have led the world in field survey technology and spatial database applications for the management of hydrographic information, geographic data manipulation and display techniques.

During the next decade the Hydrographer will be expected to provide additional support for various new defence projects, including the replacement submarines, the new surface combatants, the Australian Surface Ship Towed Array Sonar System (ASSTASS), the on-board sonar range prediction system, and various marine command and control systems. Shore facilities such as the Maritime Command Centre will require a significant level of support. In the civilian area, cooperation with agencies in the coordination of data now being collected within the various land information systems will become necessary and the development of the international electronic chart will have a profound effect.

The implications of the international electronic chart is currently being addressed by both the International Maritime Organisation (IMO) and the International Hydrographic Organisation (IHO). These activities stem from the demand to integrate various navigation systems through the use of modern electronic display and communication technologies. The repercussions of the Electronic Chart Display and Information System (ECDIS) for maritime safety are being addressed at the highest international level and Australia will provide the regional information base for this technology. Various electronic chart systems are already in use today without the coordination of the information base necessary to maintain maritime safety. This capability will require the appropriate international standards for the data content to ensure international confidence and uniformity in the quality of the information obtained from the database and to provide the maximum flexibility for national industries to exploit information technology. The electronic chart system has significant implications for Defence where a higher technological level of user capability is to be expected, which will demand increased sophistication of the information base contents and structure.

## NATURE OF HYDROGRAPHIC INFORMATION

Hydrographic information provides data on an environment that is largely unknown and cannot be seen in the normal manner. The known state of information has been acquired by the slow accretion of data throughout a large geographical area and collected over an extended time period. The information content and quality varies considerably according to the technology and conditions that existed at the time the information was acquired. Advances in technology over the years have, of economic necessity, been applied to exploit areas of specific user interest which, in turn, has been conditioned by limits to the user's expectation of that technology. There are also far more gaps to the desirable state of knowledge than there is information available. This provides a dynamic characteristic to the nature of the hydrographic information base which, by necessity, must be maintained by continual revision to complete the gaps to the state of knowledge and to revise the quality of the information content as improved data becomes available through scientific expedition, survey, and advances in technology.

Hydrographic or maritime information can be distinguished from land-related geographic information by specific interests in the marine application and the different sensor technologies used to acquire the data. These relationships are illustrated in Figure 6.2. The main distinction arises from the nature of the marine environment and its affect on the technologies used for data collection and the user requirements for information to conduct marine operations. The environment affects the information by limiting the type of sensor technology which, in turn, constrains the characteristics, capacity and coverage of the information collected. The sea environment also affects data acquisition by restricting the type and operational speed of the platform used to carry the specific sensors. The logistics and environmental conditions that govern the operation of the platform and its sensors creates further complications for the acquisition of hydrographic information.

Sonar is the primary marine sensor technology which has a bearing on other defence operational requirements. The use of acoustic technology for hydrographic information provides the basic marine measurement capability as well as justification to collect oceanographic parameters to improve the understanding of sonar propagation for defence and scientific purposes. Modern

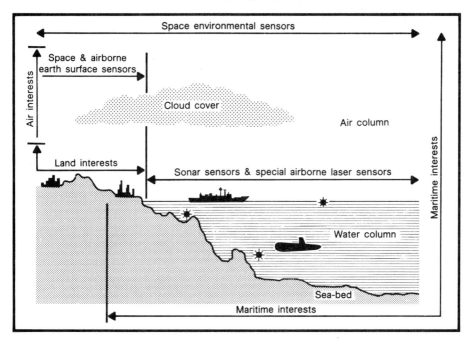

Figure 6.2   Distinctions in GIS Interests and Primary Sensor Technology.

defence requires an understanding of sonar characteristics in order to improve the accuracy and precision of basic measurement as well as the performance capabilities of underwater detection equipment. The scientific understanding of the dynamics of sonar performance within the sea-water environment is vital to submarine and mine countermeasure (MCM) activities. The collection of selected oceanographic parameters provides the information needed to refine the measurement of the sea-floor terrain and to improve other sensor capabilities (e.g., to improve bottom reflection signatures). The scientific nature of hydrographic information must be understood in the context of the marine science role of physical oceanography.

The development of a new range of swathe survey systems has enhanced the capability to provide comprehensive and detailed knowledge of the seabed. This improvement to sonar systems technology has considerable advantages over profile survey methods, in that it suits seabed modelling techniques for the widest range of user requirements. Providing the resolution is adequate, swathe survey techniques also eliminate much of the need for repeated surveying as user requirements change. The use of specialised sonar interferometer techniques coupled with advanced data processing can provide the resolution to facilitate database modelling to suit object detection with defence applications. This advance in sonar technology merges the equipment performance capability required for normal hydrographic surveying with that used for underwater obstacle detection. Other advances provide the capacity to detect sub-bottom sedimentation layers in the course of hydrographic survey. The primary information model for the user can be derived from a hydrographic information base which defines all the known physical features and scientific properties of the sea.

Other sensor technologies have been developed to meet the unique characteristics of the marine environment. The Laser Airborne Depth Sounder (LADS) is a significant development of optical sensor technology for the rapid swathe survey of maritime areas to a depth suited to general surface operations. There is also the application of electromagnetic induction sensors which can be used in combination with other sensors to increase the range of observations from a single platform and to improve the confidence in observation of the unseen environment.

The use of space- and aircraft-mounted multi-spectral scanning sensors for environmental data is common over land and sea. The use of this sensor technology can, at present, provide considerable benefit for planning, intelligence, and broad-based environmental data. Some applications also lead to the identification of seabed dynamics and characteristics in very shallow water areas, but use in the marine field can be restricted by the limitations to the sensor's capacity to penetrate water. This sensor technology does not yet have sufficient penetration to provide underwater data for detailed marine requirements or to support confidence for precise navigation. There is significant potential for linking the multi-spectral scanner technology with the precise water penetration characteristics of the optical laser airborne technology in order to provide ground truth information for the analysis of remotely sensed data to improve the information gathered by this type of sensor.

The need to provide operational safety for navigation at sea has driven most hydrographic effort. The primary end use of hydrographic information has traditionally been the production of navigation charts. The initial hydrographic charter was to conduct surveys and produce navigation charts, which are a legal and practical requirement for operations at sea. In the process of conducting hydrographic activities it is necessary to acquire and continue to hold ready all the relevant source information throughout the region of interest, in order to satisfy legal obligations and to evaluate changes to previously published material in the light of new information and changes in user requirements. The operational deployment in a defence role calls for a higher level of hydrographic information than that required for normal civilian shipping.

All hydrographic information defines the shape and composition of the seabed and the properties of the water mass, together with supporting coastal landform detail and intelligence. The Hydrographer is a national lead agency for the coordination of hydrographic information. It is important to distinguish the primary or source information from the more commonly accepted information displayed on user products such as charts, publications and environmental forecasts. The primary geographic information base represents the total state of hydrographic knowledge. User products represent a very small selec-

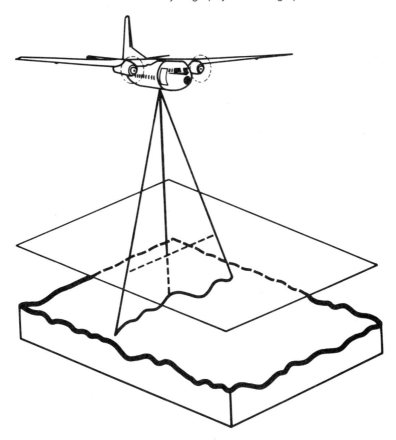

*Figure 6.3   Laser Airborne Depth Sounder (LADS).*

tion of available data, which is not the level desired for defence geographic information systems. The user selection supports the needs of the general maritime community and the significance to defence of the source database is obscured by the traditional view of hydrographic activity. The source database provides the single coordinated view of the ocean at the highest resolution available. The Hydrographer holds national responsibility for this source of marine science and geographic information and has international links to other national maritime agencies to provide the national hydrographic information base. A brief discussion of the characteristics of hydrographic information groups follows.

## Seabed terrain data

This data describes the seabed bathymetry and composition at the highest resolution available. Modern hydrographic survey technology can now provide saturation area coverage at a resolution capable of defining objects on or above the seabed. This is a significant application for geographic information, where static historic data can be used in conjunction with similar real-time sensors (e.g., high resolution swath sounding systems using advanced multi-dimensional sonar interferometer techniques) to identify variations to detail that may disclose a mine or submarine. The area seabed model defined at this level of resolution also avoids the need to conduct expensive re-survey for normal surface navigation as shipping needs change.

However, it must be recognised that there is no comprehensive or coherent information coverage for most of the sea. The speed at which surveys can be undertaken across some 40 million square kilometres of ocean is very slow and much of the area outside the continental shelf remains unsurveyed. Even the information within the continental shelf is limited by the technology available when the survey was conducted and some coverage dates back to the nineteenth century. More modern survey has been limited for the defence role by the use of profile survey techniques, where the lines of survey have been run, in certain cases, up to one nautical mile apart and the use of sonar sweeping, when it is conducted, is not always conclusive.

The disadvantage of a significant lack of knowledge within the information base (in terms of coverage and quality) is compensated for by the comprehensive knowledge of the limitations to surface and submerged operations provided by the polygon boundaries of the effective areas of survey coverage. This reinforces the need to qualify the data within the information base to provide important guidance to corridors of safe deployment. This is critical intelligence for the conduct of marine operations. Against substantial deficiencies in the desirable level of detailed survey coverage is set the knowledge of where to deploy modern systems to provide safe passage corridors and where more detailed survey of selected areas may be conducted to take advantage of unique geographically positioned scientific phenomenon of strategic importance; for example, thermal fronts provide sonar havens for submarines.

## Physical oceanographic data

This hydrographic information base is the result of the coordination of marine science activities in surrounding oceans. Scientific studies by Defence together with studies by national and international agencies, are coordinated and held for selected physical oceanographic parameters of interest to the Navy. This information is assessed and structured under the organisation of the Australian Oceanographic Data Centre (AODC) which, through the Hydrographer, forms an integral part of the marine science structure within Australia. AODC holds various digital databases and is a national lead agency in the supply of physical oceanographic data. The parameters coordinated include bathythermal observations and sea-water salinity profiles.

## Water-body and ocean dynamics

Tidal levels, tidal streams, and ocean currents form part of the information acquired and coordinated for the publication of national tide tables and chart-ing. Water-body movement generated through thermal variation (geostrophic current) and other environmental factors form part of the hydrographic scien-tific program.

## Environmental data

The interrelationship of meteorological conditions and the sea environment form an integral part of hydrographic activities. This requires the coordination of the marine environmental database with meteorological forecasting for maritime operational deployment.

## Navigation Chart Base

This database provides the information for safe navigation at sea. It contains selected topographic and terrain detail, held to hydrographic specification, of the land and near-surface features which provides part of the base for nautical charting. The information is now being managed in digital form to suit current chart production practices and will provide a basis for the international electro-nic chart display and information systems. This, together with selected digital bathymetric data, navigation data, and remotely sensed information, forms part of an integrated international hydrographic arrangement for the coordin-ated supply of a geographic navigation information for the maritime user. The national charting scheme with the hydrographic information as its base, ser-vices the defence surface navigation requirement away from the main shipping routes. The application of such an extensive geographic information system coverage to maritime defence systems will probably become a necessary exten-sion of ECDIS and will be required earlier than other GIS applications because of the relationship to the essential safety aspects of navigation. The electronic chart base will also provide the means of coordinating operations conducted in foreign waters and provide compatible information links with vessels of other nations.

## Maritime Intelligence

In the process of hydrography, the intelligence-gathering role provides signifi-cant supplementary information to the primary collection of raw scientific data. When in support of normal surface navigation, this information is provided in the form of supplementary publications (e.g., sailing directions, radio lists, notices to mariners, port facilities, etc.). Such publications are available to all maritime users and provide only a selection of the geographically related intelligence information available for strategic or defence needs (beach gra-dients, beach intelligence, non-submarine contacts, gravity and magnetic ano-malies, speed of sound variations, etc.).

# DATA ORGANISATION

There is great diversity in the range and type of geographically related information held by the Hydrographic Service. In the past it has been necessary to organise the data in support of specific user products and various field survey activities. Changes to user requirements and the technology of data collection have made it necessary to revise data organisation practices in order to respond to the growth in information from numerous sources and to meet expected response requirements for efficient information management.

The method of acquisition of hydrographic information will continue to pose significant problems for data organisation and information management. The sea provides a formidable barrier to the rapid acquisition of detailed information and sea-borne survey resources are costly to deploy and allow only a relatively slow acquisition of data compared to that which can be gathered over land. The process of nationally coordinating relatively small data sets, obtained in a piecemeal fashion over many years, is important to understanding the dynamic nature of hydrographic information. These processes are not of a simple cumulative nature and management requires a transactional and interactive approach to continually revise and re-assess the information coverage and keep track of where information must be updated on derived products. This is particularly true for information affecting maritime safety and is a prerequisite to support any defence information network which must rely upon accurate and current assessment for operational decision-making. The rationale for this approach to data organisation is inherent in the way data is acquired on a national basis and the purpose for which it is used, and dictates the manner in which marine information should be managed, whether it be maintained for charting, defence or national archival purposes. Centralised management of a national hydrographic information set is a prerequisite to providing the necessary coordination for specific defence user requirements, such as support of an operational facility, like an MCM database, or, a defence survey capability for data acquisition and immediate production of user requirements during the conduct of operations at sea.

To keep track on user products and evaluate new data sets for incorporation into the main information base, a systems database approach to information management has been used. Because of the high dependency on geographic information, the modern spatial database technology has been adopted within the Hydrographic Service. The GIS application serves as a tool for data organisation and information management. The GIS management of primary information is a necessary precursor to the GIS management and transmission of secondary, and user-simplified, geographic information.

Problems arising from variations in quality and density of hydrographic information acquired from different sources over time, require all incoming primary data to be analysed and integrated into a single unified geographic model. Current data-logging systems can supply millions of significant data points over a relatively small area. The merging of many large data sets over the considerable geographic area of Australia's strategic interest has created problems involving the capacity and response limitations of current spatial database systems technology. The problems associated with handling ultra-high information densities are significant, both in terms of processing and data reduction, particularly with spatial geographic databases on a world-wide basis and the general complexities of systems graphics display techniques. Solutions to the problems arising from handling of the level of information densities considered necessary to providing meaningful, say, command and control facilities, would be an urgent and critical requirement to achieving an effective maritime GIS for Defence.

Much of the primary hydrographic information is in manuscript format, which makes it difficult for intelligent systems inquiry. Electronic display for this type of information can be achieved through video or raster scanning techniques, but this is not an entirely satisfactory solution. The coordination of manuscript information is achieved by bringing the polygon boundaries of the effective areas of survey under control of spatial database technology. In turn this will facilitate the linking of expert systems techniques to determine optimal zones of operational confidence or to assist in planning strategy and operational decision-making.

The principle behind the organisation of hydrographic information is to hold the data set at the highest resolution available in a primary GIS structure and to have the data qualified in order to establish its relevance in relation to other data sets. Higher levels of structure will then be used to integrate other digital data sets into secondary data for user-orientated GIS requirements.

## IMPORTANCE OF RELATIVE GEOGRAPHIC POSITION AND DATA QUALIFICATION

The relationship between the position datum and the relative accuracy of the various sets of data that comprise a unified database is significant for geographically related information, particularly when the base data is synchronised with real-time data. Outside a range of specialised professionals and navigators, there is no strong appreciation for the impact of positional accuracy and the need to relate geographic information to a common datum. The advent of highly accurate position-fixing devices poses real problems for information management to meet user requirements of the data. This is of particular importance for defence where access to high accuracy, dynamic position-fixing systems is possible. It is hardly appropriate for a modern naval vessel to be accurately navigating into a mine field, because the datum of the static geographic information was different from the datum of the real-time data, or the error ellipse of the original survey data was, say, twice the width of the mine-cleared route!

Improvement in the precision of position fixing is one of the most significant factors affecting the hydrographic community. While all types of navigation (and surveying) systems remain important, global positioning systems have potentially the most significant impact on information management and hence GIS applications. While relative accuracy remains adequate for normal navigation using current charts, the absolute accuracy of high precision real-time earth-centred satellite positioning systems will impact on information provided by geographic information systems. Future navigation systems will require the systematic knowledge of the relative positional accuracy of the information base if integration with real-time sensors is to be achieved. In situations where greater emphasis is placed on dynamic command and control type systems, navigation will require more from source geographic information than can probably be supplied unless greater emphasis is placed on identifying the variation in position datum and other qualifications on the information.

The positional accuracy obtained from the direct copying of existing paper information bases (charts, maps, etc.) is not adequate for any base required to produce large-scale display on dynamic navigation control systems. Information provided for the ECDIS must be able to indicate the precision or any qualifications of the data that can provide the basis for adjustment in the real-time user display. The non-expert user must not be able to imply an order of accuracy of the static data that does not exist. Given the wide variety of circumstances under which surveys for geographic information are conducted, it is necessary to place greater emphasis on the relative accuracies of all survey data, even to subsets of data within the boundary of a single survey. While practical judgments are made on the quality of information collected during surveying, it is only commensurate with the understanding of the technology used at that point in time and must be continually re-evaluated for relevance to modern requirements. In future there must be greater consideration given to the manner in which information is assessed and qualified for later user evaluation and this calls for renewed thought on comprehensive and uniform standards for the assessment of the quality of geographic data.

The necessity to provide uniform standards to qualify information has significant implications for the use of geographic information. A database holding, say, depth soundings, grouped in survey sets and subsets of potential user qualification, permits the longer term goal of linking with other data sets to provide the basis for future system-aided decision-making processes. It is the notion of data qualification that will provide the basis of system-aided choices for decision-making through the applicaton of rule-based or expert systems technology.

## CURRENT HYDROGRAPHIC ACTIVITIES IN GIS

The Hydrographer is currently installing two computer-based geographic information systems. These systems have been adapted from an existing spatial information system currently used in land information applications. The initial hydrographic application of GIS technology provides a tool for information management of selected areas of oceanography and hydrography. There is potential for further development of these systems to allow access by other defence users, but the initial application must be contained until the practical issues involved in the implementation of this new technology have been determined. Aspects of higher level coordination and management will be pursued in subsequent stages.

The basic arrangements for each system is a main computer to service the database function with a series of high capacity graphic workstations on a local area network (LAN). These workstations can copy the database selection and operate as a local database system for analysis. The initial acquisition provides mini-computer hardware for the main base and this can be re-configured for a mainframe installation. System compatibility is maintained throughout by similar architecture on both systems and a common link on the LAN for the necessary communication and transfer of data sets.

There were a number of characteristics in the design of the spatial information base which were considered necessary for hydrography. The spatial coordinate structure had to be able to accommodate geographic position anywhere on the earth's surface at a high resolution. Desirably this structure should have full three-dimensional flexibility on inquiry. The coordinate structure had to be neutral (desirably angular for two-dimension) and not favour any particular output display or map projection. This was important where data was to be used for many purposes as well as for transfer between different user systems. Coordinate structures that favour a particular graphic representation of a curved surface on a two-dimension plane tend to become complicated in transformation in polar regions and with relative position techniques that may become more commonplace with integrated displays using real-time sensors. The failure of many existing systems to recognise these needs has probably been the result of certain limitations in the current state of development and the commercial market for land information systems, where area coverage requirements tend to be small in comparison with global requirements and the applications tend to service internal organisation application at the expense of wider user access.

To access hydrographic information, a universal view on all information is a prerequisite to any inquiry. An inquiry for a random polygon of interest should not be limited by boundaries or pages within the information. There is a problem in this approach with the volume of information that may be accessed, particularly if the polygon covers an extensive regional area. Design implications for hydrography have led to the stratification of information into summary layers within the main structure (not to be confused with normal GIS layers). This allows user access to a broader view of the information which is probably more relevant to detailed display. (See Figure 6.4)

The summary layering technique is necessary to support the non-homogeneous nature of the hydrographic information (particularly seabed modelling data). There are extreme variations in the density of primary information over relatively small geographic areas depending on the technology of the source information. The level of detail is not always required and the summary layers

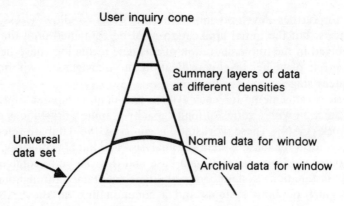

*Figure 6.4   Concept of Database Summary Layers.*

allow high-level filtering of the information density in the display.

The initial application for one GIS is to manage the hydrographic survey model of Australia. This GIS also accommodates the processing of digital survey data. The main database management facilities facilitate coordination of the growing volume of survey data, in all different formats, within the Australian region of interest and provide facilities to plan and revise hydrographic activities. Information that defines the seabed varies widely in content, quality and format, and the information structure will store the polygon and sub-polygon boundaries of different information content and quality. The concept of these polygon boundaries within a single survey is illustrated in Figure 6.5.

The structuring of incoming survey data into the main information base must

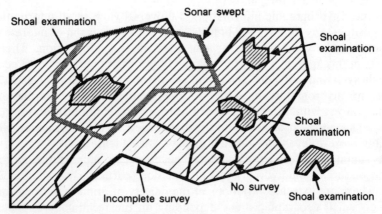

*Figure 6.5   Concept of Polygon Boundaries in a Hydrographic Survey.*

allow for the interaction of overlapping survey data sets. The final resolution of this overlap provides the reference polygons of the General Integrated Survey Model of the Ocean (GISMO). The interrelationship of polygons is more complex than explained here but the principle of continuous refinement and adjustment of the GISMO continues as information is acquired.

At the level of the reference polygons it is not necessary to hold the actual sounding data. Sounding data is only held within the base if it has been digitised or when it becomes available from automatic field data logging systems. The management polygons are analysed for all information (digital or manuscript) and resolved for competing data sets and referenced for quality. This provides an effective management tool for surveying planning and coordination of the navigation chart revision and production program. It can also provide information on safety corridors for planning and the conduct of maritime operations. This aspect of the base can be established and maintained irrespective of the format of the source information and therefore provides a total management capability for hydrography.

When specific digital sounding data is available it forms part of the actual base data for seabed modelling and specific production purposes. The management aspects of the base are supplemented with applications packages for manipulation of data. At a simple level, the task of reducing a set of one million observations to a viewable set based on certain criteria can be accomplished through the spatial data reduction and selection facilities. When there is a requirement to analyse incoming digital survey returns and reconcile with previous digital data, the GIS database can be used to model alternative representations of the seabed in the area of survey overlap and produce interference models to determine the degree of variation. For surveys conducted by the marine science force this resolution may be performed in the field, from information supplied and analysed on the GISMO. The GIS is a management facility for quality assessment of all new data independent of any specific field equipment.

The GIS provides the opportunity to integrate some digital charting techniques by transferring certain existing digital charting information into the summary layers. Where the charted soundings are available from source digital data within the base, the promotion of this observation to the charting level is linked through the database. Thus the GIS application provides a key link in the management of the seabed model information with that required for maritime operational deployment (charting and route planning). The information is enhanced by providing the operational corridors that are not obvious on the normal chart. The extension of GIS to cover all aspects of charting and maritime intelligence requires further consideration based on the implications of the electronic chart (ECDIS) and experience with the implementation of current GIS facilities. Considerations for future phases include the storage and interactive recall, in raster format, of information not available in digital form; increased scope of mass storage for archival data; development and integration of selected navigation bases and the facilitation of direct external access.

The application of the second GIS for oceanographic processes has been separated from the hydrographic base. The current state of development of GIS application does not warrant the risks involved with joint development of a common base. Conformity is maintained by using the same system architecture and common database characteristics, operating through a common LAN. When oceanographic analysis requires seabed terrain data, the information can be passed from the hydrographic base to the oceanographic workstation for integration with other geographic data. Similarly tidal analysis or seabed geological samples can be accessed for hydrographic operations from the oceanographic data set.

The current use of GIS facilities by the Hydrographer provides a tool for information manipulation and management. This does not obscure the use for wider information management and data transfer to other users. The development of this aspect will depend upon the availability of appropriate volumes of suitable digital information and the resolution of suitable data transfer structures. However, it must be recognised that the current spatial information technology is relatively new and there remain many system and procedural problems to be overcome at the organisational level before the real impact of a geographic data support base for other users can be addressed.

## DEFENCE GIS ASPECTS

The deployment of high technology defence weapons systems and platforms requires refined scientific information and intelligence of the marine environment to be effective and to achieve maximum efficiency. The *Review of Australia's Defence Capabilities*[3] and the White Paper on *The Defence of Australia 1987*[4] place emphasis on the collection and holding of information to support defence maritime operations. The technological capabilities now exist to exploit the collection of appropriate levels of information required to support such activities. The same information required for, say, MCM activities, is a logical part of the base required for the coordination of hydrographic information that must exceed the need of any single-Service project. The deployment of expensive sea-borne resources, over and above the marine science force, to service defence information needs, requires the coordination of resources and the establishment of coherent information-holding policies if appropriate resource economies and a Service-wide use of relevant aspects of the data is to be achieved. Information sets of the same generic nature, obtained for specific projects, must be coordinated and managed with the appropriate professional responsibility in order to achieve uniform coordination of information at a national level for both defence and civil needs. This factor is emphasised with the advent of high-precision, earth-centred, satellite position-fixing equipment for military use. If the position of the known, but unseen, hazards of the sea cannot be co-related to the position-fixing capabilities of the modern defence technology, then defence technology will be rendered impotent and operations will be placed at considerable risk.

The current hydrographic application of GIS manages high-volume digital data on a world-wide basis and is being developed to meet international obligations. This GIS application is, at present, internal to the information management needs of the Hydrographer in order to effectively coordinate the primary coverage of hydrographic survey and scientific observations. In turn, the structure of secondary or user geographic information can be linked and processed from the primary data through GIS technology.

The hydrographic application of GIS technology provides a microcosm of maritime defence GIS requirements, which are seen to include:

- World-wide or at least extensive regional coverage.
- The ability to move between detailed and generalised information content.
- Reduction of information to a common geographic datum.
- Qualification of information content.
- Information coordination and maintenance services.
- Rapid communication links.
- High-level GIS coordination and management facilities.

GIS coverage must reflect the operational needs of defence. The areas of interest for the Navy should be world-wide or at least cover the Indian, Pacific, and Southern Ocean regions. This, in turn, requires serious consideration of the interrelationships of information from various sources which should be reduced to a uniformed geographic datum, particularly when the correlation to real-time data is required (e.g., for navigation, weapon deployment, etc.). The spatial coordinate system for world coverage must be removed from local or national coordinate systems often encountered in mapping of utilities information systems. Likewise, tendencies to favour specific cartographic map projection displays must be removed from the information structure where display may be preferred to match the real-time relationship of geographic information to the dynamics of a ship or aircraft movement. The neutralising of coordinate structure is vital to defence requirements that calls for deployment from the equator to the polar regions.

To be of specific defence value, information densities must be available to suit both detailed and general regional views. Depending upon requirements, this could involve ultra-high system storage and retrieval capabilities. The GIS applications within the Hydrographic Service calls for billions of information points within sometimes relatively small geographic areas. Information required for operational systems at sea is not necessarily uniform and techniques must be developed to meet the practical constraints of handling a wide variety of different data characteristics. Ultra-high data densities may require the networking of GIS systems to provide the linking of the analysis of complex density structures and the variety of relevant geographic aspects required in operational situations.

In order to coordinate the relevant information between different systems the qualification and structure across any GIS network becomes imperative.

The qualification of database elements and sets provides the basis of selective inquiry necessary to link super-sets of interest and to facilitate search and display time. In turn, this requires effective standards for the structuring and communication of information across the network. Changes to information content within any GIS node on a network must be able to be transferred quickly and effectively. Information management practices become an important component of GIS operation. The scale of integration for the types and geographic range of information required for defence activities indicates a layered structure of GIS groups, each being coordinated by higher level GIS application. The management, specification and coordination of such a network structure is probably the most challenging aspect of defence information systems.

## DEFENCE PLANNING CONSIDERATIONS FOR GIS

A high level of coordination for the development of component GIS facilities and the structuring of GIS groups into networks is considered essential if excessive cost overruns are to be avoided. The defence requirement probably has one of the highest needs for coordinated geographic information which must draw upon a diverse range of organisations with specific expertise. If appropriate coordination practices are not quickly implemented at a national level the ultimate cost of the information age may be prohibitive. To achieve this, it is considered there is a requirement to foster study and research into:

- Very large-scale integrated information networks.
- Spatial database information systems.
- Information processing and transfer standards.
- Real-time inquiry and transfer communications.
- High-level information coordination and security.
- Data qualification structure and standards.
- System-aided decision processes (rule-based and expert systems).
- Development of a national strategic plan for information management in accord with realistic rate of development in defence technology.

The national development of Land Information Systems (LIS) and general extension of this application under the generic notion of GIS requires high-level coordination if efficiencies are to be maintained at a national level. Isolated development of LIS that may suit urban utility organisations (e.g., water supply, electricity distribution, etc.) may create problems for the wider use of sections of that information, unless coordinated planning is undertaken. The use of GIS for defence suggests high level of coordination in terms of:

- The variety of information bases required.
- The variation in information densities and the response rate required for different GIS sets.

- Security aspects related to making necessary enquiry of a GIS not specifically held by defence units.
- The need for operational information of a GIS nature to suit specific equipment.

Geographic information for defence covers a broad range of physical, environmental and intelligence data on a global basis. This information is universal and responsibilities usually lie across many agencies. The implications of advanced technology for defence have particular significance for the use of geographical information where very large equipment acquisition programs can affect coordination. Matching information to suit specific project technology can disrupt other legitimate defence functions and affect national responsibilities if proper coordination for information is not established. Specific project requirements for geographic information will usually not keep pace with advances in information technology which continue to develop in order to serve other needs. Project application of information can also become outdated and potentially render the equipment ineffective. The very high budgets of single acquisition programs often create the climate that lead to command decisions, in ensuring the supplier meets contractual arrangements, which can largely ignore the wider implications of geographic information. There is a special need in the use of geographic information in defence to ensure that capital equipment projects having a GIS requirement are properly assessed for the real costs of the data and meet higher level coordination that reflects the multiplicity of GIS functions and responsibilities. There must be thorough testing of each project for reliance upon specific geographic data for the lifetime of the project and information costs that are necessary for the effective operation of the asset must be appropriated against that project from the outset.

Defence is particularly vulnerable to vested professional and technology-based interests, within the ADF as well as the defence industry sector. In considering the implications of defence needs for geographic information there must be suitable processes to ensure that the objectives are feasible; that suitable information exists or can be obtained within the scope of the requirement; that existing functional responsibilities are not displaced; and that the need can be met on a realistic economic basis in accord with the consequences of not having geographic information for the defence of Australia.

# NOTES

1  Department of Defence, Navy Office, *Organisation of the Office of the Deputy Chief of Naval Staff*, DI(N)ADMIN 2–2, No. 16/83 (Department of Defence, Canberra, 1983).

2  Department of Defence, Navy Office, *Oceanography in the RAN — Policy, Responsibilities and Ship Programming*, DI(N)OPS 45–1, No. 12/80 (Department of Defence, Canberra, 1980).

3   Paul Dibb, *Review of Australia's Defence Capabilities*, Report to the Minister for Defence (Australian Government Publishing Service, Canberra, 1986).

4   Department of Defence, *The Defence of Australia 1987*, White Paper presented to Parliament by the Minister for Defence, the Hon. Kim C. Beazley, March 1987 (Australian Government Publishing Service, Canberra, 1987).

*Plate 1  SPOT Imagery over Adelaide City.*

Source: © CNES 1986. Distributed by the Australian Centre for Remote Sensing under a SPOT Image R Licence.

Plate 2 *SPOT Imagery — Adelaide Airport zoomed × 2*

Source © CNES 1986. Distributed by the Australian Centre for Remote Sensing under a SPOT Image R Licence.

Plate 3 *Airborne MSS Image — Nerang River Entrance.*

Source: Landsat Imagery provided by the Australian Centre for Remote Sensing, Australian Surveying and Land Information Group, Department of Administrative Services.

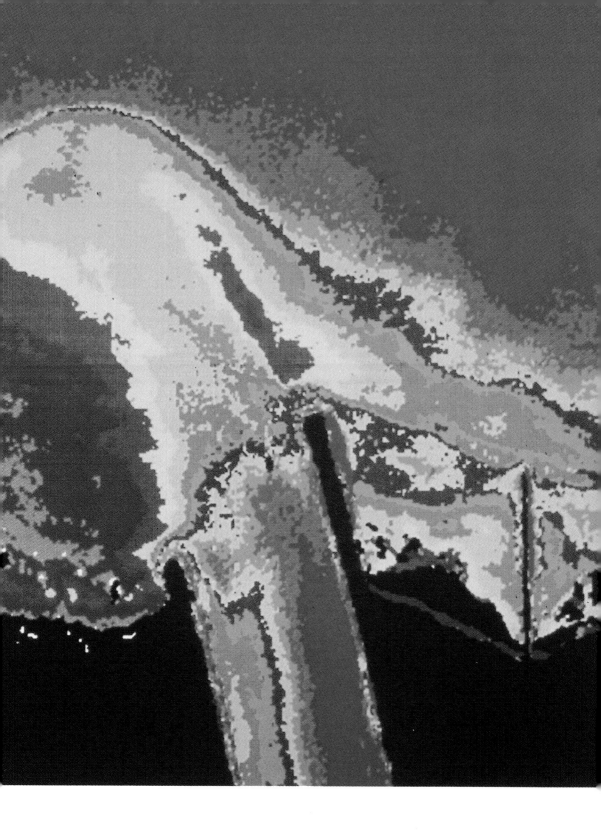

*Plate 4   Landsat Imagery, Cape York. North-western quadrant of a Landsat image showing the Weipa district. Weipa is the white area in the centre of the peninsula; the rectilinear light blue areas are the cleared mining sites; the reddish areas along the coastal streams are mangroves; the light brown represents the open forest, whose margin coincides with the limits of the bauxite deposits; the mottled yellow area is open woodland and grassland; the stream pattern is characterised by brown lines of denser eucalypts.*

Source: Landsat Imagery provided by the Australian Centre for Remote Sensing, Australian Surveying and Land Information Group, Department of Administrative Services.

# CHAPTER SEVEN

# ARIS: A Working Geographic Information System for Continental Australia

### K.D. Cocks

### P.A. Walker

The Australian Resources Information System (ARIS) is a continental-scale computerised geographic information system (GIS) first described by Cocks and Walker in 1980[1]. Developed in the Commonwealth Scientific and Industrial Research Organisation (CSIRO) Division of Water and Land Resources and now located in the Division of Wildlife and Ecology, it is a facility for storing, recalling, searching, manipulating and displaying data on Australia's bio-physical and socio-economic resources. ARIS commands a range of data and map manipulation capabilities as well as a range of analytical procedures useful for policy analyses and decision-support studies. It is a national system in the sense that all data items are referenced against sets of locations covering the whole country. Accordingly, its primary use is for small-scale (national, state, sub-state) rather than large-scale (regional, local, site) description and analysis.

ARIS began with an in-house requirement during the mid-1970s to be able to display local government data graphically. Many of the first maps produced within the ARIS project were simply maps of population census or utility data by enumeration district, for example, electricity consumption, road network conditions.[2] A major expansion in computer mapping activities occurred in 1978, when the Division of National Mapping (NATMAP), the principal government mapping organisation in Australia, released digital files describing the boundaries of all local government areas in Australia.

When first acquired in late 1978, these files were seen as providing a digital spatial base for a continental study of geographic aspects of human settlements in Australia. By late 1979, however, this digital mapbase was being seen as a foundation for developing a continental-scale geographic information system commanding a range of analytical capabilities. By then, software which enabled digital map files to be manipulated had been obtained and was being used with confidence. The name ARIS was coined, reflecting a hope of establishing a comprehensive central repository of quantitative natural and other resource data about Australia. It was hoped that, when fully developed, ARIS would provide authorities and individuals wishing to study the use of the nation's natural resources with a central source of relevant data, a computerised mapping system, and a bibliography which would cover Australia. By the end of 1980, goals of guiding development of ARIS had been established:

(a) to create a spatially coordinated resource data base which can be used to generate continental perspectives for regional land use studies;

(b) to explore and report on the opportunities and problems associated with setting up a small-scale large area general-purpose resource information system in the Australian data/institutional environment;

(c) to evaluate the hypothesis that, when developed, such a system will prove extremely helpful in the carrying out of a range of socially and scientifically significant analyses of the Australian resource base.[3]

The first three years of ARIS data collection were based on a principle of collating existing publicly available computer-readable data sources. System development involved adapting existing software to requirements and providing interfaces between data sets, data manipulation capabilities, and mapping software. Little research was conducted on spatial data structures or on new sources of data.

Since transfer to a new computer in 1982, the basic features of ARIS, as implemented during establishment, have remained unchanged. However, the concept of ARIS as a database nationally available to government and the private sector has been shelved. ARIS is still seen as a central repository of consistently geocoded data about the resources of Australia, but the servicing role envisaged in the first phase of development will not be expanded until the power and utility of a national GIS have been demonstrated more clearly. To this end, current research is largely directed towards developing capabilities for regional description and modelling spatial relationships between different resources.

This chapter is organised around the following themes:

- Hardware supporting the system.

- Data, including mapbases, available to the system.

- Technical capabilities for manipulating and analysing geographic (i.e. mappable) data.

- Research tasks for which ARIS is being used.

- Some applications of ARIS to practical problems.

- ARIS and the defence task.

# HARDWARE

ARIS development in the first three years (1979–82) was on a CYBER 7600 of the CSIRO computing network, with most in-house software development being in Fortran. A large format digitising table and large format pen plotter were available. Maps were previewed on a high resolution monochrome graphics terminal prior to plotting. The media options for display of mapped data, although exclusively monochrome, included microfilm, bromide paper, large and small plot paper, clear film, as well as 35mm and 16mm film. The majority of maps were produced on 35mm film, primarily because of the low cost of production, but also because of its reliability and quality control. Device independent plotting software gave users considerable flexibility and control of mapping. Colour mapping became possible in 1981 with the purchase of a large format ink jet plotter and associated basic graphic subroutines and mapping utilities.

ARIS was transferred to a VAX 11/750 computer in 1982 where a reasonably wide range of peripherals remains available to the system. Most maps now are plotted either on a pen plotter, or on a small or large format ink jet colour plotter. In late 1987 ARIS was transferred again, this time to a Micro-VAX 2.

# DATA

## Initial data holdings

Two nation-wide mapbases were initially developed, both from the previously noted digitisation of local government boundaries from NATMAP.[4] The first mapbase, called the adjusted local government mapbase (741 polygons), differed from local government areas only in that local government areas within each major urban or metropolitan area were amalgamated to form a single polygon. The second mapbase, the basic mapping unit mapbase (876 polygons, see Figure 7.1) differed from the adjusted local government base only in that geographically large local governments were subdivided by latitude and longitude and/or watersheds. The former mapbase was designed to allow mapping of local government data while accepting that intra-urban detail was unnecessary for a national perspective. The latter base was seen as providing mapping units small enough to map flexibly a variety of resource data country-wide.

A single integrated database was set up to be the major repository of ARIS data. Geographically, data was referenced against the basic mapping units described above. This allowed the large quantities of local government data routinely produced by the Australian Bureau of Statistics and other organisations to be rapidly and easily associated with a mapbase.

By the end of 1982 this database contained some 1925 bio-physical and socio-economic attributes for each basic mapping unit. Data included soils, natural vegetation, climate, lithology, landcover, population, coastal land use, water usage, transport statistics and terrain. Data recorded against the adjusted local government area mapbase was largely derived from the Census of Population and Housing.[5]

Late in 1982, a third mapbase was developed describing the electoral divisions of the federal parliament. Some 1900 census and political variables were stored for each division. This was the first time that Australian federal electoral boundaries had been compiled in digital form, and allowed mapping of voting and socio-economic data by electorates.[6]

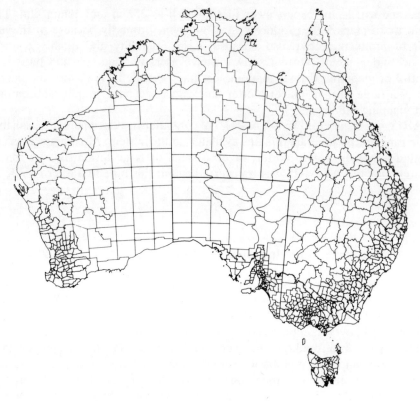

*Figure 7.1   The ARIS 'Basic Mapping Unit' Mapbase.*

## Current data holding

Currently, all ARIS data sets are stored under the VAX 11/750 Datatrieve package[7]. Some ten separate spatial databases have been established, including those carried over from the first phase of development. All are open-ended, in that new data sets can be added at will. The contents of each of these is briefly described in the following sections.

## (i) GRID025

Development of this first grid cell database was commenced in 1983. Initially this resulted in a database of some 20 data items for over 11 000 grid cells covering the continent. Each grid cell is a quarter of a degree in extent in latitude and longitude. Subsequently, mapbases corresponding to subdivisions and aggregations of these grid cells have been developed.

GRID025 was developed to assist in mapping bio-physical and socio-economic influences on the grazing industry in the arid and semi-arid range-lands of Australia. Being the first grid cell data set developed, it was the basis for testing Datatrieve as a data manipulation package. GRID025 holds data on elevation, location, soil, upper and lower storey vegetation, land use, grazing density, land administration, climate, and distances to capital cities and export ports.

## (ii) GRID05

GRID05 holds data against some 3000 grid cells collectively covering the continent (see Figure 7.2). Each cell is half a degree in extent in latitude and longitude. The primary source of data for this base was an aggregation of Census of Population and Housing enumeration district data to half degree grid cells. Data on the number of males, females, and dwellings are stored by type of settlement (e.g., major urban, minor urban, rural). In addition, data on proximate populations is stored.[8] Summary data computed via Datatrieve and available to users, but not stored in the database, include total males, females, dwellings, urban and rural population. Data on feral animal populations are also stored in this database.

*Figure 7.2   The ARIS Half by Half Degree Mapbase.*

## (iii) EIGHT

Only a limited number of data items are stored in EIGHT, a recently developed grid cell database focusing on eighth degree grid cells. For each of some 50000 grid cells covering the continent, data are stored on soil, underlying lithology, topography, and superficial lithology. Parts of south-west and south-east Australia (approximately one-seventh of the continent) also have data on evaporation, precipitation, and forest cover at this resolution.

## (iv) CONVERT

CONVERT is a converter (set of geocode equivalence files) between various small-scale geographic regions and half-degree grid cells. It holds, for instance, the conversions between grid cells and physiographic regions, agricultural survey regions, biogeographic regions, urban regions, topographic mapsheets, and bioclimatic zones.

## (v) GAZETTEER

GAZETTEER is based on the NATMAP 1:250000 Gazetteer.[9] GAZETTEER stores the name, feature type, latitude-longitude, and map sheet (equivalent to half-degree grid cell) for over 60000 geographic features named on the 1:250000 topographic map series of Australia. Features recorded in GAZETTEER include airfields, farms, dams, homesteads, lakes, mines, reserves and forests. GAZETTEER could be used, for instance, to provide a list of all named properties (homesteads) in a region, by linking this database with the CONVERT database.

## (vi) LGA81

LGA81 contains 1981 Census statistics for each local government area (LGA) in Australia. Data stored include total males and females, Australian-born population, number employed and unemployed, number of dwellings, educational status, income, occupation and industry statistics. This database also stores the results of a national survey of local authorities to identify important resource and environmental management issues.[10]

## (vii) AGSTATS

AGSTATS contains data on agricultural enterprises from several of the biennial agricultural censuses conducted by the Australian Bureau of Statistics. The number of farming establishments, area, and, where appropriate, tonnage of over 100 different types of produce are held for each local government area. Data is held for the agricultural censuses of 1982–83 and 1984–85.

A converter between the LGA identifiers used in the Census of Population and Housing and those used in the Agricultural Census is also held so that users can combine data from these two major official statistical series.

AGSTATS has been boosted recently with the acquisition from the Australian Wool Corporation of full details of the Australian wool clip for their 153 wool statistical areas.

## (viii) Australian Resources Data Bank (ARDB)

Some 400 bio-physical data items stored by basic mapping units in the establishment phase have subsequently been made available under Datatrieve. These data are described by Wood[11] and Wood and Cocks,[12] and include data on terrain, elevation, vegetation stratum, and growth forms, soil types, climatic zones, lithology, land cover, degree of modification of vegetation, coastal landforms, coastal vegetation, forest plantations and soil degradation.

## (ix) ELECT81

Selected data items from the federal electorate database established in the first phase of development have subsequently been made available under Datatrieve.

## (x) NATPK

This database contains descriptions of all conservation reserves in Australia. It is based on a register of reserves maintained by NATMAP. It contains the name, identification code, area, location, and type of more than 4200 reserves. Reserve types include Aboriginal land, alpine reserve, coastal park, fauna reserve, forest park, historical reserve, national park, roadside reserve and wildlife sanctuary.

Currently the entire ARIS database holds some 40–50Mb of data on the country-wide distribution of a wide range of socio-economic and bio-physical resources. Most data is from sources at scales of 1:2.5m and smaller. Data on the boundary coordinates for the polygon mapbases occupies approximately 9Mb of storage.

# TECHNICAL CAPABILITIES OF AUSTRALIAN RESOURCES INFORMATION SYSTEM

## Data retrieval

VAX-11 Datatrieve is a versatile data management language developed by Digital Equipment Corporation.[13] It retrieves data stored in key-indexed data files and allows the user to produce sorted reports using simple English-like syntax commands. It can process both relational and hierarchically structured records and contains a limited set of business graphics plotting functions.

In ARIS, Datatrieve is used to produce files formatted for input into a range of specialist packages for carrying out geographic and non-geographic operations. The language used in Datatrieve enables moderately complex models to be developed without increasing the quantity of data stored since global or computed variables can be declared and evaluated only as required. An example of the language is as follows:

FIND GRIDS 025 WITH SOIL = 12, 13, 14 AND LAT BT —35.0 AND —34.0

This command would find all grid cells in GRID025 which had the nominated soil codes and which were located between latitudes −34 and −35 degrees.

A manual for first versions of several databases has been published[14] but full documentation of all files is not yet complete.[15] An example of the level of data documentation that is considered desirable is provided by Wood and Cocks.[16]

## Analytical capabilities

A majority of the analytical tasks confronting users of geographic information systems can be viewed as regionalisation problems. Essentially, such problems require the subdivision of geographic space into regions which are then to be described.[17] In some cases, regionalisation is based on geographic adjacency; in other cases the similarity of locations in terms of their attributes can be used to group locations into region sets. Procedures have also been developed for regionalising on the basis of both proximity and attribute similarity.[18]

Software assembled to assist in regionalisation exercises includes:

(1) Minitab[19] — a popular and powerful statistical package designed for users with little experience of computer systems who need to manipulate moderately large data sets. It operates on a worksheet basis and, in addition to the usual commands for manipulating columns and rows of the worksheet (e.g., read, print, copy, add, multiply), it has plotting (histogram, plot), regression, analysis of variance, correlation, chi-square, and other functions. It is also useful for exploratory data analysis. This package provides routine statistical capabilities for ARIS.

(2) Numerical Taxonomy Package (now called PATN) — developed in CSIRO Division of Water and Land Resources,[20] PATN is a suite of algorithms for data reduction and exploration, hypothesis generation and prediction based on groups. The package can, for instance, be used to reformat data files, produce basic statistics, define and calculate measures of association between elements, group elements and examine minimum spanning trees and principal components in a data set. In total, more than 50 analytical algorithms are available within the PATN package.

(3) LUPLAN[21] — a land use planning package developed by the CSIRO Division of Water and Land Resources. LUPLAN allows users to allocate one of a number of allocands (usually land uses) to each location on the basis of a set of allocative decision rules.

Young et al. illustrate the use of PATN and LUPLAN to regionalise the Australian rangelands in terms of factors affecting pastoral viability.[22]

(4) REGION[23] — an in-house package for identifying all sets of contiguous

cells identically categorised in a grid cell image. REGION also generates measures of region size and boundary length.

(5) CART[24] — a new and extremely powerful package for sequentially splitting a set of observations into subsets based on nominated attributes. CART does this by constructing a binary tree which can be expressed as a set of decision rules stated in terms of the attributes used for subsetting, for example:

If the annual temperature range is greater than 20 degrees C and if precipitation in the driest quarter is greater than 64mm and if mean temperature of the wettest quarter is less than 13.7 degrees, then you will find Eastern Grey kangaroos.

The error associated with this rule is 6.7 per cent; that is, it predicts Eastern Greys in 45 of 641 cells when they are actually present in 42 cells.

Because surrogate variables can be included in an analysis, CART also allows rules to be inferred when data is missing or uncertain.

In addition to these main programs, software has been developed for:

- Distance and area calculations using geodetic grid cells
- Proximity analysis
- Region labelling
- Data aggregation
- Establishing hierarchical data structures
- Profiling nominated regions
- Sieve mapping
- Point, line and polygon intersections
- Overlay of polygon with geodetic grid cells
- Run length encoding
- Coordinate transformations.

## Mapping capabilities

Prior to 1982, after retrieving data from the database, the user would invoke an interactive procedure which, by question and answer, established the control commands necessary to create a thematic map. This procedure allowed manipulation of title, legend, class intervals, type of cross hatching, scale of output etc., but created the map in batch mode. MAPROJ was used to produce transparent map overlays and to plot accurately the boundaries recorded in the mapbases.[25] POLYVRT was used for some mapping functions prior to 1982, principally for line generalisation and mapbase creation.[26]

Removal of ARIS from the CSIRO Cyber 7600 computer in 1982 imposed the not insignificant task of developing equivalent software for the VAX 11/750. POLYVRT was replaced with in-house software for mapbase creation and line generalisation. The procedures for map generation were made fully interactive although many users still prefer to create maps using previously stored sets of control commands. New mapping software which provided advanced graphic subroutines, including 2D and 3D imaging, spatial interpolation, and perspective views were purchased.[27] MAPROJ is still used to produce point and line maps.

## RESEARCH INTO THE NATURE AND USE OF DATA IN GEOGRAPHIC INFORMATION SYSTEMS

As ARIS evolved, it became apparent that there were many issues related to the design and operation of a geographic information system that required more detailed research. Since 1982 the main areas of research that have been addressed are:

- Methods of capturing complex and simple thematic maps
- Methods of structuring large quantities of geographically referenced data
- Assessing the accuracy of gridded data
- New data sources
- Decision-support modelling
- Region creation, search, and description procedures.

Progress on each of these themes is now reviewed briefly.

### Methods of capturing complex and simple thematic maps

Although much ARIS data comes from existing digital sources (e.g. census tapes), some has come from in-house digitising of analogue data (e.g. contour data) and from manual encoding (e.g. of thematic maps).

It has been recognised that identical methods are not appropriate for capturing thematic data from both complex and simple thematic maps. Complex maps (i.e., containing many highly contorted regions), if they are to be represented and manipulated digitally, require a full topological specification of region boundaries whereas simple maps can be specified adequately as a collection of free-standing closed polygons.

Further, simple maps can be encoded rapidly to grid cells using, for instance, manual data capture based on run-length encoding.[28] For more complex maps, the cost-effectiveness of optical scanning is being investigated.

### Methods of structuring large quantities of geographically referenced data

ARIS currently contains point, line and area data. For polygon boundary data, topological storage structures are employed, that is, each polygon has all its neighbours explicitly identified. In the field of spatial data structures, linear quadtrees are the subject of much current research.[29] In particular, we have conducted investigations into their use as a way of archiving grid cell data sets.[30] Basically, a map is converted to a linear quadtree by (i) dividing it into quadrants, (ii) examining each quadrant for thematic purity and, if it is impure, (iii) dividing it again. The result is a mosaic of thematically pure grid cells of different sizes (i.e., a variable size grid cell system). A unique key (often termed a Morton key) can be assigned to each cell such that cells close in space have a numerically close key.

By linking cell keys to an attribute database, rapid methods of windowing any part of a large and complex image are being developed. Investigations have been undertaken into alternative ways of formulating this key and the effect this has on data storage and retrieval. The work could lead, for instance, to an 'image archive' for scanned thematic maps, where each map would be stored in linear quadtree form and stored maps could be windowed and overlaid efficiently using key access methods.

## Assessing the accuracy of gridded data

Grid cells are becoming increasingly popular for GIS, partly as a result of the increasing use of scanners which produce data by pixels, but also because of the ease of establishing modelling procedures (see below) and of geographic processing (e.g. neighbourhood and proximity calculations) of such data. When free-form data is encoded to grid cells, some type of spatial and/or categorical generalisation necessarily occurs. Since the choice of grid cell size affects the accuracy of encoded geographical data, it is practically important to be able to determine the largest size of grid cell which provides an acceptable level of spatial accuracy. This reduces data storage requirements and the cost of manual data capture.

Research has also been conducted on the quantification of spatial generalisation from a theoretical viewpoint; Crapper *et al.* developed a model which estimated the spatial accuracy of grid cell coded thematic data from measures of the size and shape of source regions.[31]

## New data sources

A promising new data source currently being investigated for ARIS is photography from a large format camera (LFC) mounted in a space shuttle.[32] NASA constructed such a camera for the shuttle mission of October 1984. The camera has a focal length of 30.5cm, a $23 \times 46$cm format and operates with up to 80 per cent overlap, allowing stereo interpretation. Of the 2160 photographs taken by the mission, 209 were over Australia. Each photograph covers approximately $350 \times 175$km ($55\,000$–$67\,000$km$^2$) at photo scales between 1:740 000–810 000 (depending on altitude) with between 60 and 80 per cent overlap.[33] This permits the photographs to be interpreted using standard stereoscopic and photogrammetric equipment giving a photographic resolution of 14m (approximately 7m Landsat pixel equivalent) in black and white and 25m in colour.

In preliminary investigations of these products Parvey *et al.* reproduced LFC photographs with 1:1m world map series features superimposed to allow stereo viewing of relief and vegetation with locational reference points.[34] In addition, photographs have been photogrammetrically rectified to produce 1:250 000 photomap sheets of the same area from overlapping frames. Elevation data can thus be extracted for previously unmapped and uncontoured areas.

However, as a future data source of ARIS, LFC photography is limited. The 209 photographs cover only a quarter of the country and, following the *Challenger* disaster of February 1986, the likelihood of further LFC coverage appears slight at this stage.

## Decision-support modelling within a geographic information system

A recent initiative has been to consider alternative methods of developing application models which allow comparative evaluation of sites for some purpose. One technique starts with an expert's judgments about values of some matter of interest at a sample of sites and models the relationships between those judgments and sets of site attributes identified by the expert. This allows the expert's judgments to be extended to sites he has not visited. Cocks *et al.* have demonstrated the use of such a linear judgment model.[35]

An alternative approach currently under investigation is to use numerical classification techniques, such as Automatic Interaction Detection (AID) or classification or decision-tree analysis[36] to identify predictors of gestalt judgments. Decision-tree analysis is seen to be a way of efficiently developing production rules for geographically oriented decision modelling. For developing, redesigning, and recomputing simple models, however, DEC Datatrieve is proving an adequate tool.

### Region creation, search and description procedures

The tasks of identifying and describing region attributes (e.g. size and shape) and the statistical distribution of each region's themes (e.g. soil types) are probably the most common operation undertaken within ARIS. Datatrieve and the two in-house programs, GRIDLIST[37] and REGION[38], provide the main capability for developing descriptions of nominated geographic regions and descriptions of individual/grouped cells satisfying nominated conditions.

The numerical taxonomy package, PATN can be used to create regionalisations reflecting co-variances between grid cell attributes.[39] Consider the problem of establishing a sampling frame over most of Australia as required by Cocks *et al.* [40] PATN was used to assign each of 8000 grid cells to one of 15 categories based on similarity with respect to nine nominal (e.g. soil type) and cardinal (e.g. extreme temperatures) attributes. Each set of contiguous cells falling into the same category implies a region and the set of such regions can be processed through REGION and GRIDLIST.

# APPLICATIONS OF ARIS

## Applications in the establishment phase

Most of the first three years were devoted to system development and data acquisition. Apart from occasional servicing of user requests for thematic maps of the continent's resources only four major projects were undertaken in this period;

- Cartographic modelling of sites for new cites
- Profiling and mapping AUSSAT communications regions
- A 30-map atlas using an electoral mapbase
- Mapping tree loss and priority replanting areas.

The first two of these are discussed in more detail below.

(1) Sites for new cities. One early project, presented as a poster paper at the 1982 International Cartography Conference in Warsaw, involved using ARIS for 'cartographic modelling' with logical and arithmetic operations performed on thematic data describing individual locations.[41] Dangermond described a similar exercise for part of California using ESRI's GRIPS (grid from polygon) system on some 48 000 grid cells.[42]

The project involved nominating what might characterise a suitable location for a major new city to accommodate some of the six million extra Australians expected over the next twenty years. Each basic mapping unit was rated for some twenty factors judged important to choosing a location for major urban development (e.g. pleasant climate, current population, water resources, terrain, energy supply, environmental fragility). This data was used to produce:

(a) Exclusion policy maps identifying areas where the presence of some overriding locality deficiency or problem makes it highly unlikely that urbanisation would be allowed to occur, for example, do not consider sites with very low surface water resources.

(b) Preference policy maps identifying areas where there is some good but not overwhelming reason why a city might be developed in the locality, for example, give preference to sites with pleasant climates.

(c) Avoidance policy maps highlighting where there are good but not overwhelming reasons why city growth might not be encouraged, for example, avoid areas known to be environmentally fragile.

By a process of compositing and weighting component maps, a final map was produced showing an overall suitability class for each unexcluded mapping unit.[43]

(2) Mapping the effect of the location and orientation of the AUSSAT communications satellite on viewing audience and the quality of television reception. The Department of Communications provided, in digital form, sets of reception quality contours for different locations and orientations of the then-planned AUSSAT satellite. Point-in-polygon and polygon intersection algorithms were used to identify local government areas and populations in each reception quality zone. This project was essentially a computer mapping exercise although some limited manipulation of geographic data was required. It is a good example of one of the basic tasks of a geographic information system, namely the description or profiling of nominated geographic regions.

## Recent projects

Since 1982 some 20 further projects have been based around ARIS capabilities. Four of the more recent projects are described in some detail below, and a further five are noted.

(1) Road costs.
Which local authorities in Australia are likely to require augmented funding on the grounds of experiencing high costs per kilometre when constructing new roads?

An in-house geotechnical map of integrated soils-lithology-topography spatial units was manually encoded against ARIS basic mapping units.[44] Simple expert judgment models of relative difficulty with respect to earthworks, paving, and sealing phases of road construction were constructed as a function of soil type, lithology, and topography, and extrapolated to all basic mapping units. These three separate models have been reported[45] but not as yet combined into an overall index of road construction difficulty. This exercise was our first attempt to apply formal decision-support modelling to data stored in ARIS.

(2) Urban regions.
Identify the set of $n$ (where $n$ can be any number nominated by the client) regions of 150 kilometres radius which collectively contain a maximum number of Australians.

Census collection district data was aggregated to half-degree grid cells by a 'centroid-in-cell' procedure[46] and a 150 kilometre catchment population calculated for each of 3000 half-degree grid cells in Australia. The heuristic developed for defining catchment regions involved the sequential selection of a node cell for each region, namely, that with the highest proximate population. All cells within the catchment of the node cell were then 'allocated' to that region and removed from further consideration. Proximate populations for all cells affected by this removal were recalculated and the cell with the highest proximate population selected as the node for the next region. After 18 iterations of this procedure (i.e. 18 regions) 92.8 per cent of the Australian population had been allocated to an urban region.[47]

In this problem, the solution space was too large to explore exhaustively and the exercise is an example of the need to use heuristic methods to approach combinatorially large regionalisation problems as will be encountered with continental-scale GIS.

(3) High-speed ground transport system.
Locate a high-speed ground transport system for eastern Australia so as to service a 'maximum' number of people by the construction of a 'minimal' length network.

For practical reasons, this large, combinatorial problem was approached as a design exercise of linking the 18 urban regions identified in the previous application. Initially, the primary network was defined to link the geographic centroid of each urban region, although the option of locating these 'main stations' at population-weighted centroids was also evaluated. Feeder links were then added to provide a service from each heavily populated grid cell to its nearest 'main station'. The resulting design implied some 5000 kilometres of primary and 10000 kilometres of feeder track. Some 11.7 million people were within a maximum of 150 kilometres of the network and some 10.9 million people (75 per cent of the Australian population) within 30 kilometres of the network.[48] Topographic and lithologic data stored in ARIS was used to estimate the relative difficulty of constructing each primary link.

This exercise shows ARIS being used as an intuitive design aid without making any formal attempt to specify and compare a range of alternative systems. In calculating relative construction difficulty, ARIS is being used for post-design impact assessment.

(4) Rainforest formations.
Identify parts of Australia which support vegetation formations containing or likely to contain patches of rainforest.

The vegetation source map for ARIS, encoded to quarter-degree cells, shows 51 formations, some of which are likely to contain unmappably small patches of rainforest. An ecologist client selected four vegetation formations highly likely and two vegetation formations moderately likely to contain patches of rainforest. These groups of formations were each mapped collectively to illustrate rainforest-indicative formations.[49] The project illustrates the use of a GIS to reclassify and map stored attributes.

A comparable exercise was to highlight parts of Australia with large areas of soils potentially suited to the growing of the latex crop guayule.[50] Data on dominant soil type (29 categories) is held against each grid cell in GRID025. By pre-classifying each of these soil categories according to its suitability as a growth medium for this crop and mapping the resultant categories, a map was produced showing the relative suitability of each grid cell for guayule cultivation.

## Other projects which have been undertaken include:

(1) Rangeland environments.
Describe and map the distribution of the main environmental factors (soils,

vegetation, climate) affecting the Australian pastoral industry and identify parts of the rangelands which are environmentally similar.

The project is documented in *Management of Australia's Rangelands*.[51] The exercise consolidated the interfacing of ARIS to a numerical classification package and developed skills in establishing data collection procedures, the use of small-scale surface fitting techniques and the production of thematic maps suitable for publication.

(2) Soil-vegetation combinations.

Identify those parts of Australia which, because of their unusual combinations of soil and vegetation, are candidates for inclusion in some future national parks system.

This is an on-going exercise which illustrates the usefulness of interfacing ARIS to powerful analytical tools. Classification tree analysis, in particular, provides a promising method for both eliciting and formalising expert judgments and 'explaining' objective phenomena.

(3) Viability of pastoralism.

Identify currently ungrazed parts of Australia's rangelands that might be made available for pastoral use on the basis of their good viability prospects and currently grazed parts that might be withdrawn on the basis of their poor viability prospects.

In this project an exploratory linear model of an expert's judgments of medium-term prospects of financial survival for pastoral enterprises in Australia's rangelands was developed and applied.[52] This exercise demonstrated the use of ARIS for policy analysis and also the interfacing of a geo-data system to models of expert personal judgment. The project utilised a diversity of ARIS analytical capabilities including numerical classification and statistical modelling.

(4) Land use issues.

Map and analyse the results of a survey of land use issues perceived by Australian local government authorities.

ARIS was used by Parvey *et al.* to map local governments where the 20 major land use issues identified by Cocks *et al.* were seen to be important.[53] Parvey *et al.* compared these perceptions of soil erosion with ARIS data on soil erodibility.[54] Comparably, Davis and Parvey used ARIS to aggregate community perceptions of water-related issues to 39 'water basins' in the populated areas of Australia.[55]

Whilst in no way technically innovative, these exercises highlight the way in which a national resources information system can contribute to policy debate and analysis of emerging resource issues.

(5) Biosphere reserves.

Identify, map, and evaluate the locations of the eleven Australian national parks currently designated as biosphere reserves in relation to biogeographical provinces/bioclimatic zones.

At the request of the Australian Man and Biosphere Committee, a map showing the location of biosphere reserves in relation to bioclimatic and biogeographic regions was produced.[56] The exercise illustrates the power of being able to bring disparate data sources together to complete a task which otherwise would not be contemplated.

## ARIS AND THE DEFENCE TASK

ARIS has reached the stage of being a working geographic information system able to support users concerned with the small-scale description, evaluation, analysis and management of Australia's spatially distributed natural and anthropogenic resources. It has produced useful material for a range of extramural and in-house clients and continues to attract inquiries for its further use.

Development of a continental geographic information system clearly demands compromises; for example, between the ability to answer questions about small areas at acceptable resolution and Australia-wide questions; and between acquiring a wide range of general-purpose data and a narrower range of more specialised data. In ARIS we have pursued breadth in spatial coverage and in the range of data held. On occasions this policy has led to criticism from potential clients with local/sub-regional interests but, conversely, it has attracted several clients welcoming the capability to provide and combine a number of national data sets.

What this means in military terms is that an ARIS-type GIS is more likely to be able to support strategic rather than tactical decision-making. The 'Cobar project' provides an example.[57] In 1986 the Department of Defence was studying various areas in New South Wales to determine their suitability as Army training areas and they were asked, at short notice, by the Senate Standing Committee on Foreign Affairs and Defence to provide evidence of the extent to which one of these sites, that at Cobar, was representative of the Australian biological and physical environment.

ARIS was interrogated to identify the types of soils, vegetation, topography and climate at the proposed site. All grid cells in Australia were then tested to see whether they had biophysical attributes matching one or more parts of the Cobar site. Within 48 hours they were able to produce four maps showing areas of Australia similar to at least part of the Cobar area in terms of soils, vegetation, climate and topography (Figure 7.3). It can be noted in passing that the related problem of identifying and evaluating a large range of potential training sites would itself have been a task well suited to ARIS.

The Cobar project is a simple example of the sequential use of a GIS to firstly characterise a nominated location and then to find other locations with similar attributes. A reasonably rapid response was only possible because appropriate data were stored in the system at the time the request was made. A more sophisticated response to this request would have been well within ARIS capabilities, but with slower response time. For example, the PATN package could have been used to classify all grid cells over soil, climate, vegetation and topography simultaneously into, say, 15 similarity groups. Re-

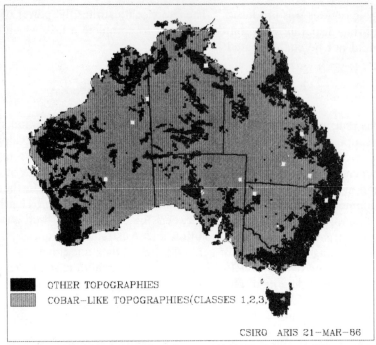

CSIRO   ARIS 21—MAR—86

*Figure 7.3   Cobar-like Topographies. Areas with topography similar to at least one part of the proposed Army training area (smooth plainlands to 6 m relief, undulating or irregular plainlands of 6–30 m relief, dissected plateaux of 30–90 m relief, escarpments and ranges of 90–180 m relief).*

gions containing cells classified as similar to one or more Cobar cells could then have been delineated.

User demands of a tactical level GIS (e.g. to support deployment decisions) would be markedly higher than in the Cobar project. Superficially, a tactical system needs capabilities for such things as real-time responses, access to large-scale topographic databases, and feature analysis and comparison capabilities, for example within five seconds identify and map all outcrops commanding a middle ground view of a particular river crossing. Such systems are feasible but substantially more expensive. The areas where large-scale tactical GIS are to be established would need to be selected very carefully and one promising use of an ARIS-type GIS would be to support such decisions by systematically evaluating relevant attributes of numerous candidate localities.

Moreover, investigation is likely to reveal a range of strategic tasks amenable to the slower, small-scale capabilities of an ARIS-type GIS. Examples which immediately suggest themselves (without requiring new data sets) include:

(1) Coastal surveillance strategy. ARIS contains quite extensive data on each 10 kilometres section of Australia's 30 000 kilometres coastline for example, beaches, rockiness, estuaries, vegetation type.[58] This information could be combined with ARIS data on population distribution, homestead location, etc. to identify low, medium, and high priority sections for regular surveillance (and for building high-resolution tactical GIS).

(2) Long-distance traversing. Whilst far from the scale of Laut and Davis's study of trafficability of Cape York (Chapter 9) the 1:2.5m geotechnical map of Australia[59] stored in ARIS at eighth-degree resolution could be a useful aid for planning stages and stopovers in long cross-country traverses of any part of Australia.[60] Maps showing corridors to be avoided or favoured because of soil, terrain, and superficial or underlying lithology, plus potential stopovers such as watering points, homesteads, etc. (from the GAZETTEER database) could be produced relatively easily.

(3) On-line regional handbooks. Laing and Puniard (Chapter 4) describe the generic contents of a series of regional-scale defence land information handbooks. ARIS already contains a significant part of the information planned to be included in these and has the capabilities for aggregating such material to match any set of boundaries nominated by Army Office. New editions could be produced immediately or at any required frequency following updating. Electronic access to relevant cadastrally-based land information systems would facilitate this undertaking. It is perhaps worth commenting at this point that an awareness of the existence of many useful machine-readable data sets only develops as the task of building a GIS proceeds. The message is that it is important for Defence to begin acquiring experience with GIS as soon as possible after a decision to proceed is taken, even if this is initially only with a strategic-type system.

(4) Servicing civil defence/counter disaster needs. The Natural Disasters Organisation (NDO) in the Department of Defence has a planning and coordinating responsibility in relation to natural and man-made disasters and civil defence[61] throughout the whole country, not just northern Australia. NDO information systems have not been automated, despite a recognised need for this within the Organisation. A simple system for profiling all population centres in the country in terms of civil defence/counter disaster resources could be developed within ARIS, drawing initially on GAZETTEER and population census data. It would be a mistake to develop an NDO GIS in isolation from a military GIS.

The above examples all illustrate a point of fundamental importance about constructing geographic information systems. Whether the technology is reasonably established as for strategic systems or at the frontier as for tactical systems, it is data sets which are all-important. Even making full use of mechanically acquired data such as satellite imagery, data acquisition and validation is an extremely expensive business and likely to be the pivot on which the cost-effectiveness of a military GIS is eventually judged. Even if it is decided not to proceed with the development of a defence GIS at this stage, all land-related data currently being collected should be held in a form facilitating its eventual transfer into a GIS.

# NOTES

1   K.D. Cocks and P.A. Walker, *An Introduction to the Australian Resources Information System*, Technical Memorandum No. 80/19 (CSIRO Division of Land Use Research, Canberra, 1980).

2   See P.A. Walker and J.R. Davis, *The Nelligen Geographic Processing System: System Design*, Technical Memorandum No. 78/11 (CSIRO Division of Land Use Research, Canberra, 1978).

3   K.D. Cocks and P.A. Walker, *An Introduction to the Australian Resources Information System*, p. 1.

4   See C.A. Parvey and N.H. Wood, *Spatial Units in the Australian Resources Information System*, Technical Memorandum No. 80/27 (CSIRO Division of Land Use Research, Canberra, 1980).

5   Australian Bureau of Statistics, 1976 Census of Population and Housing. LGAO Summary Data Computer File, Tables LG002 to LG049.

6   See C.A. Parvey, *The Federal Electorate Divisions Information System: Its Spatial Base and Mapping System*, Technical Memorandum No. 82/6 (CSIRO Division of Land Use Research, Canberra, 1982).

7   Described in Digital Equipment Corporation (DEC), *VAX-11 Datatrieve Reference Manual* (Digital Equipment Corporation, Maynard, Massachusetts, 1981).

8   K.D. Cocks and P.A. Walker, 'Estimating Proximate Populations for an Extensive Set of Locations in Australia', *Australian Geographer*, Vol. 16, 1985, pp. 295–300.

9   Division of National Mapping, Department of Minerals and Energy, *Australia 1:250 000 Map Series Gazetteer* (Australian Government Publishing Service, Canberra, 1975).

10  See C.A. Parvey, H.D. Blain and P.A. Walker, *A Register and Atlas of Local Government Land Use Issues*, Technical Memorandum No.83/21 (CSIRO Division of Water and Land Resources, Canberra, 1983); and C.A. Parvey, P.A. Walker and H.D. Blain, 'Local Government Land Use Issues: A Data Set for a Geographic Information System', in B. Pathe (ed.), *Proceedings*, URPIS 11 Conference, Brisbane, 1983 (AURISA, Sydney, 1984), s. 9A, pp. 12–13.

11  N. Wood, *Procedures for Selectively Listing Data from the Australian Resources Data Bank*, Technical Memorandum No. 83/12 (CSIRO Division of Land Use Research, Canberra, 1983).

12  N.H. Wood and K.D. Cocks, *Microfiche of Data held against Basic Mapping Units in the Australian Resources Data Bank*, Technical Memorandum No. 84/31 (CSIRO Division of Water and Land Resources, Canberra, 1984).

13  See Digital Equipment Corporation (DEC), *VAX-11 Datatrieve Reference Manual*.

14  P.A. Walker, *GRIDBANK: A Guide to the Database Using DEC VAX-11 DATATRIEVE*,

Technical Memorandum No. 85/10 (CSIRO Division of Water and Land Resources, Canberra, 1985).

15   P.A. Walker, ARIS — A Guide to the Database Using DEC Datatrieve. In preparation.

16   N.H. Wood and K.D. Cocks, *GRIDLIST: A Procedure for Accessing GRIDBANK on the VAX 11–750*, Technical Memorandum No. 85/20 (CSIRO Division of Water and Land Resources, Canberra, 1985).

17   See, for example, K.D. Cocks and P.A. Walker, 'Using the Australian Resources Information System to Describe Extensive Regions', *Applied Geography*, Vol. 7, No. 1, January 1987, pp. 17–27.

18   See C.R. Margules, D.P. Faith and L. Belbin, 'An Adjacency Constraint in Agglomerative Hierarchical Classifications of Geographic Data', *Environment and Planning A*, Vol. 17, No. 3, March 1985, pp. 397–412.

19   See T.A. Ryan, B.L. Joiner and B.F. Ryan, *Minitab Reference Manual* (Statistics Department, Pennsylvania State University, Pennsylvania, 1982).

20   See L.L. Belbin, D.P. Faith and P.R. Minchin, *Some Algorithms in the Numerical Taxonomy Package NTP*, Technical Memorandum No. 84/23 (CSIRO Division of Water and Land Resources, Canberra, 1984).

21   See J.R. Ive and K.D. Cocks, 'SIRO-PLAN and LUPLAN: An Australian Approach to Land-Use Planning. 2. The LUPLAN Land-use Planning Package', *Environment and Planning B: Planning and Design*, Vol. 10, No. 3, September 1983, pp. 346–354; and J.R. Ive, *LUPLAN: MICROSOFT BASIC, CP/M User's Manual*, Technical Memorandum No. 84/5 (CSIRO Division of Water and Land Resources, Canberra, 1984).

22   M.D. Young, P.A. Walker and K.D. Cocks, 'Distribution of Influences on Rangeland Management' in G.N. Harrington, A.D. Wilson and M.D. Young (eds), *Management of Australia's Rangelands* (CSIRO, Melbourne, 1984).

23   See P.M. Nanninga and P.A. Walker, *Regionalisation of Grid Cell Data: REGION — a Maximally Connected Components Algorith*, Technical Memorandum No. 83/19 (CSIRO Division of Water and Land Resources, Canberra, 1983).

24   See L. Breiman, J.H. Friedman, R.A. Olshen and C.J. Stone, *Classification and Regression Trees*, Wadsworth Statistics/Probability Series (Wadsworth, Belmont, California, 1984).

25   See M.F. Hutchinson, *MAPROJ — A Computer Map Projection System*, Technical Paper No. 39 (CSIRO Division of Land Use Research, Melbourne, 1981).

26   See Harvard University, Laboratory for Computer Graphics and Spatial Analysis, *POLYVRT: A Program to Convert Geographic Base Files, Manual* (Laboratory for Computer Graphics and Spatial Analysis, Harvard University, Cambridge, Massachusetts, 1974).

27   Described in European Software Contractors, *GEOPAK Users Manual*, Version 83.1 (European Software Contractors A/S, Gentofte, Denmark, 1982).

28   See C.A. Parvey, *Grid Cell Data Capture for a National Resources Information System*, Technical Memorandum No. 86/16 (CSIRO Division of Water and Land Resources, Canberra, 1986).

29   For example, see D.J. Abel, 'Some Elemental Operations on Linear Quadtrees for Geographic Information Systems', *Computing Journal*, Vol. 48, No. 1, 1985, pp. 73–77.

30   See P.A. Walker and I.W. Grant, 'Quadtree: A Fortran Program to Extract the Quadtree Structure of a Raster Format Multi-coloured Image', *Computers and Geosciences*, Vol. 12, No. 4, 1986, pp. 401–410.

31   P.F. Crapper, P.A. Walker and P.M. Nanninga, 'Theoretical Prediction of the Effect of Aggregation on Grid Cell Data Sets', *Geoprocessing*, Vol. 3, No. 2, 1986, pp. 155–166.

32   See F.J. Doyle, 'A Large Format Camera for Shuttle', *Photogrammetric Engineering and Remote Sensing*, Vol. 45, 1979, pp. 73–78.

33   See C.A. Parvey and P.A. Walker, 'Coverage of Australia by Large Format Camera Space Shuttle Photography', *Cartography*, Vol. 14, No. 2, 1985, pp. 108–111.

34   C.A. Parvey, K.C. Hynson and P.A. Walker, 'The Potential of Space Shuttle Photography for Regional Resource Mapping and Evaluation', in P.J. Hocking (ed.), *Proceedings, URPIS 13 Conference*, Adelaide, 1985 (AURISA, Sydney, 1986), pp. 327–331.

35   K.D. Cocks, M.D. Young and P.A. Walker, 'Mapping Viability Prospects for Pastoralism in Australia', *Agricultural Systems*, Vol. 20, 1986, pp. 175–193.

36   For example, see L. Breiman, J.H. Friedman, R.A. Olshen and C.J. Stone, *Classification and Regression Trees*.

37   N.H. Wood and K.D. Cocks, *GRIDLIST*.

38   P.M. Nanninga and P.A. Walker, *Regionalisation of Grid Cell Data*.

39   See L.L. Belbin, D.P. Faith and P.R. Minchin, *Some Algorithms in the Numerical Taxonomy Package NTP*.

40   K.D. Cocks, M.D. Young and P.A. Walker, 'Mapping Viability Prospects for Pastoralism in Australia'.

41   Described in C.D. Tomlin and J.K. Berry, 'A Mathematical Structure for Cartographic Modelling in Environmental Analysis', in *Proceedings*, 39th American Congress on Surveying and Mapping, Washington DC, 1979, pp. 269–284.

42   J. Dangermond, 'Selecting New Town Sites in the United States Using Regional Data Base', in E. Teichoz and J.L. Berry (eds), *Computer Graphics and Environmental Planning* (Prentice-Hall, New York, 1983).

43   See L.D. Hopkins, 'Methods for Generating Land Suitability Maps', *Journal of the American Institute of Planners*, Vol. 43, 1977, pp. 386–400.

44   See K. Grant, J.R. Davis and C. de Visser, *A Geotechnical Landscape Map of Australia*, Divisional Report No. 84/1 (CSIRO Division of Water and Land Resources, Canberra, 1984).

45   See J.R. Davis, K. Grant and C.A. Parvey, 'Assessing the Geotechnical Component of Road Construction Suitability Across Australia', *Australian Geographical Studies*, Vol. 24, No. 2, 1986, pp. 244–258.

46   Compare, for example, D. Rhind and H. Mounsey, 'The Land and People of Britain: A Domesday Record', *Transactions*, Institute of British Geographers, New Series 11, 1986, pp. 315–325.

47   See K.D. Cocks and P.A. Walker, 'Estimating Proximate Populations . . .'.

48   See K.D. Cocks, P.A. Walker and C.A. Parvey, 'Using Information Technology to Examine
      ᵗ᷾        ᵗation of a High Speed Ground Transport System for Australia', Australian Institution
              neers, Civil Engineering Section, *Transactions*, Vol. 27, No. 3, 1985, pp. 321–327.

                    . Cocks, Using ARIS to Map Rainforest Formations. CSIRO Division of Water and
                  sources, Land Use Planning Group Working Document No. 86/7, Canberra, 1986.

              Cocks and P.A. Walker, Using ARIS to Identify Soils Suitable for Guayule. CSIRO

Division of Water and Land Resources, Land Use Planning Group Working Document No. 86/1, Canberra, 1986.

51   M.D. Young, P.A. Walker and K.D. Cocks, 'Distribution of Influences on Rangeland Management'.

52   See K.D. Cocks, M.D. Young and P.A. Walker, 'Mapping Viability Prospects for Pastoralism in Australia'.

53   C.A. Parvey, H.D. Blain and P.A. Walker, *A Register and Atlas of Local Government Land Use Issues*; and K.D. Cocks, G. McConnell and P.A. Walker, *Matters for Concern — Tomorrow's Land Use Issues*, Divisional Report No. 80/1 (CSIRO Division of Land Use Research, Canberra, 1980).

54   C.A. Parvey, P.A. Walker and H.D. Blain, 'Local Government Land Use Issues . . .'.

55   J.R. Davis and C.A. Parvey, 'Local Government Perceptions of Water Related Issues in Rural Australia', *Australian Geographical Studies*, Vol. 24, No. 1, 1986, pp. 72–87.

56   K.D. Cocks and P.A. Walker, *Using ARIS to Evaluate the Biogeographical Spread of Australia's Biosphere Reserves*, Technical Memorandum No. 86/22 (CSIRO Division of Water and Land Resources, Canberra, 1986).

57   K.D. Cocks, Representativeness of the Proposed Army Training Area at Cobar, CSIRO Division of Water and Land Resources, Land Use Planning Group Working Document No. 86/3, Canberra, 1986.

58   See R.W. Galloway, R. Story, R. Cooper and G.A. Yapp, *Coastal Lands of Australia*, Natural Resources Series No. 1 (CSIRO Division of Water and Land Resources, Melbourne, 1984).

59   See K. Grant, J.R. Davis nd C. de Visser, *A Geotechnical Landscape Map of Australia*.

60   See, for example, Colonel P.M. Jeffrey, 'Initial Thoughts on an Australian Land Surveillance Force', *Defence Force Journal*, No. 21, March–April 1980, pp. 24–34.

61   Air Vice-Marshal J.D.G. Lessels, 'Counter Disaster Organisation in Australia' in *Natural Disasters in Australia*, Proceedings of the Ninth Invitation Symposium of the Australian Academy of Technological Sciences, Sydney, 1985 (Australian Academy of Technological Sciences, Parkville, Melbourne, 1985), pp. 15–23.

# CHAPTER EIGHT

# Overview of LIS Activities in Queensland

**P. Perrett   K.J. Lyons**

**O.F. Moss**

Current LIS activities throughout Australia have been outlined in Chapter 2 where it was seen that activities are occurring at the state government level in all states. It is now proposed to look at some projects which have or are being undertaken in Queensland. Queensland has been selected because the projects:

- Represent a non-centralised approach.
- Contain not only land administration data, but also a range of other geographic information and remotely sensed data; that is, topographic, utility, resource, environment, marine, socio-economic, etc.
- Cover an area of defence interest.

## BACKGROUND

To assist in understanding where LIS is at present, and where it could go, it is useful to understand the history of LIS development in Queensland. The background of other various states is not dissimilar.

In 1978, a senior government delegation visited the United Kingdom, the United States and Canada. A subsequent report[1] recommended that a steering committee be established to report to Cabinet on the possible development of a land information system for Queensland. The Land Data Bank Steering Committee was subsequently appointed by Cabinet to review land information flows between government organisations.

The Committee identified many inefficiencies within the existing manual systems, prompting the establishment of a project team to investigate the development of a land data bank for Queensland. The *Land Data Bank Project Report*[2] was produced in 1982, resulting in a Cabinet decision establishing the Land Information Steering Committee (LISC) to replace the Land Data Bank Steering Committee.

The task of the LISC is to monitor and coordinate the development of the State Government LIS activities.

# LEVELS OF LIS DEVELOPMENT IN QUEENSLAND

In Queensland, three levels of LIS development may be identified:
(1) Development of computer-based data systems in individual state government departments to meet their own responsibilities.
(2) Integration of those systems across departments.
(3) Establishment of a user-responsive LIS framework for all public sector and
private sector users throughout the State. (Note: the data held by government would be only one part of the total available data sets.)

At present most progress has been made in level (1), some initial progress in
level (2) but very little in level (3).

Achievement of (3) is very desirable. It is also in keeping with the philosophy of the State development strategy. To achieve optimal results it is not
suitable to approach these three levels as separate exercises.

While the charter of the LISC, as it is presently constituted, is to focus on
levels (1) and (2), it is envisaged that a framework will be developed to address
the issues relevant to level (3). The issues which are to be addressed under this
new structure include:
(a) Promoting and coordinating development of an LIS to cover government
departments, and overall advising on LIS matters to Cabinet (e.g. on
communication standards to be established).
(b) Positive facilitation to achieve the wider development of LIS throughout
the State. A body of wide public and private representation — such as a
state land information council — might be appropriate. As great a level of
self-determination as possible would be desirable for the body. Sub-
committees dealing with particular industry sectors or special interests
might also be useful. (NB There could well be a high-level defence representation on the state council and a special subcommittee of defence and
civil representation dealing with, for example, defence needs for infrastructure information.)
(c) Coordinating the resolution of more detailed technical and functional
issues — both in government and private LIS arenas (i.e., a support role to
both (a) and (b)). Topics requiring consideration include communication
standards, privacy, charging arrangements, training, maintaining flexibility
to cater for technological change, etc. To this could be added areas of
defence interest.

To successfully implement a level (2) and (3) LIS for Queensland a concept
plan is to be developed which will address, in addition to the types of issues
raised above, essential policy matters such as:

● Who are the land information generators and users throughout the community?

● What balance should there be between a publicly operated LIS for internal
government information and privately sponsored LISs marketing information to particular user groups?

- To what extent and by what mechanisms should the private groups' operations be regulated and interfacing between different groups be controlled?
- How should the government LIS be structured — e.g. the extent of centralisation/decentralisation, and the role of a HUB in this regard?

## CURRENT STATUS

The current status at each level of development in Queensland is described below. While most activity has occurred at levels (1) and (2) and little at level (3), it will be seen that most attention will be given to those projects which may be considered as providing a major contribution to future developments at level (3).

### LEVEL (1)

At the level (1) stage significant progress has been made by many State government departments. Of these, the Lot on Plan Descriptor and the Digital Cadastral Data Base (DCDB) are of major importance.

The Lot on Plan Descriptor is a unique land parcel identifier. It is the common primary key which enables the linking of different land-related data sets held by the various land administration and mapping authorities (such as the Department of the Valuer-General, the Titles Office, Department of Mapping and Surveying (DMS) and Lands Department).

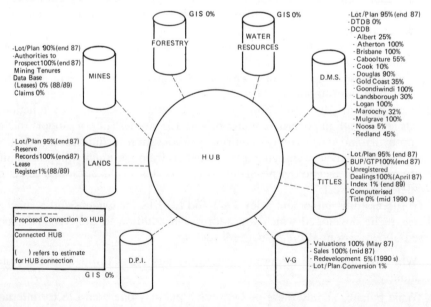

*Figure 8.1   Completion Status of State Government Systems for HUB Connection, as at February 1987.*

The DCDB developed by the DMS includes the spatial base to which much land-related information may be referenced. This spatial base consists of all cadastral property boundaries and uses the Lot on Plan Descriptor as the unique property identifier.

## LEVEL (2)

The integration of those systems developed at level (1) is to be facilitated through the level (2) development of the HUB system by the State Government Computer Centre (SGCC). The HUB project is designing a system to provide inquiry access to different land-related data sets from a single inquiry point. Figure 8.1 shows schematically the concept of the HUB and indicates the completion status of many level (1) projects by the various State Government departments and authorities involved.

## LEVEL (3)

Through the various level (1) and level (2) projects a broad range of land-related data sets are made available. At the level (3) stage concepts are being tested and prototypes are being developed which draw on different groupings or combinations of these data sets which may be used to form various sub-systems of an overall LIS.

The developments to be described here concern three major projects. The first one, the Coopers Plains pilot project (1984–85) tested basic concepts over a small Brisbane suburban area. Of the other two, one deals with land administration and associated data (the Corporate Working Map project) and the other applies the concepts developed to a large regional area (the Regional Geographic Information System (REGIS) program).

These three major activities are now discussed in more detail giving most attention to those which are currently under way.

## The Coopers Plains Pilot Project (1984–85)

The aim of the project was to bring together onto a single system graphic and attribute data from a number of different organisations for part of a Brisbane suburb (Coopers Plains). Interactive computer graphics equipment was used to display attribute and graphic data, in response to user-defined requests. Whilst successfully demonstrating the potential of interactive graphics systems for land information systems the project was not designed to allow donor organisations to maintain their data routinely.

The evaluation of the Coopers Plains pilot project identified the need for the two other projects. These projects are currently under way. The first of these, which is being undertaken during 1986/87, is the Corporate Working Map (CWM) project. The other is the Regional Geographic Information System (REGIS) program.

## The Corporate Working Map (CWM) Project

Currently, Queensland authorities involved in the registering and examining of land ownership each make use of separately-maintained paper-based departmental 'working cadastral maps' for the display of spatially related data. A departmental working map can be defined as a copy of the latest published cadastral map that is continually kept up-to-date by noting and charting tenure and administrative information as it becomes available from the day-to-day business of land administration. There are approximately 3100 of these working maps in daily use.

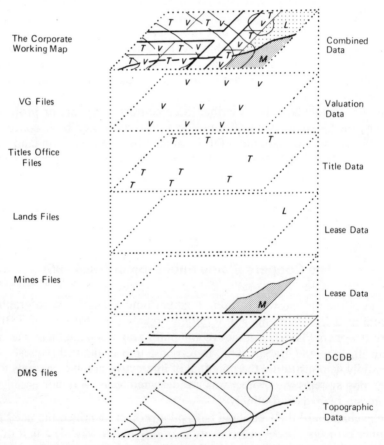

*Figure 8.2   Corporate Working Map Concept.*

Source: D. Hebblethwaite and R.J. Eden, 'The Corporate Working Map', in S.D. Hunter (ed.), *Proceedings*, URPIS 14 Conference, Melbourne, 1986 (AURISA, Sydney, 1986).

In Queensland, the Department of Mapping and Surveying, Lands Department, the Valuer-General's Department, and the Titles Office all use the same base cadastral data for their working maps. A number of other departments also maintain copies of the working maps.

It was proposed that the working map requirements of each organisation be examined with the view to producing a single digital graphical Corporate Working Map (CWM) which will be linked to associated attribute data already held on separate mainframe computers to form a Land Tenure Information System (LATIS).

As described by Hebblethwaite and Eden[3] each organisation providing data for the Corporate Working Map would have its own graphics files which it, and it alone, would maintain, but each would be able to view the other organisations' files. The collective set of files when overlaid would form the Corporate Working Map.

The corporate working map concept is illustrated in Figure 8.2 and brings together several level (1) projects, that is, DCDB, Lot on Plan Descriptions, etc.

Users of the corporate working map are considered by Hebblethwaite and Eden in terms of three categories, their data links within the system depending on their data access requirements:

- *Category 1* — Required by groups of organisations with a common purpose and which need interactive access to a common, or corporate, pool of data, the currency of which is continually kept up-to-date by the members of the group. An example of such a group, or processing cluster, is that which includes DMS (the Department of Mapping and Surveying), Lands, Titles, Valuer-General, and Mines all using and maintaining the Corporate Working Map and associated attribute data.

- *Category 2* — Required by organisations which need interactive use of specific data provided by other organisations but, for some reason, cannot be a Category 1 user of the data or which can tolerate a lesser degree of currency. It is expected that such organisations will use a copy of the data which will be revised at regular intervals by the donor organisations. The frequency of revision would depend on the degree of currency required. An example would be the use of the Corporate Working Map data by Local Authorities.

- *Category 3* — Users requiring data from other organisations on an ad hoc basis or in the nature of simple standard form type inquiries. This type might cover use of the Corporate Working Map data by such groups as solicitors and the real estate industry.[4]

Defence needs for this type of data could well make it a Category 3 user. Conceptually, Category 1 users could also be Category 2 and 3 users, etc. These three categories of user are schematically illustrated in Table 8.1.

Possible data links between users are summarised in Figure 8.3 where the CWM system is illustrated.

This is a pilot project. If it is successful (and it is anticipated it will be) then adoption on a large scale would have the following impact on civil operations:

Table 8.1   CORPORATE WORKING MAP USER CATEGORIES

| Category | Graphics Data Use | Access Method | Data Currency |
|---|---|---|---|
| 1 | On-line interactive<br>Remote interactive | Direct or LAN<br>Remote (Telecom<br>data line) | Current<br><br>Current |
| 2 | Off-line interactive<br>on a copy | Copy obtained by<br>—   magnetic tape<br>or optical discs<br>—   dial-up-modem<br>or microwave<br>links<br>(possibly through<br>the HUB) | Periodic update or<br>on request |
| 3 | Off-line inquiry | Dial-up-modem or<br>microwave link<br>through the HUB | Current (if<br>connected to a Cat<br>1 User) or perhaps<br>less-than-current (if<br>connected to a Cat<br>2 User) |

*Source*: Hebblethwaite and Eden (1986)

- Elimination of time spent in passing working maps between departments for use and maintenance.
- Significant reduction of resources used by Mines, Titles and the Valuer-General's Department in maintaining working maps. (Some Titles Office resources may advantageously be used to digitise survey plans).
- A reduction in search time for verification of new titles and leases by being able to view other organisations' data immediately.
- The ability to issue documents much more quickly.

The main benefit from the introduction of such a system is considered to be improved service to customers due to increased efficiency and more current, accurate, and accessible data. The project will solve some of the problems related to the incorporation of attribute data on one computer system with the graphic data held on another computer system. This is considered essential for subsequent data analysis and efficient product generation. It will also further define the nature and the role of the HUB. The procedures developed in this project will pave the way for the generation of viable revenue-earning products. These procedures should be transportable to other systems operating in the LIS environment.

It would offer the following benefits for the defence user:

- Selection of training and exercise areas.
- Contacting the owner of a parcel of land quickly.
- Providing one layer of a LIS which is a primary key to others.

The wide participation from the organisations involved in the supply and use of land tenure data will provide a sound basis for the further development towards an operational system.

## The Regional Geographic Information System (REGIS) Program

While the Coopers Plains pilot project and the Corporate Working Map project are significant steps in the development of a Queensland LIS, many further issues need to be addressed. These include:

- Administrative cooperation and financial/technical management for a geographically dispersed project.
- The transfer of data over long distances (up to 1500 km).
- The integration of a wide variety of data, held by different agencies at different levels of government.
- The provision of LIS data to widely dispersed user nodes, which will vary in the sophistication of hardware, software, and operators and who will add the supplied data to their own data.

The Regional Geographic Information System (REGIS) program has addressed these issues by:

- Selecting a test area at some distance from Brisbane.
- Selecting an area with a wide variety of terrain types and land uses, and in which rapid change was occurring.
- Incorporating a significant amount of resource data.

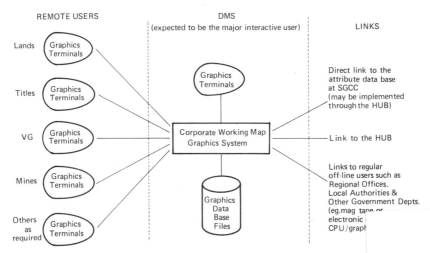

*Figure 8.3   Corporate Working Map System.*

Source: D. Hebblethwaite and R.J. Eden. (1986).

- Including as participants a number of agencies which maintain various data sets.
- Establishing a number of projects within the REGIS program (see Figure 8.4).

## Concepts to be Tested

Concepts to be tested under the REGIS program include:

- Different data sets can be merged.
- Remotely sensed data can be merged.
- Databases can be maintained remotely from data sources.
- LIS development will be expedited by:
  - providing key data sets in areas of economic importance;
  - having regionally located systems.
- Cooperation is possible between different data custodians.

## Program Aims

To test the REGIS concept it was necessary to define a number of aims. Since there will be many different organisations participating it was convenient to consider three types of aim:

- General
- Technical
- Individual participant.

### General Aims

These relate to the common interests of the participating bodies and include:

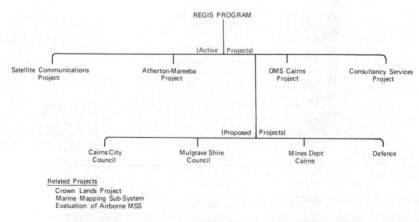

Figure 8.4   Projects in the REGIS Program

- Determining the methods necessary to integrate land-related data from a wide range of sources.
- Identifying data sets that cannot be integrated in their present form and identifying possible changes to the data structure to allow integration.
- Determining the characteristics and parameters of the geographical region that can be serviced adequately by the REGIS processors and communication network.
- Determining the usefulness of the integrated data to a variety of users.
- Estimating:
  - the volume of GIS business generated;
  - the cost differential of this output as against previous methods.
- Developing cooperation among program participants.
- Examining problems of maintaining the data in as current and accurate state as possible.

### Technical Aims

These aims refer to the characteristics of the system hardware and software, the equipment, and the communication links. Some aims are to:
- Design, create, maintain, and use a GIS over a defined geographic area where:
  - the system design work can be used in the development of future GIS;
  - the experience gained by personnel on this program can be used in the development of future GIS;
  - a single query can access different databases;
  - system parameters (e.g. data retrieval time, database size and query time) and costs will be determined.
- Establish a computer network that will allow evaluation of:
  - the performance characteristics of a range of peripherals (e.g. terminals and plotters);
  - the problems of users whose workstations are distant from the central processing units;
  - the available data communications systems (Q-NET, Wide Area Network and Netplex);
  - workstation storage of data, supplemented by transmitted update data.
- Solve the communication problems between different computers and between different databases.
- Establish standards for the interchange of data, if such standards still do not exist when the regional system is operational.

### Individual Participant Aims

These refer to the specific applications that each participant wishes to test.

There may be many cooperating agencies in the program with each having its own set of objectives.

For many of the participants, these aims may be directed towards education in, and a greater understanding of, GIS technology. For others, who may be well advanced in this area, reasons for involvement may include development of GIS-related products for the community.

A number of projects closely related to the REGIS program are already in existence, while the aims stated above may subsequently give rise to further projects considered as actual sub-projects of the REGIS program (see Figure 8.4). Some of these projects will be outlined below.

## Area of Operation

The general area is Cairns and its hinterland, which is outlined in Figure 8.5. The location has been chosen because of:

- The variability of terrain (reefs, islands, beaches, rivers, valleys, mountains).
- The diversity of land use (agriculture, urban areas, mining, national parks, forestry).
- Rapid changes in land use (tourism developments, changeover to different crops).
- Its intrinsic and specific interest to many organisations.
- The clarity of tropical waters (e.g. for shallow water mapping).
- Its remoteness from Brisbane (1500 km).

However, this should not be interpreted as defining the location. Areas within this location that are not specifically requested by participants will have little, if any, data. For example, if no participants wish to use marine data, the REGIS database will not cover coastal waters. On the other hand, if participants requested coverage of a limited area of North Queensland that does not conform to the above boundaries, such an area would be included.

## Data Types Being Used

### Digital, Graphical and Textual Data

The usefulness of a GIS increases dramatically as the number of data sets available increases. There should thus be a significant amount of digital data covering the area of operation of the REGIS program.

Table 8.2 indicates some of the data that may be available (at least in part) over the program area and notes data sets already being used in the Crown Lands Inventory project (a sub-project of the REGIS program). The LAND-SEARCH Directory, produced by the Australian Survey Office, contains details of the Commonwealth held data sets. It is anticipated that data sets will be drawn from this source.

In general, user organisations are required to convert their own data sets to a compatible digital form and send it to the computer centre for loading into the system. Once on the system, users will be responsible for maintaining and keeping up-to-date the data sets supplied by them. Each user of the system may access all data sets held, subject to any security restrictions. Where users

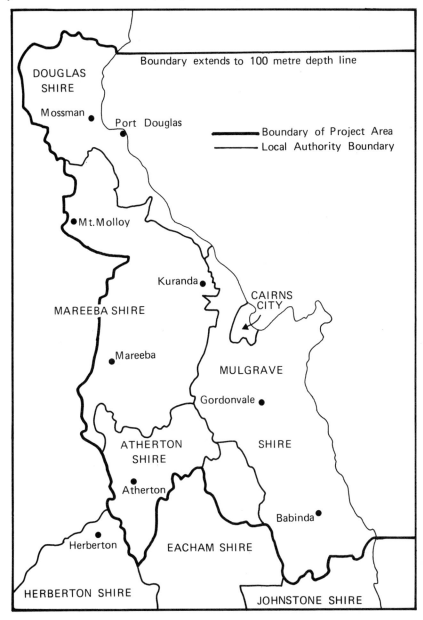

Figure 8.5   REGIS Program Area.

Table 8.2   POTENTIAL DATA SOURCES — REGIS PROGRAM

| Data Details | Data Source |
| --- | --- |
| **Digital** | |
| Census | ABS* |
| AUTOMAP (cultural, drainage, relief, vegetaton) | Army* |
| Grid base of climate, geology and topography | CSIRO (Canberra) |
| DCDB (property IDs, centroids, edge points) | DMS* |
| Administrative boundaries | DMS* |
| Engineering details (roads and structures) | MRD |
| Census boundaries | Natmap* |
| Transmission line routes | QEC |
| Valuation, zoning, owner, land use | VG* |
| Crown reserve data | Lands* |
| | |
| **Graphical** | |
| Zoning resource maps | GBRMPA |
| Soil type | CSIRO (Townsville) |
| Cane classification areas | DPI* |
| Mains maps | FNQEB |
| State forest, timber reserve boundaries | Forestry* |
| Zoning maps | Local Government |
| Authorities to prospect, leases | Mines* |
| Park boundaries, ecotypes | QNPWS |
| Dams, irrigation channels | QWRC |
| Railways | Railways Department |
| Bathymetric data | Natmap |
| | |
| **Textual** | |
| Resource inventories | GBRMPA |
| Soil characteristics, description | CSIRO (Townsville) |
| Plantation species, age, treatment | Forestry |
| Pole and transformer data | FNQEB |
| Property owners, addresses, rates | Local Government |
| Tower data (tension, height, etc.) | QEC |
| Stream flow rates, licence owners | QWRC |
| Lessees, lease dates | Mines* |
| Crown land data | Lands* |

\* Already included in the Crown Lands Project.

Table 8.3   SOURCES OF REMOTELY SENSED DATA BEING UTILISED

Aerial Photography
   Black and white aerial photography
   Colour aerial photography
   Colour Infrared aerial photography

Space Shuttle
   Large Format Camera
   Shuttle Imaging Radar

Airborne Scanner
   NASA NS001
   TIMS (Thermal Infrared Multi-Spectral Scanner)
   AIS (Airborne Imaging Spectrometer)

Satellite Data
   LANDSAT MSS (Multi-Spectral Scanner)
   LANDSAT TM (Thematic Mapping)
   LANDSAT RBV (Return Beam)
   SPOT
   AVHRR (Advanced Very-High Resolution)
   CZCS (Coastal Zone Colour Scanner)
   SEASAT

have not had the facilities or skills necessary to convert data to digital format, assistance has been given by the Australian Key Centre in Land Information Studies.

### Remote Sensing Data

The application and importance of remote sensing data to a GIS has been described in Chapter 3. Remote sensing forms an important data source for the REGIS program. Sensor platforms listed in Table 8.3 provide digital data on a regular basis. This facilitates rapid computer processing, change analysis, and simple integration into the other data sets.

The natural resource inventory database will process both polygonal and raster formats. Data will be obtained primarily from existing maps and participating agencies. However, remotely sensed data will also be processed for land use/cover applications and for shallow water mapping.

## Processing System

Data sets for use by REGIS participants are stored on computer systems located at the State Government Computing Centre, the Department of Mapping and Surveying, and the University of Queensland. The spatial analysis and mapping software used mostly is Universal System's CARIS.

Local users will have their own computing facilities (of varying sophistication) and be connected to the REGIS database using the Q-NET satellite communications system (see Figure 8.11).

## Program Timings

The program has commenced and will continue for about two years.

The implications of the REGIS program are wide-ranging and may be considered in terms of the implications of the individual sub-projects of the program.

## Sub-Projects of the REGIS Program

A number of projects closely related to the REGIS program have already been conducted or are nearly complete, that is, the Crown Lands Inventory project and the Shallow Water Imagery Mapping (SWIM) project. Further projects to be included within the REGIS program have been or are being proposed following discussions with possible participants in North Queensland. Because of participant enthusiasm some of these projects have commenced and are well advanced. It is anticipated that more projects will be included as the program gathers momentum (see Figure 8.4).

To indicate the diversity of these related projects and sub-projects of the REGIS program some details of four of them are provided below (i.e., the Crown Lands Inventory project, the Mareeba project, the Shallow Water Mapping project and the Satellite Communications project).

### The Crown Lands Inventory Project

During 1985, the Department of Lands commenced a project to examine the current and future use of Crown land in the northern coastal areas of Queensland.

The purpose of the study was to examine all land-related data for a particular area and produce recommendations that would assist the administrators of Crown land to achieve maximum efficiency of land use. The study concerned land of which the Department of Lands has either full control of or a major influence on its use.

Two project areas were selected. The first, an area surrounding the city of Mackay, was completed by collecting information from the existing paper-based records of the Department of Lands, the Department of Mapping and Surveying, and other organisations. For the second area, extending northwards from the town of Babinda to the Daintree River excluding the City of Cairns, it was decided to explore the use of computer graphics to overcome the problems associated with the previously used manual methods. This second area was later extended to include Cook Shire in the project area, effectively covering most of Cape York.

The main objectives of the project are:

- To demonstrate the value of computer graphics in assisting the assessment and administration of Crown land.

- To provide a model for determining future resource requirements to complete the Crown lands projects using computer graphics.

Table 8.4 CROWN LANDS INVENTORY PROJECT DATA

---

(i)    Digital Cadastral Data Base (DCDB) (Department of Mapping and Surveying)*

(ii)   Computerised ownership and sales data (Department of the Valuer General)*

(iii)  Reserve file (Lands Department)*

(iv)   Mining lease data (Mines Department)

(v)    Beach protection authority administrative boundaries (Beach Protection Authority)

(vi)   LANDSAT data (Department of Mapping and Surveying)*

(vii)  AUTOMAP digital database (Royal Australian Survey Corps)*

(viii) Census collection district boundaries (Division of National Mapping)*

(ix)   Socioeconomic data (Australian Bureau of Statistics)*

(x)    Land suitability studies (Department of Primary Industries)

---

*Supplied in computer-readable format

- To compare computer graphics systems with manual methods for decision-making.

Data sets which are being included or investigated in the Crown Lands Inventory Project are indicated in Table 8.4.

The Crown Lands Inventory project is now complete and has proven extremely valuable as a contribution towards the overall goals of the REGIS program. It has demonstrated the versatility of computer graphics in merging, converting and manipulating data from different sources.

The capability of storing information on different layers and then recalling layers as desired has been of great assistance to the planning staff of the Department of Lands — far more efficient than the paper-based manual methods traditionally employed.

The computer-based techniques used allow quick response in updating much of the data held in the database. Up-to-date hard copy maps which combine various themes may be plotted quickly and at very low cost compared to traditional methods.

## Application of Road Network Infrastructure Data

This project is a sub-project of the Crown Lands Inventory project and investigates the establishment of a road network infrastructure database. To date it has involved investigating the type and availability of attribute information pertaining to road networks and bridges. Organisations at the three levels of government were contacted, namely:

Federal: Department of Transport — Canberra
State:   Main Roads Department — Cairns
Local:   Mulgrave Shire Council — Cairns

It was found that infrastructure data relating to roads in any given area is not, as a general rule, held by the Department of Transport. Only limited information is kept. The Main Roads Department is responsible for 'main' and 'secondary' roads within the state of Queensland. Local shire councils are then responsible for the remaining road classifications. Infrastructure data for a particular road classification is maintained by the respective organisation responsible for that road classification.

The organisations which supplied data for this project were the Main Roads Department — Cairns, and the Mulgrave Shire Council — Cairns.

The types of information provided included:

- Road name.
- The distance of the road within the Mulgrave Shire. (This category was classified as sealed, unsealed, gravel, formed or unformed roads).
- The authority responsible for the maintenance of the road.
- The width of the road.
- The number of bridges on the road within the Mulgrave Shire.
- The bridge reference number.
- Bridge lengths and widths.
- Bridge construction type.
- The authority responsible for the maintenance of the bridge, etc.

A complete list of data items can be found in Table 8.5, as well as a description of the Main Roads Department's and Mulgrave Shire Council's inventory codes in Table 8.6.

The graphical road network data was extracted from the digital topographic database (AUTOMAP) provided by the Royal Australian Survey Corps. This allowed the road infrastructure data (attribute data) to be correlated with graphical data and viewed together on a computer graphics terminal (the Computervision Workstation at the University of Queensland).

The attribute database can then be interrogated to perform such tasks as listing properties held against specific graphical entities and searched for a given situation (e.g. locate all roads with a stretch of gravel incorporated in their length).

This is an excellent example of the benefits gained by merging data from different organisations, that is, Army graphical road pattern data and the state road attribute data.

It is believed that merged data sets would be of significant use to defence, particularly when enhanced with network analysis and modelling software.

## Application of Statistical Data

This is another sub-project of the Crown Lands Inventory project in which the development of a socio-economic database is investigated. The objectives of the project include:

Table 8.5   DATA ITEMS — ROAD NETWORKS

| Road classifications. | |
| --- | --- |
| Categories | Types of Classification |
| Local road class | Arterial<br>Distributor<br>Collector<br>Other |
| Local Government Act class | Main road<br>Secondary road<br>Deemed residential roads<br>Deemed pathways<br>Deemed lanes<br>Residential roads<br>Pathways<br>Lanes |
| Main roads classification | Main road<br>Secondary road<br>Not classified<br>Expressway<br>State highway |
| Functional classification | National highways<br>Connections between capital cities<br>Connections between key towns<br>Connections between important cities<br>Provide access to abutting property (rural)<br>Miscellaneous rural<br>Commun. for massive traffic movements<br>Distrib. traffic to local streets<br>Provide access to abutting property (urban)<br>Miscellaneous urban |
| Legislative status | Urban arterial road<br>Urban local road<br>Rural arterial road<br>Rural local road<br>National highway<br>Export road<br>Major commercial road |
| Operational restriction | Undivided (two-way traffic)<br>Divided<br>Undivided (one-way traffic)<br>Undivided light traffic only<br>Divided light traffic only<br>Split level<br>Service roads |

*Source*:   Mulgrave Shire Council

## Table 8.6   LIST OF ROAD NETWORK INFRASTRUCTURE INFORMATION

---

### Road Infrastructure Data — Main Roads Department

---

Information maintained by the Main Roads Department includes:

Roads

> Formation type
> Pavement type
> Surface type
> Shoulder type
> Commonwealth legal class
> State legal class
> Functional class
> Surface width
> Pavement width
> Formation width
> Road reference number
> Carriageway

Bridges

> Local authority number
> Bridge name
> Bridge function
> Bridge class
> Bridge length
> Bridge width
> Number of spans
> Description code — Super-structure type
>                   — Deck material
>                   — Super-structure material
>                   — Sub-structure material
> %T44 capacity
> Date constructed
> Horizontal clearance
> Vertical clearance
> Average height
> Sign-post capacity

---

### Road Infrastructure Data — Mulgrave Shire Council

---

Information maintained by the Mulgrave Shire Council includes:

Roads

> Road name
> Road reference number
> Local authority responsible for road
> Road width
> Length of road — sealed (km)
> Length of road — unsealed (km)
> Length of road — gravel (km)
> Length of road — formed (km)

Length of road — unformed (km)
Total length of road in shire (km)
Status of road (e.g. all weather)
Number of bridges crossing the road
Classification of road (e.g. primary road)

Bridges

Road name
Bridge reference number
Local authority responsible for bridge
Bridge width (m)
Bridge length (m)
Bridge type (e.g. timber)
Remarks about the bridge

Source: Burden P., 'Application of Statistical Data to a GIS', Queensland Department of Mapping and Surveying, PRP 87/004, 1987.

- Investigating the sources of socio-economic data.
- Determining user needs for this data within the Crown Land Inventory project, that is, land use planners.
- Acquiring and loading suitable socio-economic data onto the Crown Lands Inventory project database.
- Examining methods of graphically presenting the acquired data.

The spatial component of this project consists of the statistical boundaries forming the areas to which the relevant attribute data (socioeconomic in this case) will be linked. These are the 1981 Census Collection District (CCD) boundaries and were obtained in digital form from the Division of National Mapping.

While a broad range of socio-economic data was examined, only data from the 1981 Census of Population and Housing was included in the project at this stage. This attribute data, housed on a separate mainframe computer at the University of Queensland, was linked to the CCDs held on a graphics work-station and includes aspects of population, age, income, employment, occupation and private dwellings.

The statistical data held in the project database may be interrogated in two basic ways — those which identify a single graphical entity and those used to enhance a polygon.

Information pertaining to a particular CCD may be interrogated; for example CCDs with a total male population greater than 200, with a CCD area less than one square kilometre, can be listed. CCDs identified in this manner can also be highlighted.

Various methods of graphically presenting the statistical data are available. Some examples are shown in Figure 8.6 to 8.9.[5]

This project has developed a base upon which further investigation into the inclusion of socioeconomic data in a GIS may be made. It has demonstrated how statistical data may be quickly presented in an easily interpreted manner.

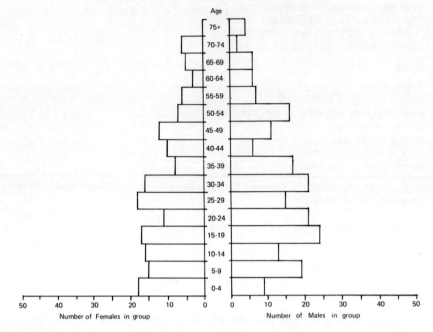

Figure 8.6

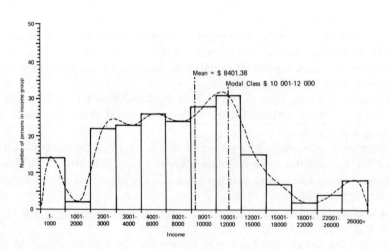

Figure 8.7

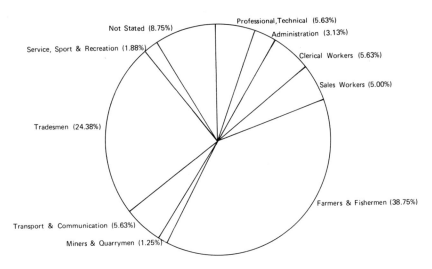

OCCUPATION DISTRIBUTION : TOTAL (CD = 03012603).
Not Stated (8.75%)
Professional,Technical (5.63%)
Administration (3.13%)
Service, Sport & Recreation (1.88%)
Clerical Workers (5.63%)
Sales Workers (5.00%)
Tradesmen (24.38%)
Farmers & Fishermen (38.75%)
Transport & Communication (5.63%)
Miners & Quarrymen (1.25%)

*Figure 8.8*

1981 CENSUS COLLECTION DISTRICTS OF THE MULGRAVE SHIRE, DIVISION 3
INSET
3012605
3012607
3012606
3012608
not to scale
3012602
Palmer Point
3012601
Constantine Point
3012603
CORAL SEA
3012604
SEE INSET
3012605
3012606
17° 21'S
3012607
BABINDA
Mirriwinni
3012608
3012610
Cooper Point
RATIO OF MALES TO FEMALES, JUNE 1981
3012609
0.951-1.023
1.024-1.096
1.097-1.169
1.170-1.242
1.243-1.315
3012610 Census Collection District
Census Collection District boundaries
Mulgrave Shire, Division 3 boundary
0 5 10 km.
145° 55'E

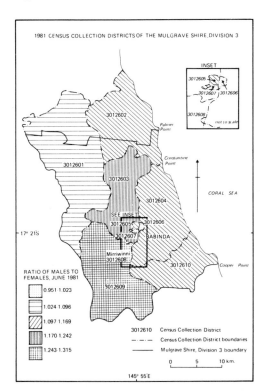

*Figure 8.9*

*Figures 8.6–8.9 Examples of Graphical Presentation of Statistical Data.*

**Source: P. Burden, Application of Statistical Data to a GIS, Queensland Department of Mapping and Surveying, PRP 87/004, 1987.**

## The Mareeba Project

The aim of this project is to assist the Mareeba Shire Council in their planning and development by evaluating the appropriateness of changing land used for irrigation farming to higher density rural residential or suburban development, while still retaining farms assessed as viable, on soil, water, shape, size, and other considerations. The balancing of the varying needs of the community will also be determined through the development of a long-term management plan.

A feature of the project will be the participation of local organisations with an interest in the outcome of the project.

In the first stage of the project, it is envisaged that the following data sets will be used:

(a) Digital cadastral database (DMS)
(b) Soil classifications and boundaries (QWRC/DPI)
(c) (i) Contours and slope (QWRC/DMS)
    (ii) Digital topographic data (Army)
(d) Crop areas and type (DPI)
(e) Irrigation channel network (QWRC)
(f) Survey bench mark network (QWRC/DMS)
(g) LANDSAT TM data (DMS)
(h) Local authority data (ASC/MSC)

At a later stage, land administration records and other information relevant to the project area may be included.

Following the Crown Lands Inventory project, this project will demonstrate the ability of local users, for example, the shires (remote from Brisbane) to interact with a Brisbane database quicker and more efficiently. It will also show how, as more users pool their data, greater benefits to all participants will be gained.

The project has commenced and is planned to finish by the end of 1987.

## Shallow Water Mapping Project

There are numerous offshore shallow water areas around the Australian coast and in neighbouring countries where coverage by existing maps and charts is poor. The Shallow Water Imagery Mapping (SWIM) pilot project covering the Trobriand Islands area of Papua New Guinea, conducted in 1984–85, re-searched means of overcoming these deficiencies. It showed that it was possible to use digital methods instead of traditional cartographic methods to merge hydrographic chart and map data with LANDSAT imagery. The digital method of combination was shown to be faster and more flexible.

Remote sensors can be used to determine water depths of up to 15 metres in tropical seas. LANDSAT MSS data can be rectified and formatted to produce effective map products. Four advantages were identified in using LANDSAT data for the purpose of mapping shallow water areas. These related to:

● Positional accuracy — once rectified, the position accuracy can meet National Map Accuracy Standards (MAS1) for 1:250 000 and can nearly meet accuracy standards (MAS2) for 1:100 000.[6]

- Continuous and repetitive coverage — LANDSAT provides data for all the features in its areas and can provide spatially continuous data acquisition at periods of 18 days. Since multi-temporal data is available on a large scale, it is possible to monitor changes in position of features over a period of time.
- Reconnaissance — unsurveyed areas may be evaluated prior to a more detailed study.
- Cost effective — LANDSAT data is cheaper to obtain by comparison with more conventional methods. Classical survey methods are slow and hazardous, particularly in shoal areas.

Apart from navigation, many potential applications exist for shallow water mapping, for example:

- Oil and mineral exploration
- Fishing
- Assistance in coastal development
- Defence
- Tourism and recreation.

As a part of the REGIS program the research undertaken in the SWIM pilot project was extended. This involved research into the use of new high-resolution scanners and new production techniques as part of the development of a shallow water mapping sub-system.

The objectives of this section of the REGIS program are:

- The provision of aid to navigation graphics over a 1:100 000 area, combining depth data derived from LANDSAT MSS imagery with information from hydrographic charts and topographic maps, utilising computer-assisted drafting techniques.
- Examination of the applications of other remote sensors with better spectral or spatial resolution that LANDSAT MSS for navigation graphics and provision of classification imagery for reef management. These include:
  - NS001 aircraft scanner data;
  - National Safety Council aircraft scanner data;
  - LANDSAT TM data;
  - SPOT data.
- Examination of methods of further improving the type of graphic described above, and the method of production.

Up to August 1987 activities involving investigation of shallow water mapping techniques consisted of the development of a general digital database based on LANDSAT (80m pixels) and a variety of other data sources for an area adjacent to Cairns and a pilot project using aircraft multi-spectral scanner data (5m pixels) in an area adjacent to the new Southport bar (Nerang River entrance) on the Gold Coast. This later pilot was very successful and has been reported on by the Australian Key Centre in Land Information Studies.[7]

The final products of these activities include graphics combining a LAND-

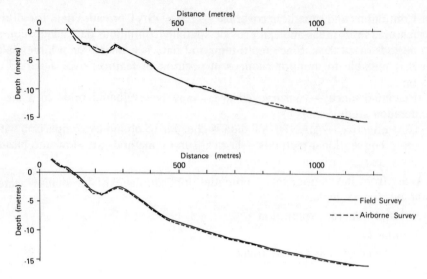

*Figure 8.10    Comparison of Remotely Sensed Data with Surveyed Cross Sections.*

SAT image showing depth information with data from hydrographic charts and topographic maps, and various maps derived from aircraft scanner and other satellite data.

The involvement of a marine mapping sub-system in the REGIS program is vital to the development of a comprehensive GIS. It applies modern computer techniques to the capture, manipulation, analysis and presentation of hydrographic and related data involving a wide range of applications.

It is considered that these applications have significant defence use as they allow defence planners to examine possible landing sites and potential submarine and surface ship corridors through the northern reef areas in a detail formerly not possible. As an example, Figure 8.10 shows the comparison of remotely sensed data with surveyed cross-sections on the exercise carried out over the Nerang River entrance (mentioned above). Plate 3 shows water depth mapping using airborne multi-spectral scanner data over the Nerang River entrance.

## Satellite Communications Project

In line with the decentralised nature of Queensland and with the REGIS database being located in Brisbane, it was decided to test the application of satellite communications to GIS.

The Queensland Department of Industry Development (DID) is developing a pilot State Government telecommunications network based on the AUSSAT 1 communications satellite. This is being developed in the form of the Q-NET Project. The REGIS Program has been accepted by DID to participate as a major component of the Q-NET project.

Five DID micro earth stations have been allocated to REGIS for use by participants remote from Brisbane. Each station has two ports and thus two participants can be connected to a single earth station. Brisbane users of the REGIS database will be connected to the REGIS processor by landline. The proposed communications system is shown in Figure 8.11.

The Q-NET aims of the REGIS program are to determine the feasibility of Q-NET to:

- Quickly update the local copy of those components of the GIS database that are of interest to a remote user (the copy being stored on the user's own computer).

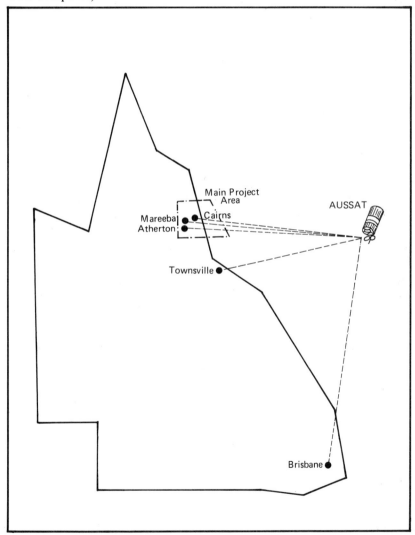

Figure 8.11  Q-NET Communications System.

- Quickly update the GIS database (most of which will be held in Brisbane) from remote locations.
- Increase the geographic dispersion of the user network.
- Provide a new decentralised information service.

Involvement in the Q-NET project provides a major input to the overall REGIS program. In a state the size of Queensland, distances and communication costs are a major concern to a state-wide GIS. Through the Q-NET project the suitability of satellite communications in the REGIS program will be evaluated.

This description of the projects contained within the REGIS program has indicated its scope and size. The activity which has occurred and is occurring within the program is laying the foundation for future GIS development. The specific aims and objectives within the program are constantly being amended to incorporate new projects and participants as they are added to those already present. This aspect reflects the user-driven nature of the program.


## CONCLUSION


The activities taking place in Queensland are developing a base from which a comprehensive LIS for the state can be developed. The projects described in this chapter have demonstrated that a broad range of land-related data can be integrated successfully. It is clear that as more participants become involved in a LIS the benefits to all users rapidly increase.

Much of the data included in these projects has a range of Defence Force applications, for example, terrain analysis, infrastructure and environmental conditions. An informed estimate is that 70–85 per cent of Defence Force needs for geographic data will come from civilian sources with about two-thirds coming from state or local government sources.

In order to incorporate the needs and requirements of a MGIS in the state developments the early involvement of the Defence Forces in the current state and local government developmental activities is vital.


## NOTES


1  Queensland, Office of the Minister for Survey and Valuation, Land Data Bank Report. Report to Cabinet by a delegation sent overseas to investigate the establishment of a Land Data Bank, accepted by Cabinet Decision No. 29409, Brisbane, 30 October 1978.

2  Queensland, Department of the Valuer-General, Land Data Bank Project: Report 1982. Report to Cabinet by Land Data Bank Steering Committee, accepted by Cabinet Decision No. 38854, Brisbane, 1 November 1982.

3  D. Hebblethwaite and R.J. Eden, 'The Corporate Working Map', in *Proceedings*, URPIS 14 Conference, Melbourne, 1986 (AURISA, Sydney, 1986), p. 369.

4  ibid.

5  P. Burden, Application of Statistical Data to a GIS, Queensland Department of Mapping and Surveying, PRP 87/004, 1987.

6  D. Jupp, P. Guerin and W. Lamond, 'Rectification of LANDSAT Data to Cartographic Bases with Application to the Great Barrier Reef Region', in D.L.B. Jupp *et al.*, *Collected Workshop and Conference Papers from the Great Barrier Reef Marine Park Project*, Technical Memorandum No. 84/8 (CSIRO Division of Water and Land Resources, Canberra, 1984), p. 37.

7  Australian Key Centre in Land Information Studies, *Airborne Multispectral Scanner Joint Research Project: Gold Coast* (Australian Key Centre in Land Information Studies, University of Queensland. St Lucia, Queensland, 1987).

CHAPTER NINE

# Cross-country Trafficability Ratings for Cape York Peninsula: A Method Based on Simple Landscape Data and Expert Systems

Peter Laut

Richard Davis

As part of the Memorandum of Understanding between the CSIRO and the Department of Defence, the Forward Planning and Environmental Sections of the Facilities Division of the Department of Defence (DoD) in November 1982 requested among other things:

> a vegetation and terrain/going map for tracked vehicles taking into account seasonal changes.

The map was to be of that portion of Cape York Peninsula between 12°30′S and 13°30′S, and was required as part of the Major Army Training Area Study (MATAS) of North East Queensland (see Figure 9.1). Work commenced on the vegetation and going map to meet this request in early 1984 but was suspended as the result of discussions between the Department of Defence and the Division of Water and Land Resources in early 1985.

The publication of the Dibb Report on future Australian defence capabilities in 1986 and the Government's Defence White Paper in 1987 set in train changes in defence priorities emphasising defence preparations in northern Australia. Because of the sparse settlement of the north, the land resources of the area are poorly known compared with southern Australia, and one consequence of the redirection of policy was the need to know more about the land resources of that part of the continent and their trafficability. It appeared appropriate to revive at least that part of the MATAS-based project concerned with mapping terrain/going conditions and to this end a proposal was made to the Environmental Section to recommence the project.

At that time, an evaluation of north Australian landscapes for livestock mustering as an input to the Brucellosis and Tuberculosis Eradication Campaign (BTEC) had recently been completed.[1] The BTEC mustering project was based on the use of expert opinion to develop a simple model to evaluate a sample of landscapes across the north of the continent in terms of livestock mustering (i.e., the degree of difficulty the landscape imposes on finding livestock and moving them to yards). This approach appeared to offer a useful analogue for providing a relatively cheap evaluation of terrain/going condi-

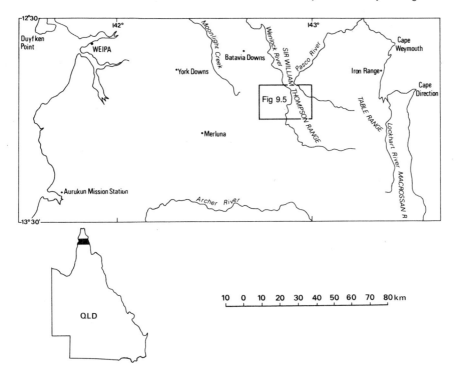

*Figure 9.1   Location of the Study Area.*

tions. This evaluation could be based mostly on readily available landscape data and expert opinion which could be applied not only to the study area of north eastern Queensland, but also elsewhere in northern Australia, and perhaps southern Australia. With the agreement of the Environmental Section, the trafficability portion of the MATAS project recommenced in mid-1986.

At the same time, a small team in the Division of Water and Land Resources was developing a geographical expert systems shell, GEM-II, which, among other applications, was being used to predict the consequences of fires in Kakadu National Park.[2] Since the distinguishing characteristic of an expert or inferencing system is the application of codified, qualitative expert knowledge to predict the likely consequences of actions under specified conditions, it appeared highly appropriate to adopt the GEM-II expert system shell for the evaluation of the landscapes of the study area for terrain/going, now redefined as Cross-Country Trafficability Rating (XCTR).

## The present situation

This chapter reports on work in progress rather than on a completed project. By late 1987, conceptual and methodological options had been explored, a methodology adopted, and research direction established (see Method below).

The study area had been mapped or divided into landscape units appropriate to XCTR; these landscape units had been described, coded, and entered in the database of the GEM-II shell; generation of rules obtained from expert sources to drive the inferencing section of GEM-II had been completed, and the rules applied to the database to infer XCTR using a scale of 1–9 (1 best, 9 worst or no-go) for the study area.

During the later half of September and early October 1987, field trials were scheduled in conjunction with the 51 Far North Queensland Regiment to provide data to calibrate XCTRs. The plan was to calibrate output in the form of a graph relating speed of vehicle movement to XCTRs for two standard types of vehicle.

## The Concept

In this study XCTR is considered to be a function of vehicle capability, driver capability, and such measurable landscape elements as landform barriers, surface slope, soil strength, local and micro-relief, vegetative cover, local drainage, stream barriers, and the prevailing seasonal conditions. The approach adopted was to delineate landscape units on 1:100 000 topographic maps representing relatively homogeneous segments of the landscape in terms of the above landscape elements; describe the landscape units in these terms; generate XCTR-rules dependent upon these terms and evaluate the XCTR of the landscape units with the rules; and, finally, to calibrate the XCTRs gradings in field trials.

This heuristic approach can be contrasted with many engineering-type trafficability models, such as that referred to as the NATO model (NATO Reference Mobility Model), which are algorithmic.[3] The NATO model is a very powerful general-purpose model which can be used to predict landscape trafficability in very precise terms for a range of vehicles. Unfortunately, such models require a comprehensive set of engineering data inputs, both for the vehicle and the landscape. Whilst the vehicle inputs are readily available from design criteria, the landscape inputs are not, and they are very costly to obtain at the spatial resolution required by the model. If these data are obtained at a coarser resolution, the resulting imprecision of model predictions renders the predictions useless in practice.

Increasing our understanding of the landscapes of northern Australia becomes particularly important now that Australia's defence system will have a much strengthened northern land-based component. In general, northern Australian landscapes are not well known in terms of traditional trafficability and engineering data. The land systems surveys carried out during the 1950s and 1960s by CSIRO provided much general information about occurrences of, and apparent ecological relationships between, landforms, lithology, and vegetation, and limited information about climatic conditions, and the effects of climate on soil strength. They were, of course, designed to provide a rapid and intelligible inventory of the land resources of some of Australia's remoter areas, and an indication of their pastoral and agricultural capabilities. Moreover, this information was provided within a limited geographical context. There may be several occurrences of land systems (which are the mapping units), but the more precisely described land units are not mapped, and not all land units which occur in a particular land system need occur in a particular occurrence of the land system. Whilst mapping land systems and not land units was a great convenience at the time, the surveys were completed with considerable geographic generalisation, which directly limits the value of these reports for evaluating trafficability. However, the land systems framework together with other published data, and the results of a massive field exercise collecting engineering data, were used in a modelling exercise commissioned by the Department of Defence and involving the Kimberley, Victoria River and Darwin regions.[4] The information derived from this exercise provides trafficability information on a probability of occurrence basis, and is particularly useful for establishing design criteria for military land vehicles. It is less useful in strategic planning, of limited use in planning exercises, and of very limited use to the commander and soldier in the field.

The major sources of landscape information about Australian northern landscapes today are the 1:100 000 topographic map series. These provide an excellent synoptic view of the terrain and the drainage systems in maps covering ½° by ½° units (i.e., approximately 3000 km$^2$), and limited information about vegetative cover and cultural features. This series was designed primarily to meet military needs but it is inadequate as a single data source for traditional trafficability models. However, the cost of providing the additional inputs such as soil strength and micro-relief over vast areas of northern Australia is very high. It is therefore important to explore alternative approaches which may not be so precise but which are at least indicative of XCTR and which depend upon data which are either readily available or could be obtained at low cost per unit area.

The work on landscape evaluation for livestock mustering capability for the northern BTEC in the early 1980s noted above suggested a type of approach which could be useful for XCTR. The livestock mustering approach depended upon reliable information from individuals within the industry rather than mathematical models. Owners and managers of northern pastoral properties and contract musterers were consulted to provide opinions as to how landscape elements hindered or assisted cattle mustering. Information was used in two ways: to identify landscape mapping units which were relatively homogeneous with respect to mustering capability, and to indicate the way data about these elements should be evaluated for livestock mustering capability. Further, this project which had a minimal budget, could not be based upon widespread field investigations and so had to be based on published sources of information such as topographic and geologic maps. Finally, as consistency of evaluation across the continent was of paramount importance, explicit procedures were adopted for evaluating landscape data within the context of these data sources.

All these features appeared analogous to those required of any extensive evaluation of XCTR.

## Expert systems

In May 1985, another group within the Division of Water and Land Resources had developed a more explicit method for using expert qualitative opinion for evaluating the consequences of actions or events as an alternative to quantitative modelling. An 'expert system' appeared to be the logical tool to use in the XCTR evaluation of the study area because of its ability to use reliable heuristic information to estimate XCTR and so obviate the need for algorithmic models. It could in fact mimic the processes Army personnel might use in traditional visual evaluation but do so in an explicit and entirely consistent fashion, thus reducing the risk of incorrect and variable interpretation.

Although numerical processing has dominated the development and application of computers since their inception in the 1940s, there has long been a minority of computer scientists interested in constructing computers that can mimic the activities of humans.[5] This field of research, artificial intelligence, includes robotics, pattern recognition, natural language systems, and expert systems. The last are computer programs used to make decisions in problem areas that are difficult enough to require significant human expertise. However, performance of these programs seldom reach levels that justify their title and they would better be termed 'knowledge intensive' or 'inferencing' programs.

Early expert systems relied upon clever algorithms to solve problems, but in the 1970s the focus of research shifted from the development of better decision-making algorithms to efficient methods for storing and applying large bodies of reliable knowledge about specific problem areas or domains. Such a body of specialist knowledge is termed a 'knowledge base' and is analogous to a database.

The knowledge base of an expert system is maintained in a separate module from that part of the system used to draw conclusions from the assembled knowledge, the inference engine. Breaking the system into these modules provides a number of advantages, the most important of which is ease of improving the performance of the system by amending the knowledge base as experience is gained in the particular problem domain. New information can be added without fear of disturbing the inferencing mechanism.

Much human expertise can only be expressed in qualitative terms and considerable research has been oriented towards devising methods for representing qualitative information on expertise in the knowledge base.[6] The most common method used to represent this type of information is to construct production rules or condition-conclusion pairs which are well suited to encoding heuristics or rules of thumb.[7] The condition and conclusion of a rule consists of a set of parameter-relation-value triplets, for example:

*If*    (slope is steep) and
       (soil surface is stony)
*Then* (vehicle movement is difficult).

The GEM expert system shell developed by Davis *et al.* has been constructed especially for geographic problems where there is a small number of well-defined solutions.[8] It has a geographic relational database for storing time-invariant facts about geographical space. Rules can be identified with specific locations and consultations may be run for selected locations. This shell also has the capability of using mathematical models if required.

It has been applied to a number of geographic problems including estimating the effects of fire on the vegetation of a large national park.[9] Experience gained from these applications indicate that the shell is especially useful in constructing prototype inferencing systems for particular problem domains, for example, cross-country trafficability grading. In such cases a prototype can be constructed rapidly since the shell contains a standard inference engine and the expert need only construct the appropriate knowledge base. However, once the utility of the approach is established using the prototype, it is advisable to construct a system specifically for the problem domain since each problem and each client inevitably has specific requirements not included in the shell. This matter is discussed below.

# METHOD

The development of this inferencing system for XCTR has involved five specific procedures beyond the initial development of the concept and the overall approach. These are:
(1)   Development of a descriptive model of XCTR.
(2)   Selection of a geographic frame apposite to the problem and the resources available.
(3)   Identification of sources and capture of landscape data items.
(4)   Application of XCTR rules to the data items on each of the units in the geographic frame.
(5)   Field calibration of XCTRs.

## Geographic frame

The conceptual frame adopted and the resources available for the project required a geographic frame or database which should have the following characteristics:
  (a) It should be readily recognised, understood, and accepted by a wide range of Department of Defence personnel.
  (b) It should identify linear features less than half a km wide and non-point, non-linear features of approximately 1km$^2$ in extent.
  (c) It should be efficient both in terms of data capture, data storage and data usage.
  (d) Each spatial unit should be as homogeneous as possible.
  (e) Spatial units must be readily identifiable on the 1:100 000 topographic mapping series.
It was concluded that irregular polygons best met each of these criteria, although it was acknowledged that given a broader mandate (e.g. XCTR for all

of northern Australia) and other constraints (e.g. that the Department of Defence adopt a grid-cell based geographic information system) it would be necessary to adapt the method to a grid-cell approach. In particular, the efficiency of the irregular polygon is outstanding in terms of manual data capture; the total area of some $21\,000km^2$ was reduced to fewer than 1500 polygons with commensurate reductions in data capture, data input, and output interpretation when compared with grid cells of even $1km^2$. Landscape units were mapped on the 1:100 000 topographic sheets in three steps. Terrain/slope units were defined by visual interpretation of contour patterns using slope guides depicting contour densities. Drainage patterns used were those identified using map symbols and generalisations of map information, for example, streams, seasonal inundation, and stream density. Selected geological boundaries derived from the 1:250 000 geological series maps which correspond to major changes in lithology were then superimposed over the terrain/slope and drainage boundaries to provide the final mapping units. These units were numerically coded by map sheets.

## Landscape data

Since XCTRs are treated as a function of driver/vehicle capability on one hand and landscape on the other, each mapping unit was described in terms of landform barriers, surface slope, soil strength, land surface texture, microrelief, vegetative cover, local drainage, and stream barriers each of which could be related to vehicle performance.

Specific performance criteria were available for some landscape elements (e.g. slopes, soil strength, and vehicle speed) but not for others, (e.g. tree trunk diameter and stem density of vegetative cover). Performance criteria require very specific inputs, and many of these were either not available with the degree of accuracy required or were only available in an indirect form. Consequently, surrogates and broad classes or categories had to be developed to replace them.

In the present study, heavy reliance has had to be placed on published sources of data, and with the exception of vegetative cover these sources have so far proved satisfactory.

The 1:100 000 topographic map series provide the best available sources of data for evaluating XCTR and were used to determine mapping units as noted above and to describe landform, common slope class, landform alignment, and the presence, cross-sections, and alignment of major and large tributary streams, and stream densities. However, the information on vegetative cover, whilst it meets the standards set for production of this map series, is entirely inadequate for assessing XCTR. This is primarily because the three classes used in the topographic map series — dense, medium, and scattered (trees) — have no strict definition and the medium and scattered classes encompass the forest, open forest, woodland, and open woodland categories of the standard vegetation structural formation classes.[10] A separate map of the vegetation structure of the study area had to be prepared. This map was based on a detailed survey of the vegetation of the study area, including stereoscopic interpretation of air photos and visual interpretation of LANDSAT images, and field sampling. Together these activities required four man-months of input. The lack of distinction between forest, open forest, woodland, and open woodland on the 1:100 000 topographic map series will require similar additional and costly investigations of the vegetative cover for any new area to which the method is applied.

Lithological information (surface rock types) is generally available in an indirect form from the standard 1:250 000 geological map series. Interpretation was easier where booklets describing the geology, lithology, and structures were available.

Soils information was derived from the *Atlas of Australian Soils*.[11] The landscape soils type map which is the basis of this publication shows the distribution of landscape soil types, but the accompanying notes give details of the various soils comprising the landscape soil types and this information may be used to interpret the spatial distribution of particular soils using contour and drainage patterns and other mapping symbols on the 1:100 000 sheets.

The data items captured and placed in the GEM-II database are shown in Appendix 1 to this chapter. Although allowance was made for three types of landforms, lithology, vegetation, and soils, in practice only the dominant form was recorded and used. Mapping units were refined to overcome the need for more than one type of landform.

## Descriptive model

An outline of the descriptive model is provided in Figure 9.2. This model is organised in a hierarchical structure, termed a decision tree. It is only one of many possible models of XCTR and its structure is determined primarily by the traditional geographical-ecological approach beginning with climate, landform, and slope, and moving through soils to vegetation. Other structures were tried, for example, an attempt was made to order the model in terms of primary limitations, that is, single landscape element restrictions, secondary limitations or two landscape element restrictions and so on, but this proved exceedingly difficult because rules tended to overlap, and the attempt was abandoned.

In northern Australia, seasonal climatic conditions and the impacts of these on landforms, soil strength, local drainage, and stream barriers are particularly important for XCTR. *Time* (Weeks 1–52) is used as a variable expressing these changes as the wet season succeeds the dry; Week 1 is the first week of the new year. To date, the model has been run (see the section on 'Application of Rules' below) for two representative weeks of the year, Week 5 for the wet season and Week 26 for the dry.

(a) *Level 1* Landform Name

In this model *landform* and *slope* are identified separately, although the latter is a major component of the former, in order to evaluate the general

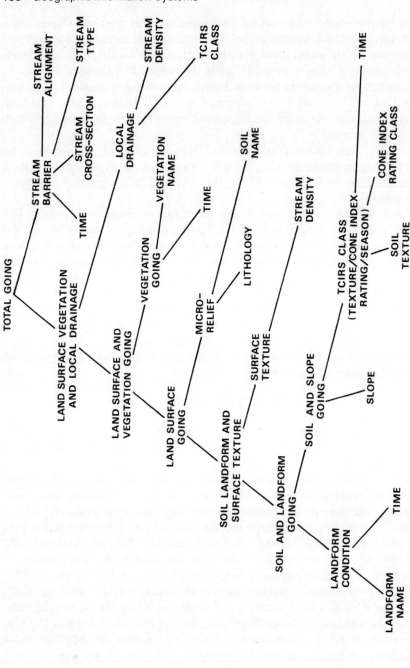

Figure 9.2   Decision Tree for Evaluating Cross-country Trafficability Ratings.

impedance to movement provided by particular landforms. Slope values alone give no indication, for example, of the greater opportunities for finding a path through hills than through mountains, or in the case of plains, the likelihood of inundation during the wet.

(b) *Level 2* Landform Condition

Together *time* and *landform* are used to infer the second level parameter, *landform condition*.

(c) *Level 3* Soil and Landform Going

The next level in the decision tree involves the use of four parameters: *soil texture, cone index rating class* and *time* to determine *TCIRS class*, a measure of soil strength and *slope*. Together with *landform condition*, these provide the major third level parameter, *soil and landform going*, which summarises the overall ability of the land surface to carry land vehicles.

(d) *Level 4* Soil Landform and Surface Texture

The fourth level of the decision tree includes a measure of the likely local relief, that is, between the standard 20 metre contours. This is based on a surrogate *stream density* which can be derived from the drainage pattern.

(e) *Level 5* Land Surface Going

The fifth level adds *micro-relief*, that is, the relief at ground level which is usually regarded as having a maximum of a metre or so. This parameter differs from the previous one in that it describes very localised conditions which affect trafficability. *Micro-relief* is related to both *lithology* and *soil name*. In any given district each rock type tends to weather in a particular manner, for example, massive sandstones may break into very large boulders whilst granites exfoliate from massive tors and then may weather directly into sands. Thus *lithology* may be used as a partial surrogate for *micro-relief*. Some soils also develop particular surface characteristics which can be expressed as *micro-relief*, for example some of the clay soils of the study area have gilgai characteristics which are typified by abrupt depressions, sometimes linear, 30 centimetres or more deep.

(f) *Level 6* Land Surface and Vegetation Going

*Vegetation going* is included in the sixth level of the decision tree. This parameter is derived from *vegetation name* and *time*. The former consists of standard vegetation structure classes[12] for example, closed forest or grassland, and the influence of *time* is mainly through the annual seasonal cycle of grass growth. The effect of vegetation on XCTR is to affect manoeuvrability of land vehicles and visibility of obstacles.

(g) *Level 7* Land Surface Vegetation and Local Drainage

The seventh level in the model adds *local drainage*, a parameter which combines assumptions about the length of the effects of the wet season on *TCIRS class* in local depressions, in combination with *stream density*. The notion is that during the early part of the dry season, depressions around local tributaries will remain moist and particular soils may bog land vehicles.

(h) *Level 8* Total Going

The final level of the tree includes an evaluation of larger tributary and major streams as *stream barriers* to vehicle movement. The contributing parameters are *stream type, stream cross-section, time*, and *stream alignment*. The last of these, *stream alignment*, is compared with information on *direction of movement*, supplied by the user, to estimate the extent to which streams will need to be crossed in the particular mapping unit. Together, these parameters and *land surface vegetation and local going* provide the final evaluation of XCTR shown on the decision tree as *total going*.

## Cross-country trafficability rules

Rules were developed in stages corresponding to the levels of the decision tree. *Landform condition* rules were based on evaluations of descriptions of each landform type for wet season and dry season conditions (examples of these are provided in Appendix 2) and represent the simplest form of evaluation used in this study. For all other parameters, XCTR rules were developed using two-dimensional matrices (see Figures 9.3 and 9.4). *Soil and slope going* were based partly on graphed relationships provided by the Engineering Development Establishment (EDE) of the Department of Defence,[13] but all other rules were based on qualitative assessments of the effects of combinations of parameter values, albeit some being based on numerical data.

The two-dimensional matrix approach has several advantages. Basically, it decomposes the problem into a number of sub-problems, each represented by a matrix. Each sub-problem can then be examined independently. The contents of the matrix can be experimented with by, for example, trying intermediate gradings through absolute changes in values or by posing slightly differing relationships between paired parameters. Paired parameters may be cumulative, partly cumulative, independent or partly cumulative, and partly independent, and describing these relationships in a matrix form allows quick inspection of the results of altering the type of parametric relationship.

Developing rules for the parameter *soil and slope going* could possibly have been undertaken using graphed information supplied by the EDE. However, this information included cone index values and these were not available for all soils in the study area. Cone Index Ratings (CIR) were approximated by a soils expert based on his experience with relatively similar soils further south.[14]

Graphed information was provided by EDE for wet and dry clays, loams, and sands on slopes at five per cent intervals for cone index ratings at 25 psi intervals for two vehicle types in two-wheel drive and four-wheel drive modes. There were distinct breaks in the slope of the cone index–per cent grade relationship at 50 psi and 100 psi, indicating that on soils having compression strengths below 50 psi, vehicle movement was restricted to very low slopes and above 100 psi vehicle movement was possible on very high slopes. Therefore, it was possible to limit cone index classes to three categories (<50 psi, 51–100 psi

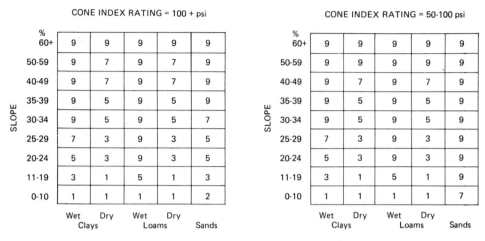

Figure 9.3   Matrices for SOIL and SLOPE GOING.

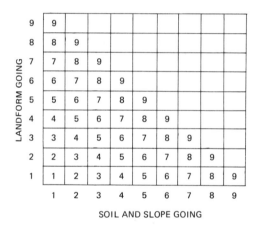

Figure 9.4   Matrix for SOIL and SLOPE and LANDFORM GOING.

and >100 psi) and to provide two-dimensional matrices for only two values, 100 psi and 50 psi. In turn this simplified the allocation of cone index ratings to the landscape soils types.

As a preliminary step, soils were allotted to one of five texture classes (clays, wet and dry; loams, wet and dry; and sands) and one of three cone index rating classes (<50 psi, 51–100 psi, >100 psi). Matrices were then constructed for each vehicle/mode for slope/texture/>100 psi CIR and slope/texture/51–100 psi CIR (see Figure 9.3 for the two matrices for the 4WD Land Rover).

The following step, combining *soil and slope going* with *landform condition* provides a typical example of the use of the two-dimensional matrix in the remainder of the evaluation of XCTR. In this case, the two parameters are largely independent in the landscape but it is doubtful if they are completely independent when considering land vehicle movement. This dependence led to these two parameters being combined partly cumulatively in the matrix (see Figure 9.4).

Production rules of the form noted above (in the discussion of 'Expert Systems') were derived directly from these matrices. In most cases, it is possible to reduce the number of rules by combining cells with similar matrix values. The rule to evaluate *soil and slope going* (see Figure 9.3) for a 4WD Land Rover on slopes of 20–24 per cent over clay soils which have a CIR of >100 in Week 5 (wet season) is as follows:

> *If vehicle* is 4WD Land Rover
> and *slope* is 20–24 per cent
> and *soil texture* is clay
> and *cone index rating* is 100
> and *time* is 5
> *then soil and slope going* is 5.

Secondary parameters used in the fourth, fifth, seventh, and eighth levels are based on qualitative data derived from surrogates. Rules for these also are derived from two-dimensional matrices but in some cases there are additional overriding rules. For example, in the fifth level the overriding rules for *microrelief* are related to whether or not a soil is characterised by gilgai formation, whether slopes are in excess of 10 per cent or, if they are not whether they are associated with skeletal soils.

The parameter *land surface and vegetation going* in the sixth level of the decision tree represents an intermediate situation, as it is based partly on quantitative data and partly on qualitative information. The standard vegetation classification procedure is based on strict field measurement and class allocation criteria. Here, these were combined with additional measurements of tree girth so that *vegetation going* rules are based on a visibility component, a manoeuvrability component, and a tree girth (can vehicles push trees over) component, and in this sense the parameter is quantitative. On the other hand, *land surface going* is a mixture of quantitative and qualitative data and rules, so that the quantitative aspects of *vegetation going* are modified by association in *land surface and vegetation going*. The relationship between the two contributing parameters is considered to be non-cumulative in the lowest (best XCTR) categories, but cumulative in the highest (worst XCTR) categories, a situation which can be readily explored using the two-dimensional matrix technique.

## Application of rules

As noted above, the GEM-II shell is an exploratory tool designed for consecutive interactive consultations rather than batch mode operation. Given the time taken to complete a single run throughout the study area (1500 units), effort has been concentrated on XCTR evaluations for the 4WD Land Rover and

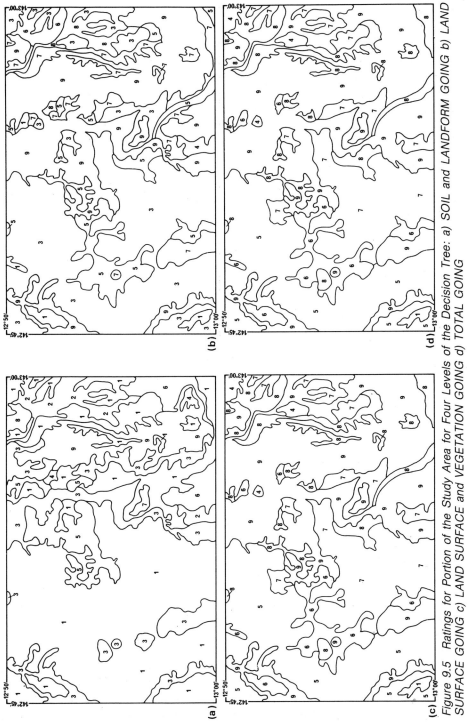

Figure 9.5    Ratings for Portion of the Study Area for Four Levels of the Decision Tree: a) SOIL and LANDFORM GOING b) LAND SURFACE GOING c) LAND SURFACE and VEGETATION GOING d) TOTAL GOING

Unimog truck in the dry season. In these runs, XCTR values have been required for each level in the decision tree. Whilst this has produced large amounts of data to be analysed and mapped, it has established confidence in the method and allowed recognition of anomalous cases for later data correction or confirmation, and possible rule changes. Some sensitivity analyses were undertaken at an early stage and as a consequence, the whole decision tree was earlier reorganised and the rules for vegetation going altered. Figure 9.5 shows the results through four levels in the decision tree, for a small part of the study area.

## Field testing

Field testing was undertaken in the late 'dry' season 1987. Through arrangement with the Department of Defence, 51 Far North Queensland Regiment provided two vehicles, a Toyota Land Cruiser and a Unimog truck, with drivers to conduct field trials over two weeks.

The major objectives of these trials were to test the assumptions used in the development of the XCTR model and to demonstrate the relationship between XCTRs and vehicle speeds. The latter relationship is needed because XCTR predictions are based on an ordinal scale whereas vehicle speed is cardinal, that is, without such a calibration it is not possible to assess whether an XCTR of 4 is twice as difficult as an XCTR of 2 or not. The former involved a wide range of phenomena from CIR classes adopted for particular landscape-soil types to the affects of stream density on driving conditions. In some cases, it was possible to obtain quantitative measures such as cone penetrometer measures of soil strength. However, in others no quick clearly defined measures could be made and these phenomena had to be judged qualitatively through discussions with drivers or through the analysis of vehicle performance. For example, the impacts of drainage lines and 'gilgai' or 'melon hole' on vehicle speed.

The second aspect, the calibration of XCTRs with vehicle speeds was completed using a modified form of random sampling. The paucity and quality of roads and tracks and consequently the limited access available within the study area precluded either random or stratified random sampling, that is, random sampling within each XCTR area of the same value. Instead, groups of sites were selected from within readily accessible XCTR areas according to the range of physical conditions expected within each area of the same XCTR value and the apparent uniformity of particular localities. The strategy was to obtain as many replicates of these representative type sites as possible within the short period available to provide reasonably reliable estimates of XCTR/vehicle speed relationships. It was not expected that a statistically valid assessment of this relationship could be obtained at this time.

It had been intended that from each selected departure point, drivers would perform a speed trial along a route approximating the boundary of 1km$^2$, with the time taken to cover each kilometre leg being recorded. In practice this proved impracticable. Drivers found it exceedingly difficult to hold a bearing whilst manoeuvring through vegetative cover and drainage lines, and the Unimog odometer did not provide readings for fractions of a kilometre. Consequently, where visibility was relatively high (e.g. 50–100m) vehicles proceeded at right-angles to the made road for 1km and returned parallel to, but not along, the entry path taking times for each leg. Where visibility was restricted to less than 50 metres, vehicles proceeded parallel to the made road, timing each kilometre. In areas of high risk of vehicle damage time-traverses were frequently limited to 0.5 kilometre.

## Field experience

The same driver/vehicle arrangements were used throughout the trials in an attempt to reduce problems arising from variations in skill and attitudes amongst drivers, and in the experience of the author conducting the trials the two drivers had average skills for cross-country driving but were generally more conservative regarding vehicle damage than might have been expected. However, it is the author's opinion that considerable variation in the performance of a given driver did occur from the beginning to the end of the trials, and during the daily routine. This was especially true immediately after vehicle damage occurred.

The results discussed below, then, have the further limitation of being derived from a very limited sample of Army drivers.

## Results

The results of the time trials are summarised in Figure 9.6. The dashed lines represent an envelope of the range of speeds which might be expected after the anomalies are accounted for and rules adjusted. For example, the eight lowest speeds recorded for XCTR1 included two sites completed during the first day, two sites with very deep gilgai, two sites where drainage lines which had not been mapped out impeded progress, whilst two had unexpected dense shrub understory. In contrast, the five highest speeds recorded for XCTR4 were on sites recently burnt with consequent improved visibility. Similarly, of the 10 highest speeds recorded for XCTR6, seven were recently burnt with the same consequence.

Whilst these results cannot be claimed to be statistically significant, they indicate that a consistent relationship exists between vehicle speed and XCTR. Analysis of the prevailing site conditions and vehicle performance suggests that some modifications could be made to the rules used in the expert system to strengthen this relationship and perhaps narrow the range of speeds which may be expected in each XCTR. For example, there is an obvious need to devise rules which take account of the effects of burnt vegetative cover, and to increase the XCTR rating for deep gilgai soils and localities with drainage lines.

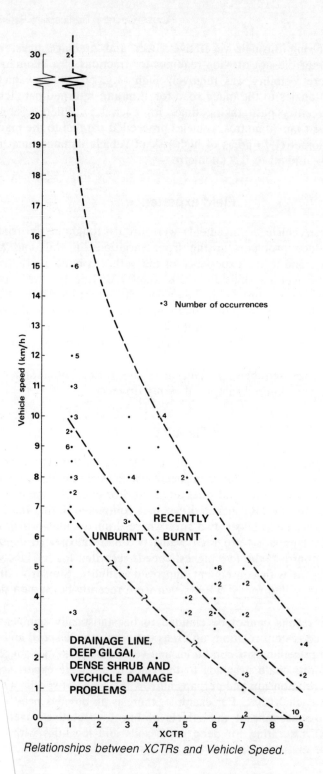

Relationships between XCTRs and Vehicle Speed.

# FUTURE DEVELOPMENT

## Short-term future development

Immediate tasks for the present stage of this project involve modification of the rules in accordance with field-trial data and other evidence to reduce the size of the envelope of the range of expected vehicle speeds as noted on Figure 9.6

The next step will be to test the method in other north Australian regions and during the dry and the wet. Given the build up of defence activities in the top end of the Northern Territory and the accessibility of some of that region during the wet, it would seem sensible to establish a second test area in that region.

Any future short-term development of this project by CSIRO will be intended to gain acceptance of the method by the Department of Defence as a standard procedure. If the method is adopted as a standard military evaluation procedure, there is then a need for some statutory agency to accept or be given the responsibility for further development.

## Long-term future developments

The method outlined for XCTR may be regarded as at the beginning rather than the end of its development. Possible methodological developments fall into four categories: (1) those associated with improving the rules, especially as performance data for the wet season become available, or adapting them for other vehicles to be employed in northern Australia; (2) those related to upgrading the XCTR system to real-time prediction capability; (3) those relating to adapting the concept to whatever geographic information system (GIS) is adopted by the Department of Defence and to remotely sensed data sources; and (4) those related to improving the expert system's structure and capabilities for this particular task.

The first group of development activities is associated with extension of the present XCTR system to accommodate other types of vehicles and to improve its prediction of wet season conditions. The former, although time-consuming, would merely involve field testing of new vehicles and recalibration of the rules. The latter is much more complex and time-consuming and involves climatological/hydrological research crucial to the improvement of any north Australian trafficability methodologies. This is research oriented towards an adequate understanding of the relationships between catchment rainfall and mid- and lower-stream hydrologic performance, in order to predict on a real-time basis the effect of cumulative rainfall on local reaches of rivers. Currently, there are no such models and very little stream flow data available and only a very limited set of meteorological and stream gauging stations available to contribute these data.

Considerable research is now being devoted to the use of digital forms of data storage for map information. In particular, this work has been oriented towards the development of Digital Terrain Models (DTMs) to reconstruct this data into acceptable terrain and drainage images. At present, it is not clear exactly how DTM research will fit with the development of the Department of Defence GIS, but if there is to be a strong DTM–GIS relationship then there will need to be further modifications to the rule base to accommodate them. Similarly, the possibilities of using LANDSAT or similar land resource satellite digital data as direct inputs to the XCTR system will not be a trivial task and will require continuation of current research on satellite data interpretation and modifications to the XCTR rules.

The type of GIS adopted by the Department of Defence and such details as the basic spatial units and landscape inputs are central to the future development of the XCTR system. Should the GIS be based on irregular polygons as the basic spatial units, it would be merely a matter of ensuring that XCTR landscape units were compatible with those of the GIS. However, if the spatial units of the GIS were some form of grid cell, then it would be necessary to adapt the XCTR system to a grid cell landscape base. Whilst this would certainly make the XCTR system larger and slower, it should be a relatively straightforward matter to make the necessary changes.

It seems inevitable that with the development of a Department of Defence GIS there will be a need for a dynamic XCTR system which will predict real-time conditions. The present system includes most of the elements required to do this, but lacks dynamic climatological/hydrological inputs. As noted above, the derivation of these is not trivial and will require a considerable research input to develop a suite of models. Without these tools, it will not be possible to establish an effective real-time XCTR system.

It was noted in the section introducing expert systems that the GEM-II shell whilst suitable for demonstrating the utility of an inferencing system for XCTR is not ideal for the final product. Thus there is a need to tailor an inferencing system to meet the specific needs of the XCTR approach. Further, as a step towards a real-time approach within an extended GIS frame, it seems desirable to establish the XCTR system as an interactive module, capable on one hand of interfacing with GIS and graphics systems and on the other of exploring possible paths across a defined region using search algorithms. These capabilities could prove particularly useful in training programs as well as in planning exercises, such as the calculation of fuel requirements, as preparation for a future integrated GIS/XCTR/logistics system.

## SUMMARY

The methods employed to evaluate the land resources of the study area are not dependent upon new or untried technology (See Plate 4). The mapping technique is readily transferable, and, with the exception of vegetation cover, the sources of landscape element data are readily available; the GEM-II shell is a proven expert system and works on a variety of microcomputers; and, finally, overprinting is a standard printing technique which could be used to display XCTR values over other 1:100 000 series information. In these respects, and anticipating the success of the field calibration procedure, XCTR is operational and could be applied as soon as a suitable agency such as the Royal Australian Survey Corps is prepared to undertake the task and train the necessary personnel. However, there is a need to test the approach in other parts of northern Australia, and especially to calibrate it for wet season conditions.

In its present form the XCTR could be used to complement the present 1:100 000 map series or perhaps the new 1:50 000 series as a manual tool for planning and field use over the next 10–15 years before more complex GIS-type appraisal systems are in place. However, the approach is capable of considerable but gradual refinement as better data and tools become available.

Many of these potential refinements are dependent upon the form any future Department of Defence GIS takes, but there are certain developments which can be anticipated. Among these are the need for a specialist inferencing system for XCTR, graphics and GIS interfaces and the development of a real-time XCTR system. The last will require enormous improvements in the available climatological/hydrological models in order to support a real-time trafficability model for northern Australia.

# APPENDIX 1

# Landscape items for database

1.  Map sheet:
2.  UMA:

3.  Landform 1:
4.  Landform 2:
5.  Landform 3:

6.  Common slope class:
7.  Steepest slope class:

8.  Drainage density:
9.  Presence of major stream:
10. Alignment:
11. Type of cross-section:
12. Presence of large tributary stream:
13. Alignment:
14. Type of cross-section:
15. Stream density:

16. Lithology 1                          (   % area)
17. Lithology 2                          (   % area)
18. Lithology 3                          (   % area)

| 19. | Vegetation 1 | (    % area) |
| 20. | Vegetation 2 | (    % area) |
| 21. | Vegetation 3 | (    % area) |
|     |              |              |
| 22. | Soil 1       | (    % area) |
| 23. | Soil 2       | (    % area) |
| 24. | Soil 3       | (    % area) |

# APPENDIX 2

# Examples of landform descriptions and cross-country trafficability ratings

|  |  | Wet | Dry |
|---|---|---|---|
| Tidal flat<br>(3) | — tidal flats of study area occur in two types of locations:<br>(a) adjacent to the shoreline or near off-shore<br>(b) in the estuaries | | |
| | — those tidal flats which occur adjacent to the shoreline or further off-shore are mostly saturated and would not support a land vehicle — inter-tidal zone | | |
| | — these tidal flats do not vary in capacity from season to season | 9 | 9 |
| | — estuarine tidal flats consists of three subgroups which are distinguished by the height and frequency of salt-water inundation — fortunately, these can be characterised by their vegetative cover | | |
| | — mangrove tidal flats are the deepest and receive regular tidal salt-water inundations — the silts which form these are fully saturated and will not support a vehicle | 9 | 9 |
| | — behind the mangrove swamps are areas which are higher, receive less frequent inundations of salt-water and sometimes run on of fresh water during the 'wet' — sediments generally include some wind-blown materials (siliceous and calcareous particles) and have a grassy or herbaceous cover, both of which provide limited vehicle support | | |

|  | | 1–20 | 50–52 | 21–49 |
|---|---|---|---|---|

during the dry season — they have vegetative cover descriptions of 'marine swamps' on topographic sheets    1–20  50–52  21–49 / 9 / 7

— higher still are tidal flats which are only infrequently inundated by salt-water — sediments frequently include wind-blown materials (siliceous and calcareous particles) and occasionally have strata of shell remains — vegetative cover is characterised by salt-tolerant spp. including grasses and forbs but notable areas have no vegetative cover and there are numerous 'salt' flats — in the wet these are mostly covered with fresh water, in the period of 'king' tides by salt-water, and for the remainder of the year are trafficable    1–20  50–52  21–49 / 9 / 2

**Reef**
**(4)**

— in this study area, reefs are predominantly coral beds which may be adjacent to the shoreline or surrounded by tidal flats or off-shore — they are inundated by each high tide and are unlikely to be used by land vehicles because of this daily inundation except along shorelines    9    9

**Occasional dunes**
**(5)**

— these occur on higher tidal plains or sand plains and are more accurately described as *sand plains with occasional dunes* — shallow waters commonly cover the lower sand plains in the 'wet' — dunes can mostly be avoided    1–15  50–52  16–49 / 5 / 1

**Lake (or other fresh water body)**
**(6)**

— there are few of these in the study area
— characterised by permanent non-flowing water and have a high length to width ratio    9    9

**Swamp**
**(8)**

— apart from estuarine swamps, the fresh-water swamps of the study area are mostly shallow and dry during the 'dry' — in general, the larger the area of the swamp, the longer it retains its water

— west of the divide they are usually less than a square kilometre and occur widely, scattered across the plains — they occur as groups of

| | | 1–20 | 50–52 | 21–49 |
|---|---|---|---|---|
| | small swamps in larger depressions and commonly have a vegetative cover of ti-tree (*Leptospermum* spp.) shown as dense tree vegetation on the topographic sheets | 8 | | 1 |
| Plain and inclined plain (9) and (12) | — these landforms are characterised by surfaces with little relief — if this relief is less than 20m/1km it cannot be detected on the 1:100 000 topographic sheets — lesser local relief as does occur can only be deduced by the presence and density of drainage lines (see parameter *stream density*) | 1 | | 1 |
| | — inclined plains vary in altitude from one boundary to another but otherwise have the same characteristics as plains with the exception that drainage lines/streams parallel to the incline have somewhat greater energy and drain somewhat faster | 1 | | 1 |
| Undulating plain and inclined undulating plain (13) | — the surfaces of such plains commonly have a maximum of 20m–40m of relief per kilometre — in the study area such areas are commonly associated with more rapid run-off and narrower flood plains — they are also associated with incision of streams within their flood plains which can make vehicular movement difficult — in general, however, these landforms are hardly more difficult to cross than plains or inclined plains and where an incised stream is obvious from the contours, this will be evaluated under the parameter *stream cross-section* | 2 | | 2 |

# NOTES

1  Peter Laut, 'Land Evaluation for Bovine Tuberculosis Eradication in Northern Australia', *Australian Geography Studies*, Vol. 24, No. 2, October 1986, pp. 259–271.

2  J.R. Davis, J.R.L. Hoare and P.M. Nanninga, 'Developing a Fire Management Expert System for Kakadu National Park, Australia', *Journal of Environmental Management*, No. 22, 1986, pp. 215–217.

3  See W.E. Gabrau, J.K. Stoll and B.G. Stinson, *A Plan for Quantitative Evaluation of the Cross Country Performance of Prototype Vehicles*, Miscellaneous Paper M–70–7 (US Army Corps of Engineers, Waterways Experiment Station, Vicksburg, Mississippi, 1970).

4   ESRI-Australia Pty Ltd. Terrain Studies for Army. Report Prepared for Director of Operational Analysis (Army), Department of Defence, Canberra, Authority CAPO W.180168, January 1983.

5   See, for example, Pamela McCorduck, *Machines Who Think: A Personal Inquiry into the History and Prospects of Artificial Intelligence* (W.H. Freeman, San Francisco, 1979).

6   See A. Barr and E.A. Feigenbaum, *The Handbook of Artificial Intelligence*, Vol. I (Heuristech Press, Stanford, California, 1981).

7   R. Davis and J. King, 'An Overview of Production Systems', in E.W. Elcock and D. Michie (eds), *Machine Intelligence* (John Wiley and Sons, New York, 1977), pp. 300–332.

8   J.R. Davis, J.R.L. Hoare and P.M. Nanninga, 'Developing a Fire Management Expert System for Kakadu National Park, Australia'.

9   ibid.

10  J. Walker and M.S. Hopkins, 'Vegetation', in R.C. McDonald *et al.* (eds), *Australian Soil and Land Survey: Field Handbook* (Inkata Press, Melbourne, 1984), pp. 44–67.

11  K.H. Northcote, R.F. Isbell, G.G. Murtha and A.A. Webb, *Atlas of Australian Soils*. Sheet 7: Townsville – Normanton – Cooktown – Mitchell River – Torres Strait Area (CSIRO and Melbourne University Press, Melbourne, 1968).

12  See J. Walker and M.S. Hopkins, 'Vegetation'.

13  Personal communication to P. Laut from T. Duell, Canberra, March, 1987.

14  Personal communication to P. Laut from R.F. Isbell, Canberra, April, 1987.

CHAPTER TEN

# The Chrysalis Project: A Regional GIS Over Jervis Bay

**Michael Phillips**

**John Blackburn***

Those in the traditional land-oriented fields of endeavour could be forgiven for believing that so-called Land Information Systems (LIS) and, more recently, Geographic Information Systems (GIS) would be the answer to their management dreams. Such has been the level of interest, even euphoria, surrounding them.

The wash from this interest has now lapped many related and even not so related areas. It seems that LIS/GIS is almost the flavour of the month. Is the interest justified? Do LIS/GIS live up to the expectations?

In late 1986 the then Australian Survey Office (now combined with the former Division of National Mapping to form the Surveying and Land Information Group) decided to look in detail at GIS by undertaking a practical test exercise — the development of a geographic database and applications covering the Jervis Bay region of NSW.

The exercise was dubbed the 'Chrysalis' project. Chrysalis means 'preparation for transition', which accurately described the Australian Survey Office's (ASO) rationale for undertaking the project. This chapter details the issues and experiences of developing a regional GIS.

## THE CONCEPTUAL FRAMEWORK

Prior to conducting the Chrysalis project, if someone had asked the ASO what its concept of a GIS was, it would probably have illustrated its concept by showing something like Figure 10.1.

What Figure 10.1 illustrates is the technical composition of a GIS, not the operational form. This distinction is significant, in that it highlights one of the main lessons learnt from the project — that in ignorance people often think of GIS purely in terms of the hardware and software, the glossy salesman's brochures but, in reality, this technical component requires far less attention than the procedural component.

* The authors wish to thank the Australian Survey Office management for their support in the preparation of this paper. The views expressed by the authors do not necessarily reflect the views of the Department of Administrative Services.

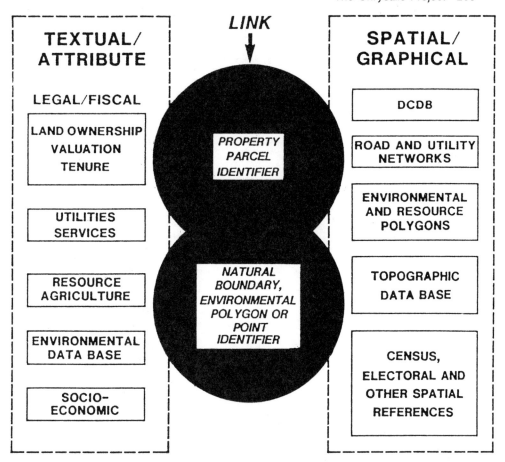

Figure 10.1 Traditional Concept of a GIS

By 'GIS procedures' is meant the mechanisms, arrangements, organisation, and human communications required to acquire and use successfully multi-disciplinary expertise and data, essential for a viable GIS. So, having been through the project, the ASO now has a far different model of a GIS. It is represented in Figure 10.2.

The different emphasis of this second model is obvious. It concentrates on the way a GIS operates at a procedural level rather than a technical level.

As this model is derived from the experience of the Chrysalis project, it will now be used to analyse the project. For the analysis, the model can be considered to have three aspects:

- The *establishment* of the GIS
- *Customers* and *Sources*, and
- The *operation* of the *system*.

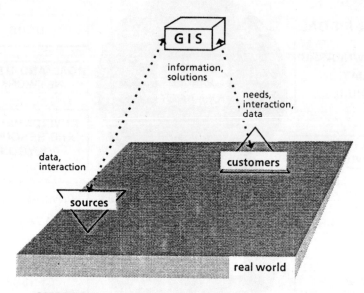

OPERATION:

- - the GIS attempts to model the customer's world
  as realistically as possible within the context of
  the overall real world

- - to do this GIS draws on data and expertise,
  (interactions) from the customer and other
  relevant sources of the real world

*Figure 10.2   Post-CHRYSALIS Project Concept of a GIS.*

The following sections of this chapter examine the issues involved in each of
these three aspects and the practical outcomes from the project.

# THE ESTABLISHMENT OF A GIS

## Issues

- ● Doing the groundwork:
  - — Learning about GIS and its operation.
  - — Reaching a point where the construction of a GIS can be attempted.

- Not 're-inventing the wheel':
  - — Finding out about and tapping the existing expertise.
  - — Being prepared to rely on other disciplines for components, or all of the GIS requirements.
- GIS and the current organisation:
  - — What is the mode of operation of the organisation?
  - — Does it have a well-developed computing background?
  - — How used to spatial analysis is it?
  - — What is the management structure? GIS tends to cut across traditional hierarchial structures.
- Gaining support and cooperation for GIS:
  - — From management.
  - — From staff.
  - — From external customers and sources.
- Cost/benefit issues:
  - — 'Proving' viability and the difficulties involved.
  - — The need for some initial risk capital.
- 'Getting the ball rolling':
  - — What is required to even attempt a small pilot exercise? What people and equipment?
  - — When do you know you are ready?
- Appropriate organisational arrangements for a GIS:
  - — For short and long term.
  - — For perhaps an interim or evaluation phase through to full acceptance and implementation.
- Project management issues:
  - — Selecting the people and establishing the team.
  - — The need for an 'espirit de corps' and a vision/mission.
  - — Project definition, planning and control.
- Promotion:
  - — The need to sell the concepts.
  - — The need to advertise early achievements.

## Experience

### The Groundwork

Depending on the level of knowledge already existing in the organisation, the groundwork may range from studying relevant literature, visiting organisations with an involvement in land information management, attending seminars, etc., up to conducting a pilot project. The groundwork should allow the organisation to tackle new and larger projects.

This was recognised two years ago by the ASO. In 1985 an ASO working group recommended that a pilot GIS be established to assess this emerging area of technology. The working group believed that GIS could:

- Enable the development and testing of data transfer channels between Commonwealth agencies.

- Provide a mechanism (through a geographic database management system) for efficient and effective management of the ASO's corporate technical database.

- Provide flexible, responsive, and efficient tools for the provision of services to clients.

- Enable ASO and other Commonwealth agency staff involved in a GIS project to gain valuable training and education in GIS concepts, techniques, and operational procedures.

ASO management supported the recommendation and a feasibility study was undertaken in early 1986. After extensive examination of different GIS systems and consultation with clients and potential clients, a pilot GIS over Jervis Bay was proposed.

The initiative to undertake the pilot project, and in fact the working group itself, were not isolated moves, but rather two of a series of initiatives the ASO had embarked on in the area known as Land Information Management (LIM).

As far back as 1983, the ASO recognised that the evolving technology and professional coverage of surveying and mapping were leading the ASO into a more generalist information processing role. To meet the challenge of that changed role, the ASO set about strategically planning for, and tackling a number of LIM tasks. The background and details of *these* tasks are given in Appendix A, but suffice to say here that the Chrysalis project was seen as an integral component of much of what the ASO was attempting to do in LIM.

One of the early considerations for the ASO was deciding over what region the GIS ought to be developed. The intention to develop a regional GIS, rather than say a national level or specific site applicaton, had been settled on the basis of the then perceived market within the Commonwealth.

Jervis Bay was selected as the pilot project study area for the following reasons:

- Diverse physical characteristics.

- Manageable area.

- Well known and mapped.

- Considerable activity and interest.

- Pressure from development proposals.

- Integrated and coordinated information base needed.

Rather than limit the project's scope to a study area bounded by administrative boundaries (i.e., Commonwealth Territory), the view was taken to look at the project as a 'joint venture' so that various related interests in other organisations and human and environmental factors in the region could be addressed holistically. Although an overhead, as much participation as possible from Commonwealth, state, and local government organisations was sought during the project definition phase.

## Not re-inventing the Wheel

In Australia there has been a significant amount of work and research in GIS carried out. Some organisations have operational GIS in some form, others have thorough designs developed. These leaders or pioneers in the GIS field, whether theoretical or practical, should be studied so that the development of a new GIS project does not 're-invent the wheel'. Through consultation and cross-fertilisation of ideas with other industry practitioners, many of the development pains can be avoided. The ASO experienced through its preliminary consultations a fraternity that was willing to share lessons and experiences, and indeed more formal mechanisms now exist for the exchange of ideas through the Australian Land Information Council, ALIC (again, refer Appendix A).

## GIS and the Current Organisation

GIS has many characteristics which can have a potentially significant effect on an organisation considering its use. For example, being reliant on multi-disciplinary input it tends to cut across traditional hierarchal organisational structures and boundaries, particularly if its implementation is to be successful. GIS is also pervasive. The facilities it offers can cover a wide range of applications, from specific graphic products to database management, and so presents a management problem of how to organisationally control its application. Obviously, GIS today is a 'high-tech' tool which alone can be a major challenge to an organisation without a well-developed computing background. Thus, recognising the mode of operation of an organisation is an important issue.

The ASO as a project-oriented surveying and mapping organisation has traditionally provided land-related data on a 'site' basis. In the past the emphasis has been placed on the requirement to produce plans. This emphasis is now changing. The shift is from products to processes.

The ASO entered the computer age like many other mapping and surveying organisations by first automating general mathematical calculations which were either complex, extensive, or laborious. Computerisation evolved from survey calculations to automating cartography and generating digital map data.

Computers are now fundamental to the ASO's operations, and changing perceptions reflect recognition of the information age. These changing perceptions have directed attention to the integration of data from field surveying, photogrammetry and, more recently, remote sensing. One simplistic solution to this integration problem was physically to overlay the maps or graphics produced from the various data systems. But it was obvious that the full potential of computerisation and the digital data generated was not being realised.

New technology is reinforcing the trend towards a broadened perception of 'geographic' data use. Technology has increased the range and sophistication of primary data collection methods available, but it has also provided the means to use secondary data sources. Secondary data sources that are held by other organisations can be accessed and shared to augment primary data collections and to service wider client demands or decision-support requirements. GIS offers operational solutions to this 'data integration' requirement.

In recent years, with more clients requiring digital data and the LIS/GIS philosophy gaining wider acceptance, the ASO's response has been to broaden its approach from information gathering to information management.

## Gaining Support and Cooperation

Many factors influence the success or otherwise of gaining support and cooperation. Quite often the issue can boil down to politics, personality, and power plays. These factors must obviously be considered, but perhaps in the first instance the arguments for support should be cast in terms which are readily understood and applied as relevant to the organisational objectives of those being solicited.

The pressures which the ASO management responded to were:

- Need for coordination of data sources and more efficient data management.

- Changing client needs.

- Government policy initiatives.

- Regional needs in areas of national interest.

Pressures like these must be communicated and described as opportunities rather than threats. As a result management is more likely to feel comfortable with them and take positive steps to address them.

The pilot project should have an open door to interested onlookers. The view to be presented to staff, for example, should be that GIS (at least in an organisation like the ASO) is being developed as an extension to, and an improvement of, the current mode of operation, not a radical change or the creation of a new select group of specialists using new technologies.

Customers and also sources (both external and internal to the organisation fostering the GIS) need to understand why a GIS and a pilot project is being developed. In the case of the Chrysalis project a fairly standard marketing approach of relating the GIS development objectives to customers' and sources' activities and interests was used. Specific needs of a customer or source may not always be identified early in a project's life. However, interests and problems can, and these can then be translated into operational GIS requirements. The operational GIS requirement can then be developed within the pilot project and presented and demonstrated as meeting a perceived need which can be scrutinised and refined. The customer's or the data source custodian's involvement at this point can be regarded as a 'joint venture' for mutual benefit. As a corollary:

- The customer reviews and influences the development of what is, in effect, his product and its appropriateness.

- The data source custodian scrutinises the application, expanded use, and value enhancement of his data.

## Cost/Benefit Issues

The process of gaining support for a new initiative will invariably run into the question of costs versus benefits. This is particularly so today where the bureaucracy is under ever-increasing pressure to do more with less.

The ASO found this reaction right across the board with the groups it approached for support. The problem was that quantitatively developing costs and benefits in a new area like GIS is difficult if not impossible to do accurately or thoroughly. In this regard, it is interesting to note that despite the proliferation of land information systems throughout Australia, there is not one succinct cost/benefit study of the area available.

This is not to say that GIS has no identifiable benefits. Costs are easily recognised — equipment, people, time — but benefits tend, perhaps, to be more subjective or intangible — better decision-making (i.e., quicker and more thorough), bigger range of services, improved operations, etc.

The net result is that those making the decisions to proceed or not must be prepared to take a risk. It is worth noting that successful private firms invest up to 10 per cent of gross earnings in research and development. The ASO spent about 0.5 per cent of its budget on the Chrysalis project.

## Getting the Ball Rolling

Having done some groundwork, gained support, etc., the time comes when the talking should stop and the action begin. That is, assemble the necessary equipment and people and begin operations. There may well be no issue at all here, if, for example, this step is just one in a totally planned exercise. In the ASO's case, they knew where they were going, but the mechanisms for getting there were not all defined beforehand. For example, whilst staffing the project team was not seen as a major hurdle, the equipment was. At the time, the ASO was looking at options such as:

- Developing its own GIS capability from the extensive range of in-house software and hardware.

- Acquiring public domain GIS software (if in fact any were suitable), or

- Perhaps a combination of both.

Fortunately through as much good luck as good management, the ASO was able to negotiate a no obligations loan of the necessary software and hardware. Discussions with other GIS practitioners indicated that a minimum of six months was required to undertake the sort of exercise the ASO envisaged and achieve realistic results. The loan was secured for that length of time. The advantages to the ASO of this approach were many.

- Immediate commencement of the pilot project.
- The ability to maintain a level of expectations amongst joint participants.
- Effective use of project team resources.
- The opportunity to identify software development needs in the long term.
- Considerably less in-house software development.
- Minimal development costs.
- Timely results to the project participants.

The equipment hurdle overcome, the other step was to actually form the team and get it operational.

People working on a project respond to an environment. They must also have a 'mission' — it may be a statement of discrete objectives or just a 'vision' which invokes initiative to challenge barriers or existing dogmas. Above all, to really get things moving and achieve, the people involved must be personally committed to the project and its mission. As succinct procedures generally do not exist, these people must use their imagination to develop solutions. In light of this, a system selected must have the resident tools and capabilities to inspire imaginative solutions.

The system's engine, that is, the hardware and software system which is the heart of the environment, should provide a high percentage of functionality required to meet the objectives of the project. It does not necessarily have to be 'flash', but if it is new and interesting, the people involved are more likely to be eager to use it.

## Organisational Arrangements

For a pilot project such as Chrysalis to succed, it needs to have a high priority and organisational commitment. The project team ideally should have a flat structure and a good measure of freedom. However, the top management of the various organisations involved must also feel they are part of the project, not to control or dictate but more to guide this freedom and coordinate the human resources.

The ASO established a GIS steering committee, made up of senior managers who had traditional responsibilities over various resources required for the project. From the ASO's experience, such a group needs to be small (a maximum of four) and should meet regularly at predicted project milestones with project advisers.

## Project Definition, Management, and Control

The aim of definition is to break the project down into its component parts so that each becomes a manageable entity. The project plan for the Chrysalis project was arranged in a hierarchy as follows:

- Overall — sequence of events, resources, and timing.
- Functional — projects to be undertaken and their interrelationships.
- Individual — monitoring of sub-projects and their progress.

The project was broken into functional components called sub-projects (see Appendix B), and each was defined and described according to the following scheme:

- Aims and objectives.
- Rationale — why this sub-project.
- Description — overview and background.
- Data sources.
- Task descriptions — data capture, management, analysis and presentation.
- Resourcing, timing.
- Relationships to other sub-projects.

Although the project team included a coordinator, project manager, and several other convenors and ancillary support members, its structure was necessarily flat, informal, and cooperative.

Project team meetings were held to discuss problems and progress on a regular and informal basis at major milestones rather than at equal intervals.

## Promotion

The need to keep those not directly involved aware of progress and, more importantly, supportive, is often critical to success. The intentions and purpose of the Chrysalis project were reported throughout the life of the project by such means as articles in internal newsletters and external publications and through seminars and open days for management and staff. Together these approaches helped develop a perspective that the project was related and pertinent to the work and functions of those people targeted for these promotional activities.

Although an overhead, the need for internal promotion throughout the project cannot be overstressed so that staff not directly involved feel there is a conscious attempt to keep them informed. Additional advantages of the promotional activity included:

- Forcing those undertaking the promotion to clarify their thinking about GIS and project.
- Injecting additional project control discipline through having to have certain results to promote.

# CUSTOMERS AND SOURCES

## Issues

- Establishing the system's regime:
  - A Geographic Database (GDB) waiting for an application, or
  - An application waiting for a GDB, or
  - Perhaps a combination of both.

As a result of this analysis,

- Clarifying the roles of customers and sources:
  - Customers define applications.
  - Sources provide input to the GDB and the interpretation of the data.
  - The complications that can arise regarding the above analysis from
    - many customers;
    - many sources; and
    - customers who are sources and vice versa.
- Soliciting customers' and sources' support:
  - 'Ownership' of data.
  - Problems with confidentiality.
  - 'Empire' protection and the perceived power of the information holder.
  - Professional rivalry.
  - Administrative barriers.
- Understanding the reasons for support:
  - Mutual benefits, for example, digital data, education.
  - Financial benefits, payment for data, expertise.
- Accurately defining needs:
  - Causes versus symptoms.
  - Short- and long-term needs.
  - Convincing participants that needs can be met.
- Developing solutions/applications:
  - How to arrange and manage input from customers and sources.
  - Need to clarify and define the differences between a customer's application definition and source data available for the GDB, and the data interpretation necessary.
  - Meeting deadlines.
- Training and education services:
  - For in-house and external participants.

## Experience

### Joint Venture Concept

From the outset the ASO recognised that a regional GIS would only work if it catered to the needs of a representative cross-section of the interests in the area. By definition, that belief meant that involvement in the project had to be multi-disciplinary in terms of both expertise and data.

As a result, the ASO adopted a 'joint venture concept' for the project encompassing:

- Multi-disciplinary and varied interests.
- Common interests in GIS, in the Jervis Bay region, or both.
- Common goals in wanting to improve organisational performance through tools such as GIS.
- Participation in project definition.
- Involvement in development and operation of the system.

## A Consultancy Approach

As much participation as possible was sought during the project definition phase to analyse thoroughly participants' interests and needs. Information obtained from participants was interpreted in terms of the problems and interests which they were addressing and then translated into requirements for a GIS.

These preliminary requirements were used to develop precursory sub-projects and systems for demonstration and learning, and to be used as a basis for further development and refinement. This approach was adopted because of the ASO's belief that it is difficult to specify, or for someone else to define, GIS system needs without something to visualise and relate to physically.

## Workshop

Midway through the project an Executive Plan Workshop was conducted in Canberra for more than 30 people from 20 organisations interested in, or participating in, the project. The workshop began with an introductory seminar to set the scene, then representatives from each organisation described their interests in brief presentations. Demonstrations of the preliminary GIS applications were conducted. With the background, issues, and a view to what was possible in the minds of the participants, three syndicate groups were convened to specify GIS development requirements by individually focusing on the three themes or major issues in Jervis Bay — conservation, development, and management. This workshop was viewed to be a success for two main reasons:

- It provided a cooperative environment for understanding various needs and interests in Jervis Bay and for GIS.
- It provided the springboard and the necessary information to further define and develop additional external participant sub-projects and to consolidate the existing sub-projects making up the Chrysalis project.

## External Participation in the Project

This was offered and occurred in several forms in the project. So-called 'joint' participants were able to:

- Provide advice and scrutiny.
- Define particular sub-projects.
- Provide data in digital and map form.
- Supervise the input and integration of data.
- Supervise and direct the analysis and presentation of data.
- Use the GIS tools with training provided by the ASO staff on the project team.
- Combine any of the above.

The ASO endeavoured to act as a facilitator by providing the system with much of the basic spatial data (e.g. topography) and the consistent spatial referencing framework required as the foundation for a truly integrated regional geographic information system. Represented in Figure 10.3 is an illustration of the relationship of these basic GIS components.

## Problems Encountered

The 'joint venture' aspect of the Jervis Bay pilot project, for all its impact and its cooperative nature, was not without problems. Indeed, preliminary expert advice did suggest that too much external user participation could be destabilising and could possibly hinder project movement in the early stages.

However, the considerable amount of interest in the first stages was encouraging and did in fact help define the project's purpose. What was apparent as work proceeded, was that despite participants being generally very supportive there were individual problems with:

- 'Empire protection'.
- Resource commitments.
- Cost/benefit analysis and justificaton.
- Senior management support.
- Inter-government and organisation relationships.
- Provision of data for a charge or on a 'quid pro quo' basis.
- Lack of participant's in-house data coordination and management.
- Concern over controlling growth and database custodianship.

## Results for Customers and Sources

The ASO regarded the Chrysalis project as being as much about experiencing and understanding problems as about assessing the positive aspects and solutions. This pilot project has shown that the positive aspects of GIS far outweigh

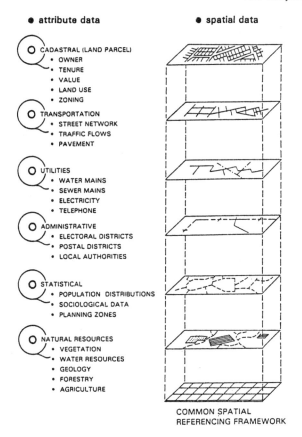

● attribute data          ● spatial data

CADASTRAL (LAND PARCEL)
• OWNER
• TENURE
• VALUE
• LAND USE
• ZONING

TRANSPORTATION
• STREET NETWORK
• TRAFFIC FLOWS
• PAVEMENT

UTILITIES
• WATER MAINS
• SEWER MAINS
• ELECTRICITY
• TELEPHONE

ADMINISTRATIVE
• ELECTORAL DISTRICTS
• POSTAL DISTRICTS
• LOCAL AUTHORITIES

STATISTICAL
• POPULATION DISTRIBUTIONS
• SOCIOLOGICAL DATA
• PLANNING ZONES

NATURAL RESOURCES
• VEGETATION
• WATER RESOURCES
• GEOLOGY
• FORESTRY
• AGRICULTURE

COMMON SPATIAL
REFERENCING FRAMEWORK

Figure 10.3   GIS Relationships (based on WALIS model).

the problems, and in fact it has been more successful than was originally anticipated because it was also possible to incorporate the Chrysalis GIS activities into a general marketing exercise which the ASO was conducting at the time of the project. This was particularly important, as the ASO is now entering a user-pays mode of operation and, like several other government agencies, is required to take a more commercial approach to its operations.

The approach which has been developed for the application of GIS for customers is:

● First of all look at the task or problem being addressed by the customer.

● Look at the analysis or presentation necessary, and then

● Work backwards to arrive at the minimum data set required and understand exactly which geographic information needs to be collected, organised, and integrated.

For land information management in Australia the Chrysalis project has further demonstrated and supports:

- The value of relating descriptive and temporal information about an issue or situation spatially to a location or area.

- The need for 'meta-data' about availability, integrity, and accessibility of land-related data. One approach to meeting this need is through directories such as the Commonwealth's LANDSEARCH Directory and the state government equivalents.

- Integration and sharing of source data requires consolidation of cooperative and coordinated institutional mechanisms for the collection and dissemination of land-related data such as the Australian Land Information Council (ALIC) (refer to Appendix A).

# OPERATION OF THE GIS SYSTEM

## Issues

- Training and education:
  — Understanding and communicating the role and significance of GIS.
  — System familiarisation and how this work sits with the role.
  — The transition from training to production.
- The 'system':
  — Salesperson's rhetoric versus reality and expectations.
  — User interface; ease of use, response, performance.
  — The geographic database management system; integrating multi-sourced, multi-faceted, multi-formatted data.
  — Raster and vector capabilities.
  — Affects of operation of the GIS on other systems; those operational, under development, or even under investigation.
  — Capabilities of the analysis/modelling tools.
  — Ease of interfacing to other systems, both internal and external.
- Operational control:
  — The project, meeting commitments.
  — Resources; people — internal and external — hardware, software.
- Data capture:
  — General, non-specific coverages.
  — Applications driven.
  — Significance of data capture as an overhead.
- Production running:
  — Incorporating GIS into an organisation. The pervasiveness of its influence.
- — Allocation of expertise to tasks, functional or job-based split of this expertise?

- The role of promotion:
    - In project control, that is, meeting milestones.
    - In developing understanding and thinking.

## Experience

A GIS is used to model the distribution in time and space of land and environmental resources, social and economic indicators, land ownership and value, etc., and the various interrelationships of these attributes. GIS is said to provide the tool to access, manipulate and display data to arrive at appropriate information for users such as planners, researchers and administrators. The hardware and software of a GIS are the visible components but to satisfy the customers far more is required.

### Training

The ASO believes that 80 per cent of GIS is the set of procedures for the integration of multi-disciplinary expertise and data, and 20 per cent the software and hardware system. To extend into an operational mode that 80 per cent is where the major training emphasis should be placed. ARC/INFO, for example (the GIS package used by the ASO), is an extensive system, well-documented and comprising many commands in several modules. It is marketed as a 'tool-box' of facilities, but in the absence of a well-developed set of procedures for their use, inevitably those expensive tools will be idle or will be ineffective in their application.

GIS challenges existing professional boundaries certainly, but it also challenges the knowledge and innovation of professional staff. GIS personnel should be selected and trained more in recognition of their personal initiative, commitment, and innovation than their organisational position. (Computer literacy is not a prerequisite, but people who understand spatial and cartographic fundamentals are essential in the team.)

The actual system training should therefore be related to the procedures required and it may arise that efficient usage (or short cuts) will be the important requirements for system training. System training for ARC/INFO was done in phases, starting with introductory level, then advanced, and finally with a fine-tuning session. Each session was of one week duration, separated by approximately three weeks familiarisation. It is very important from the outset, even though the trainer may find it difficult, that examples of the actual work to be undertaken are used in training exercises to give the training a practical focus. It is also important to start small with a simple exercise that demonstrates the fundamental capabilities of marrying spatial and non-spatial attribute data. In this regard, the ASO's first exercise was to develop an automated data index over the Jervis Bay region.

The overall emphasis should be that GIS is not a mapping or graphics system alone.

## Software

As previously mentioned the software vehicle used for the Chrysalis project has been ESRI's ARC/INFO. It was used as a representative of the current GIS technology rather than for the purpose of evaluating that particular software package itself. However, as a representative it is necessary to describe the characteristics of ARC/INFO and how it fits into a GIS role.

The ASO has already implemented interactive graphics (or Computer Aided Drafting, CAD) into an operational mode. A modern GIS needs to perform interactive graphics operations, but also needs to support a host of analytic, manipulative, and query functions based on a structure using a topological and relational Database Management System (DBMS). To develop the Jervis Bay GIS, the ASO used ARC/INFO because at the outset it addressed these functions, that is, it exceeded the basic functionality of a CAD system.

The Jervis Bay GIS now consists of a database of geographic information covering representative areas which involve both positional data about land features plus other descriptive/non-locational data about those features. ARC/INFO provides the functions to:

- Visually and numerically display selected data in the database.
- Explore relationships among spatial data sets.
- Identify locations which meet specified criteria.
- Estimate impacts through predictive modelling.

In other words, it is a system which can assist readily in the decision-making process concerning the Jervis Bay region. However, the experience of the Chrysalis project brought home several lessons to the ASO regarding software packages, but in particular a few about GIS systems:

- That whilst a system may be able to perform some operation which is needed by the organisation, it may be so inefficient at doing so that it essentially renders the facility unavailable for production running.

- That *sophisticated* analyses of geographic data which require, say, statistical processing rather than straight 'map overlay' are not generally available in GIS packages and must be developed by the user.

- That there is no escaping the simple hard fact that to be a successful user the manuals must be studied and understood. Because a lot of work is involved, the standard of documentation becomes critical to the timely introduction of production running.

## Applications

Many application solutions were developed during the project (see Appendix B), but one which is probably of particular relevance to defence was the integration of remote sensing data. Remote sensing data was seen as an important layer of information in several of the Chrysalis applications, in particular:

- Land use classification.
- Bushfire hazard analysis.
- Forest management.
- Various environmental impact analyses.

One of these projects was a geotechnical and environmental analysis of the region for the Department of Housing and Construction using several satellite — LANDSAT MSS, LANDSAT TM and SPOT — and other data sets. The satellite data sets were initially rectified using 1:25 000 topographic maps for ground control, and resampled to the Australian Map Grid (AMG) by cubic convolution and a first-order polynomial transformation. A supervised maximum likelihood classification yielded the major classes in each data set. A software interface was developed in-house to allow the transfer of this raster data between the ASO Dipix Aries 111 and the ARC/INFO systems, the interface based on the ESRI single variable file format. Finally, the raster data was converted to vector polygon format using the ARC/INFO GRID package.

At this stage of the Chrysalis project work has been undertaken on:

- Comparisons between remote sensing classifications and ancillary GIS data.
- Refinement of the remote sensing classification using ancillary GIS data (e.g. topography, slope, aspect, polygon masks).
- Overlay of ancillary GIS data onto remote sensing data for improved presentation.
- Generation of three-dimensional products incorporating remote sensing data.

The experience has highlighted:

- The problems associated with accommodating the large volume of raster data in vector systems.
- The difficulty in producing traditionally acceptable vector-based carto-graphic products from raster data.

## Incorporating GIS into the Organisation

GIS should be viewed and developed as an extension of the current mode of operation and an improvement to traditional service provision. Its conceptual and strategic incorporation should be as a 'core' or 'hub' which provides for the linkage of other land-related processing systems. Its physical incorporation should be as a 'gateway' to analytical and data integration tools which are generally available to all functional areas in the organisation to complement and supplement their operations and services. GIS should not be implemented as another specialised data processing sub-system. A diagrammatic representation of this suggested arrangement is shown in Figure 10.4.

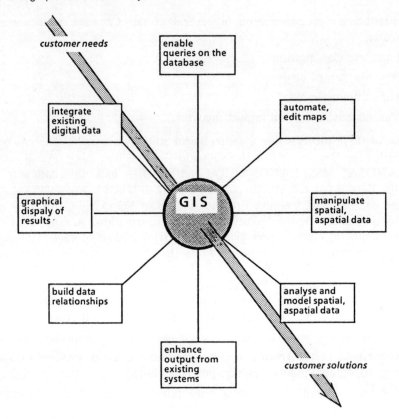

Figure 10.4   GIS in an Organisation: the Core or HUB Concept.

## Scheduling Operations

Usually a computing resource has to be shared with many other users. This is certainly the case within the ASO, where, for example, the main computer is commonly running at close to maximum capacity. A GIS requires access to several peripheral devices such as digitisers, plotters, scanners and printers. It becomes important then to recognise opportunities for cooperative processing such as downloading to microcomputers or workstations in a local area network.

Software, then, should be capable of operating in these environments. Operations should also be studied and monitored so that maximum efficiency is achieved through judicious scheduling between batch and interactive processing.

## Production Running

In practice the project's management will be faced with the following factors and problems:

- Competing daily priorities.
- Maintaining momentum — both with internal and external participants.
- Production should be 'results driven'.
- The role of promotion in project control.
- Customer satisfaction is important to project personnel as well as the host organisation and customer.

Data capture, its pitfalls and the significant resources it requires (e.g. digitisation) are often seen as negative aspects of establishing Geographic Databases (GDBs) and GISs. However the real benefits of digital data and GIS are usually downstream and therefore must be measured with this in mind and not distorted by the initial data capture overhead.

Data capture has a real impact on the system's construction but, if the top-down approach as outlined previously is followed, the necessary data capture will be kept to a minimum and subsequent data analysis and presentation will be pertinent to satisfying customer needs. However, what about future customers with different requirements? This is where data management and DBMS flexibility come into play so that the GDBs can be maintained and built on for long-term and broad benefit.

There has also been concern about the misuse of different geographic information in a GIS (i.e., various scales, resolutions, themes and classifications and its combination). But by using multi-disciplinary expertise to its best advantage, both internally and externally, the GIS can be used to improve quality, preserve integrity, and provide scrutiny of use and generation of derived products. This reinforces the importance of the procedures involved in this process.

## THE RESULTS FOR THE ASO

The ASO embarked on the development of a pilot GIS over the Jervis Bay region because it believed this was the best way to gain quickly enough GIS understanding so that strategic decisions about the ASO's future in LIM could be made confidently.

The experience (practice) derived from the Chrysalis project and described in the preceding sections is now being applied and adapted to provide the following services:

- Customised products.
- Flexibility and responsiveness in meeting client needs.
- Linking of locational and descriptive information.
- An automated map which is flexible in content, scale and time frame.
- Consistent and accurate location referencing.
- Databasing services — information is stored, updated where necessary and made available for further use.

- New information derived from new combinations and presentation of data.
- Procedures and technology for organising and analysing geographic information.

The ASO now believes it is able to facilitate the implementation of GIS technology, but understands that this role is not the domain of any one profession or discipline. The real benefits of a GIS are realised at the workface, where the engineer, planner, or administrator has a system at his or her fingertips. In view of this, the ASO will be looking to provide service options ranging from:

- A full production service, from start to end, where products include maps, plans, statistics, and other forms of answers from analyses, and an established GDB; to
- Data capture service whereby certain layers of data, for use in another organisation's GIS or data processing system, are collated, assessed, and captured digitally; to
- A facilitator service, through assisting clients in the use of land-related information in their own systems.

In addition to the benefits directly gained for the ASO, the pilot GIS exercise has also:

- Enabled the many other organisations involved to gain experience of GIS at a time when those organisations were searching for improved land-related data processing systems.
- Tested the data exchange/transfer channels and mechanisms between many organisations.
- Provided valuable insights into the political and administrative requirements involved in developing and implementing multi-disciplinary systems.

## LESSONS FOR DEFENCE

Land information management is an 'integrating' approach in that to be effective it needs:

- Multi-disciplinary data and expertise; and
- Spatial and aspatial (i.e., non-spatial or descriptive) data attributes to be combined.

Geographic information systems are a fundamental operational component of LIM. The successful implementation of GIS necessitates that the system cut across professional, organisational, and operational boundaries. The reality of this means that the GIS problem is, in the opinion of the ASO, in the order of 80 per cent procedural and 20 per cent technological.

In recognition of this split, Defence should:

- Give the administrative and conceptual framework considerable thought in the early stages of GIS development; and

- The actual development of a 'system' should begin with a small but realistic problem or application.

The above two tasks need not, and in fact should not, happen in sequence. A practical exercise is a proven way of clarifying ideas and testing strategies. However, before undertaking such an exercise some preliminary thinking and planning is essential.


# APPENDIX A

# Land Information Management and the Australian Survey Office (ASO)


The old ASO had always been a land information handler, mainly in the area of project surveying and mapping. Over recent times, however, its role has broadened. Several factors have contributed to this change.

- Changing client requirements:
    — Increased demand for digital products.
    — Increasingly sophisticated analyses of land-related data required. This sophistication has covered the types of data to be collected and stored, the type of manipulations to be done, the range of outputs and more complex timing aspects.

- The increasingly diverse base of clients who recognise the value of being able to relate different data sets spatially and portray the results graphically.

- Advances in the computer technology associated with the processing of land-related data.

- The Commonwealth Government's desire to improve the management of Australia's land resources.

- The need for increasing efficiencies in providing services due, on the one hand, to a continuing decline in the level of ASO resourcing, but on the other to a continually growing program of work.

These factors have seen the ASO move from the fairly specialised area of project surveying and mapping to what the organisaton now considers is a more general land information management (LIM) role.

LIM is defined as that body of expertise, technology, and organisation associated with the efficient, effective, and responsible application of land information technology and procedures. The ASO views LIM as encompassing a number of spatial technologies, as represented in Figure 10.5.

This role change has probably been reinforced in the Administrative Arrangement Orders changes in 1987, in which the old ASO was amalgamated with the former Division of National Mapping to form the Surveying and Land Information Group.

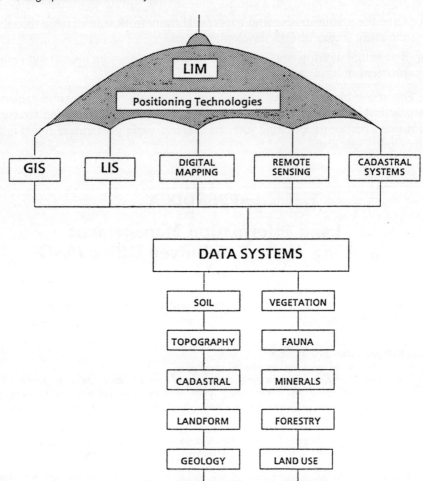

*Figure 10.5   Overview of Land Information Management (LIM).*

# LIM INITIATIVES

## Introduction

A number of LIM initiatives have been undertaken by the ASO over the past few years, concomitant with the changed role of the organisation.

# Commonwealth Coordination

## Inter-Departmental Committee

The first major step was the formation of an IDC to consider the need for coordination of Commonwealth land-related data. The IDC was convened by the Surveyor-General and ultimately, in recognition of the importance of land-related data to decision-making at all levels and the inefficiencies of the then uncoordinated approach, recommended the establishment of the Commonwealth Land Information Support Group (CLISG). CLISG was given responsibility for increasing coordination and cooperation in all aspects of the Commonwealth's involvement with land-related data.

To meet this responsibility a series of projects are formulated within an overall strategic framework. In simple terms the strategy said that in order to achieve efficiencies in the collection, storage, use, and dissemination of land-related data, Commonwealth agencies must:

- Firstly, be aware of what data exists already, where it is, whether it can be accessed, and if so how.

- Secondly, communication channels must be established between agencies to facilitate transfers of data. These channels could be physical, for example, computer links and/or 'logical', for example, people knowing who the right person is to contact for information.

- Thirdly, assessing the land-related data needs of agencies and the optimal way of meeting those needs.

## The LANDSEARCH Directory

An obvious approach to meeting the first component above was to produce a directory to the Commonwealth's land-related data holdings. The design and development of the directory was undertaken jointly by an abridged continuation of the IDC, known as the Executive Management Committee, and the CLISG. LANDSEARCH resulted. Published in late 1985, it contains details of over 800 Commonwealth-held land-related data sets.

Today, work is almost complete on the second edition of LANDSEARCH and the directory has also been made available on-line through the national CSIRONET computer communications network.

## The CHRYSALIS Project

Achieving progress in the second component of the strategy outlined above was always recognised as being difficult.

The work associated with LANDSEARCH, in particular the actual questionnaire survey, went part of the way in that it:

- Raised agencies' awareness of their data holdings, the relevance of the spatial component of those holdings, and their information management regimes.

- Let agencies know that there were other organisations with similar requirements in land-related data and that there were mechanisms available to link needs and solutions. In this respect, the GLISG saw itself as offering a clearing house or gateway service between agencies, if this was required.

However, CLISG (ASO) believed the best way to achieve real progress in establishing transfer channels was to undertake a practical exercise involving many Commonwealth agencies. This belief was one of the primary reasons for the Chrysalis pilot geographic information system (GIS) project being conceived.

# National Coordination

## LIS Development in Australasia

By the mid-1970s, government land administration agencies in both Australia and New Zealand began to experience the increasing requirement to handle efficiently large volumes of data. The traditional land administration functions of conveyancing, land taxation, rating, and land use inventories, are land parcel based. However, over recent times considerable legislation related to land use and the environment was enacted. In many cases, the new legislation necessitated the establishment of additional, geographically dispersed administrative agencies, thereby adding to the plethora of land-related information. Therefore, databases containing both traditional and contemporary land data were developed.

Computer technology developments in the same period were seen by governments as a means of better managing and disseminating land information. The primary application of this new technology was the development of information management systems which could effectively support policy and decision-making, and also enable government agencies to provide a better service to users.

The initial objectives of LIS development were to establish land databanks for legal/fiscal administrative purposes. In recent years, the trend in jurisdictions has been to expand this approach to encompass environmental, natural resource, and socio-economic applications. Therefore, the management of land information has been conceptualised in a much broader sense. That is, land information management systems should be integrated across a range of government agencies, providing both textual and graphical information for administrative, mapping, demographic, and resource/environmental purposes. Land information should be capable of analysis at not just the parcel level, but also should be capable of aggregation or generalisation on regional or geographical spatial bases.

## Early Cooperative Arrangements

Although all jurisdictions had similar goals, and were confronted by many similar legal, institutional, technical and administrative problems in developing and implementing new land information management technology, there was limited formal cooperation between jurisdictions. However, a number of informal arrangements existed between LIS professionals and decision-makers in Australasia. These arrangements included:

- URPIS conferences.
- Ad hoc meetings between LIS agency directors, professionals, academics, etc.
- Meetings, workshops, and seminars organised by academic institutions, professional bodies and local government.

During the early-1980s, an informal group called the Australasian Land Information Council evolved. This group generally comprised the director of the LIS agency in each state, the Northern Territory and the Commonwealth. Although this informal group did not operate at the policy-making level, it was the forerunner of the national coordination effort.

## The Need for National Coordination

Through the informal cooperative arrangements, many came to realise that if land information is so important to government policy and decision-makers, national cooperation to make this information more accessible was vital to all governments. In addition, the need for formal national cooperation was considered necessary because:

- The levels of government overlap geographically.
- The levels of government overlap functionally in many areas (in an operational sense, not a statutory one).
- Many land-related phenomena do not stop at administrative boundaries.
- Problems related to land and land administration are common to many jurisdictions.
- All governments are hampered by inadequate resources for land information management system research and development.
- The similarity of problems experienced by each jurisdiction in the development and implementation of land information management systems is considerable.

## Formation of the Australian Land Information Council (ALIC)

In November 1984, a national conference was convened to discuss 'Better Land-Related Information for Policy Decisions'. The conference was attended by both senior policy and decision-makers from the three tiers of Australian government, academia and private enterprise. A principal resolution of the conference was that a national coordination council be established. Subsequently, with the support of the Prime Minister, state premiers (with the exception of Queensland) and the Chief Minister of the Northern Territory, the ALIC was formed in January 1986.

The ALIC comprises the chairman of each of the LIS steering committees (generally the head of the Department of Lands or its equivalent) from each Australian state (except Queensland), the Northern Territory and the Commonwealth. New Zealand has observer status.

## Role of ALIC

The role of the ALIC is to provide a forum for debate on land information policies at the national level, and to explore the scope for adoption of compatible policies and standards.

Some specific functions of the ALIC are to:

- Plan, develop and promote a national strategy on land information exchange.
- Advise other national committees and interested groups on matters related to the collection and use of land information in Australia.
- Promote greater use of land-related information in decision-making at all levels of government.
- Promote LIS education and research in Australia.

## The Australasian Advisory Committee on Land Information (AACLI)

At the inaugural meeting of the ALIC in March 1986, it was agreed that the previous informal Australasian Land Information Council be given official recognition as the Technical Committee of the ALIC.

Subsequently, New Zealand became a member of this committee and the name was changed to the AACLI. (Queensland is not represented.)

The AACLI provides a forum for the sharing of experiences and expertise in areas such as human resources, software, technical information and policy development.

The roles of the AACLI are to provide:

- Advice to the ALIC on technical matters.
- A consultative mechanism for its own members and others in research and development of land information management systems and procedures.

### Present Activities

Specific tasks currently being undertaken by ALIC include:

- Development of a national strategy on land information exchange.
- Providing advice to national bodies and other groups on land information collection, use and dissemination.
- Promotion of the value of land-related information in decision-making.
- Provision of advice and input into land information system education and training.
- Development of a register of land information system research and development projects.

## IMPLICATIONS FOR THE COMMONWEALTH

The Commonwealth through the ASO/CLISG was a major player in the formation of the ALIC. It could see the inefficiencies of land agencies around Australia duplicating effort in the development of their systems. But the Commonwealth also realised the ultimate strategic importance to Australia of the land information systems and all they entail.

Through the Commonwealth's active involvement in ALIC it has been able to promote the needs of the Commonwealth agencies for State/Territory land-related data. The National Strategy on Land Information Exchange, currently being developed by ALIC, addresses directly many of the issues involved in the sharing of information for Australia's good.

The other benefit the Commonwealth can gain from participation in an organisation like ALIC is being in close touch with fellow-LIM practitioners. This facilitates sharing of expertise and knowledge, in theory shortening the development life cycle.

## APPENDIX B

# Chrysalis sub-projects

| Sub-project Name | Organisation Involved |
|---|---|
| 1. Geographic Data Management System | ASO |
| 2. Application System Interfacing | ASO |
| 3. Cadastral/Tenure Information System | ASO |
| 4. Remote Sensing | ASO |
| 5. Engineering/Detail | ASO, Housing and Construction |

| | |
|---|---|
| 6. Automated Cartography/Graphics System | ASO |
| 7. Territory Management Scheme | ASO, Department of Territories |
| 8. Marine/Aquatic Resource Information System | ASO, NSW Fisheries |
| 9. Socio-economic Trend Projections | ASO, University of NSW |
| 10. Landscape Architecture: Visual assessment | ASO, CCAE |
| 11. Environmental Resource Information System: Flora/fauna Geology/hydrology/soils/erosion Bushfire hazard/response | ASO, NEW NPWS Shoalhaven City Council |
| 12. Land Capability | ASO, Nowra Crown Land Office |

CHAPTER ELEVEN

# Planning the Future of Defence Geographic Information Systems

## Ross Babbage

## STIMULANTS FOR GEOGRAPHIC INFORMATION SYSTEM DEVELOPMENT

Several factors have emerged in recent years to increase greatly the attractiveness of coordinated Geographic Information System (GIS) development within the Department of Defence. The first of these factors is the fundamental change in Australia's strategic priorities.

Most of Australia's military history has involved force commitments to overseas theatres alongside the much larger deployments of our major power allies. This long history of so-called 'forward defence' strategy saw Australian forces committed to Maori Wars, the Boer War, the Boxer Rebellion, the First and Second World Wars, the Berlin Airlift, the Malayan Emergency, Korea, Indonesian Confrontation, and Vietnam.

Aside from a short period from late 1941 to early 1943, Australians were not forced to concentrate the weight of their defence investment on the direct defence of the Australian continent. Defence interest in gathering geographic data on the Australian environment reached its heights during preparations for World War II and the threat of Japanese invasion. However, after the war higher priorities were afforded to knowledge of overseas locations in which Australian forces were deployed, or could be required to operate. The study of Australia and the development of systems to support that study languished.

By the late-1960s and early-1970s Australia was moving away from its traditional 'forward defence' strategy and this trend was accelerated by significant cuts in United States and British force commitments to Southeast Asia and a marked reduction in the preparedness of these countries to become militarily engaged in this region. Australia's defence planners appreciated that it was necessary to take full account of the United States' global security obligations. While Australia's alliance connections would remain very important, they were no substitute for the development of greater self-reliance in the direct defence of Australia.[1]

This fundamental change in policy direction posed Australian defence planners with a dramatic challenge. How were they to plan for the direct defence of Australia with a high level of self-reliance when the level of national expenditure on defence was likely to remain in the 2.5–3 per cent GDP bracket?

To some extent the problem was eased by the realisation that Australia faced no imminent or foreseeable prospect of large-scale invasion. Only the two superpowers possess the numbers of ships and aircraft that would be required to land a substantial assault force on Australian territory and Moscow has little interest in attacking Australia. The prospect of the Soviet Union launching a conventional attack on Australia without stimulating a massive United States response was considered incredible. Other countries, including some in Asia, could possibly develop the substantial air and naval forces needed to launch a major attack on Australia, but this could not be done quickly and would be detected at an early stage. This should give the Australian Government time to expand the nation's defence capabilities to meet the challenge.

This logic led Australian defence planners to focus their primary immediate attention on those smaller scale potential threats, harassments, raids, and other limited military attacks that numerous countries possess the military potential to launch at short notice should a serious international dispute arise. Planning takes account of the possibility of larger scale threats emerging in the longer term by investing now in selected skills, equipments, and industry support to provide a basis for rapid force expansion should this be required in the future.

Australia faces a major challenge in preparing an effective defence of its national territory with a high level of independence. The land and offshore maritime areas of relevance are vast and the personnel and financial resources that can be devoted to the task are very limited. One very important and potentially decisive advantage that Australia can work to exploit is knowledge and understanding of the local environment.

The history of warfare is replete with examples of superior terrain and infrastructure intelligence having a disproportionate effect on battlefield outcomes. In contrast to the long forward defence era when Australian forces were committed to distant overseas locations, frequently with little notice, our defence planners are now able to define certain areas of northern and offshore Australia that would most credibly be the sites of future military operations. These endorsed planning assumptions and ease of access to the areas concerned provide Australia with a hitherto unprecedented opportunity to maximise the battlefield leverage of superb geographic intelligence.

The importance of this requirement was acknowledged in the Government's Defence White Paper:

> The availability of comprehensive and up to date military maps and charts, together with a detailed knowledge of the environment and its infrastructure, is fundamental to the effective conduct of military operations. The size of Australian sovereign territory and our area of direct military interest makes this an imposing task ...
>
> Productivity increases arising from new technology will speed up the production of military maps and related data required by the ADF (Australian Defence Force)

for military operations. Nevertheless, the mapping of the priority areas of the north will still take many years... Detailed knowledge of Australia's marine environment is fundamental not only to Australia's commercial interests and purposes but also to the safe and effective conduct of maritime operations, especially for navigation, mine and counter-mine warfare and submarine and anti-submarine operations. The task is formidable and there are few specialised ships available.[2]

A second factor that has increased greatly the attractiveness of GIS for defence use is the impressive development of new technologies and systems relevant to this function. New techniques are providing:

- New means of gathering data. Multi-spectral sensors, synthetic aperture radars, laser profilers, and other sensors mounted in aircraft and satellites are gathering vast quantities of reliable data at comparatively low unit cost.

- New means of storage and transmission. Most remotely-sensed data and nearly all other forms of geographic data is obtained in digital form which facilitates ready storage and transmission over long distances via the civil communications network.

- New data manipulation and display techniques. Digital geographic data stored on modern computers can be accessed and cross-referred to provide completely new products tailor-made to user requirements very quickly and at low cost. Many examples have been discussed in the preceding chapters, but they range from specialised map overlays indicating cross-country 'going' conditions at particular times of the year in northern Australia to three-dimensional images of the ground, sea or air approaches to particular locations.

The third major factor increasing the attractiveness of GIS for defence use is that there are many organisations that have already developed advanced GIS systems in Australia and they have gathered, or are gathering, many of the data sets likely to be required by Defence. Other Commonwealth agencies, such as the CSIRO and the Australian Survey Office, all of the Australian state and territory governments, many regional and local government authorities, and several universities and large corporations, are well advanced in this field. The Australasian Advisory Committee on Land Information has concluded that even at the current rate of progress, parcel-based land information systems will be operating in all regional jurisdictions in less than two decades.[3]

Digital databases have been, or are being, developed by these organisations containing topographic, geological, land use, land ownership, road, rail, sea, air, telecommunication and other infrastructure features, and many other characteristics. Specialists familiar with these systems believe that Defence could gain access to most of these databases fairly readily and inexpensively and that, in combination, they may satisfy 60–75 per cent of Defence's national geographic data requirements.[4] Negotiating such access would not only reduce Defence's data collection requirements dramatically, but in most cases ensure automatic access to routinely updated data as it is collected by the originating authority.

# POTENTIAL APPLICATIONS

The potential defence applications for GIS systems are vast. Many examples based on recent experience are given in the preceding chapters. Many more possibilities are likely to emerge over time.

The potential defence applications of GIS can be grouped broadly into the following three major categories:

- Strategic Applications. This involves the provision of mainly coarse, broadly based information to facilitate decision-making on matters such as the types of forces to be deployed to a region; where, when, and how they might best be deployed and the most effective methods of operation, supply, and support. GIS data could, for instance, throw light on questions such as:
  - Those waters off northern Australia that constrain submarine and/or large ship operations.
  - Those parts of northern Australia in which various categories of weapons, fighting vehicles, and transport could operate during various stages of 'the wet'.
  - A potential opponent's rates of advance and his primary logistic requirements and vulnerabilities were he to land with various force structures at given points in northern Australia.
  - The capacity of the civil infrastructure to support various types of defence operations in different locations in northern Australia.
  - The likely impact of a major natural disaster — fire, cyclone, earthquake, tsunami (tidal wave), etc. and the priorities for relief in various locations.[5]

- Tactical Applications. This category involves the supply of GIS information to support the tactical planning and execution of operations. Examples of tactical issues on which GIS could greatly facilitate decision-making include:
  - Improved prediction of sonar propagation at a given location and time of the year for submarine, surface ship, and long-range maritime patrol aircraft commanders.
  - The selection of aircraft drop zones and landing grounds in a particular operational area.
  - The selection of routes and the calculation of transport and engineering requirements for cross-country movement.
  - The identification of road and track locations likely to require priority for engineering support at different times of the year.
  - The prediction of the rates of advance of a bushfire in a particular region in specified seasonal and weather conditions.
  - The identification of the location and type of major surface water supplies in a given region at a particular time of the year.

- Facility and Equipment Management and Design Applications. This final category involves the application of GIS capacities to assist the selection, design and management of defence facilities, equipments, and other assets. GIS could be used to help resolve issues such as:

— The identification of potential training areas that satisfy specified requirements.
— Prediction of the importance of particular design features on equipments, for example, on armoured vehicles or helicopters in specified regions at particular months of the year.
— Identification of potential sites for airfield development and the local availability of aggregate and other relevant construction materials.
— Estimation of the environmental recovery rate following particular types of military movement through specified regions at indicated seasons, etc.

In broad terms, a developed GIS network has the potential, over time, to improve the efficiency of a wide range of peace and wartime defence functions. It has the potential to marshal quickly in a user-friendly way a vast array of civil and military data relevant to the issues at hand. It provides the only practical means of exploiting to the full the natural advantage possessed by the Defence Force in preparing to operate on and from Australian territory.

## DEFENCE INVOLVEMENT WITH GIS

With the redefinition of Australia's defence priorities in the early-1970s, the need for greatly improved databanks of information on conditions in northern and offshore Australia was generally appreciated. Nevertheless, numerous obstacles precluded speedy action.

Defence planners experienced difficulty adapting from the 'forward defence' era, when geographic information was an intelligence collection function, to preparing for the defence of Australia, when most information would be available from civil agencies. The Defence Force, in particular, had difficulty in adjusting to the concept of relying on a wide range of agencies beyond their direct control for information essential for operational planning and execution.

The concept of a national infrastructure directory was discussed on numerous occasions within Defence but the gathering and maintenance of such a vast data collection was rightly viewed as a daunting and expensive task. Moreover, the function did not fall readily into the allocated responsibilities of any single element of the Defence organisation as they were then defined. There was some limited and inconclusive debate concerning the advantages and disadvantages of various organisations extending their functions and staffing to move into this field.

Overall, the Defence organisation has experienced difficulty in coming to grips with the management of its geographic information requirements during the last 15 years. Various elements of the organisation appear to have perceived periodically at least parts of the overall problem but activity has been patchy, largely uncoordinated, and to limited effect.

Within Defence Central, the Strategic and International Policy Division carries responsibility for the defence aspects of national infrastructure planning, key installations, and liaison with civil authorities. In early 1984 when the Commonwealth Surveyor-General convened an interdepartmental committee to consider the need for increased coordination and cooperation in the collection, use, storage and dissemination of land-related data, the Strategic and International Policy Division represented the Defence Organisation. A Cabinet submission was subsequently produced which recommended:

- The establishment of a high-level coordinating committee.

- The establishment of a group of experts to do the work.

- The development of a strategy to achieve a coordinated approach. The first phase was to be the development of a directory to identify data resources.

Following acceptance of this submission by relevant ministers, an Executive Management Committee was created to bring together representatives from a number of Commonwealth agencies. The Strategic and International Policy Division provided a junior officer to represent Defence. In late 1985, a directory of 830 land-related data sets was published by the Australian Survey Office under the title LANDSEARCH. In the period since, neither the Executive Management Committee nor the Interdepartmental Committee has met.[6]

The Computer Services Division has carried some responsibility for preparing a master computing strategic plan for the Department of Defence and identifying aspects that require further technical or policy coordination. These functions and the existence of this division have, however, recently been the subject of a major departmental review.[7]

The Joint Intelligence Organisation and the service intelligence staffs have gathered substantial data on the regional approaches to Australia. The conventions and data sets established for this purpose are compatible with the similar systems of Australia's major allies. Their maintenance and development is likely to be of continuing high value.

Following establishment of the Headquarters Australian Defence Force in 1984, a Directorate of Joint Operational Intelligence was established with some responsibilities in this field. Part of its charter is the 'coordination, retrieval, collection and, where necessary, dissemination of infrastructure information needed for joint military planning and operations for Australia and its territories'.[8] Within this context the Directorate carries policy oversight for JSP(AS) 205(A), entitled *The Directory of Service Responsibilities for Australian Infrastructure Information*. Details of this directory are provided by Colonel Laing and Major Puniard in Chapter 4.

Within Navy Office, the RAN Hydrographer is responsible for, amongst other things:

- Formulation of hydrographic, oceanographic, and meterological policy.

- Priority, scales, and coverage of Australian charting ... hydrographic, oceanographic, and meterological organisation, administration and application, environmental matters affecting naval operations.

- Exchange and dissemination of hydrographic and oceanographic data.

The Hydrographer also represents Australia in several international hydrographic and oceanographic fora.[9]

Details of the Hydrographer's activities as they relate to GIS are explained by Mr Burrows in Chapter 6. It is perhaps enough to note here that the Navy is moving rapidly into digital data gathering, storage, and manipulation techniques relevant not only to higher standards of charting but to a wide range of broader operational, training, and support functions.

The Operations Branch of Army Office has issued a staff instruction on defence land information specifying policy responsibilities and procedures within Army for the collection, collation, storage, and dissemination of defence land information. Operations Branch also hosts an annual conference of all responsible and interested parties to review progress in defence land information, assign priorities, exchange views, and review the validity of current instructions and procedures.

Under present arrangements, the headquarters of the Army's Military Districts in each of the state capitals carry responsibility for the defence land information system within their geographic boundaries. Lack of resources within the Military Districts has hampered progress in this field, with primary emphasis being placed on identifying the major regional sources of data, should future access be required.

Since 1977 the Army Survey Regiment has been using a digital computerised mapping system called AUTOMAP.This technology has facilitated not only more rapid and higher quality map production but also the introduction of a wide range of other digital products, such as three-dimensional terrain models.

Army's Logistic Command has developed the Logistic Infrastructure Data System (LIDS) as a manual database to facilitate logistic planning. Regional reports have been produced using this system dealing with topography and terrain, transport and communication systems, civilian medical, repair and supply resources, etc.

Headquarters 1 Division has developed an extensive manual database called the Divisional Deployment Area Study. This Study material contains a wide range of information that would be required to support operations in the Pilbara, the Kimberleys, Arnhem Land, and North Queensland.

Air Force has introduced digital techniques to its Central Photographic Establishment. It also has employed advanced digital technology in its Aeronautical Information Service, which supplies current information for flight crew breifing. This system has some potential to interface with AUTOMAP data.

The Defence Science and Technology Organisation (DSTO) has performed an in-house consultancy role with many of the advanced technology information processing systems introduced into the Defence organisaton. DSTO has also developed a range of GIS-related technologies and systems. Some of the more notable examples are airborne laser profiling for shallow water mapping, multi-spectral remote sensing of terrain, airborne wide-range infra-red scanning, new techniques of remote sensor processing to suit Australian conditions, Jindalee over-the-horizon radar, and numerous sonar systems and maritime modelling and prediction techniques. The Central Studies Branch in the Force Development and Analysis Division is well advanced with a Military Movement and Support Study designed to quantify on a computer model transport and logistic support capacities for operations in northern Australia.

The overall picture of Defence GIS activity is patchy. At the Service unit level, data gathering on the Australian environment has accelerated but much of this has been undertaken by manual methods. Where digital techniques have been introduced, this appears mostly to have occurred because of a perceived need for greater in-house efficiency or, in a few instances (as was partly the case with AUTOMAP and the Hydrographer's Office), a need to generate digital data to operate advanced sensors, training systems, and new high technology weapons procured for the Defence Force.

Coordination has been limited and overall policy direction almost completely absent. Defence's interests in the GIS field have not been defined clearly or represented forcefully and coherently either within or beyond the Department.

The present ad hoc and largely uncoordinated management of Defence GIS elements can continue only at the risk of great inefficiency and waste. The most obvious dangers seem to be as follows:

- Defence GIS investments could be sub-optimised through lack of coordination. Digital data sets and systems could be developed which were incompatible or which failed to take account of broader defence interests. Manual data sets could also be proliferated in a way that was not only wasteful of resources but also used system designs that limited the scope for future digitisation and wider application.

- With the main focus in defence information systems on meeting traditional demands, albeit sometimes using new technology means, there is scope for overlooking the very substantial potential of a wide range of new, tailor-made products to improve system efficiency. The numbers of such products could be expected to grow exponentially the more defence databases were organised to interface and the more access is obtained to relevant civil databases.

- There is potential for Defence needlessly to duplicate databases already held and maintained current by civil authorities and private corporations. It would be difficult to justify Defence attempting to develop and maintain current databases on, for instance, the national road and rail networks when these are already maintained and, in most cases, updated frequently by state authorities.

There are those who might argue that Defence needs to operate an entirely independent information system in order to maintain its security and integrity. In practice it would be impossible for the Defence Force to duplicate all the databases that are already available in the civil community. Computer and communication security procedures could be instituted to prevent external access to sensitive elements of Defence data sets.

- Because Defence has not developed coordinated policy positions on most issues concerning national GIS development and it is not represented on the primary national or state GIS policy committees, there is a serious danger that its interests are not being taken into account in the development of national GIS structures, system compatibilities, standards, access arrangements, etc. Defence is also not at present in a good position to monitor closely the rapid expansion of national GIS activity. The representatives of numerous Commonwealth, state and independent authorities and organisations have privately expressed disquiet at Defence's minimal profile in this field.

## WHAT NEEDS TO BE DONE?

Three primary steps appear necessary:

(1) *Generate High-Level Awareness*. Most senior defence officers appear unaware of the potential of GIS systems to contribute substantially to the defence function. In the short term, demonstrations could be arranged of some of the civil GIS networks that have defence potential. In the longer term, pilot GIS networks developed within Defence could be used to demonstrate the future value of such systems.

(2) *Allocate Management Responsibilities*. There is a need for a senior officer to be given overall management responsibility for Defence GIS activity both within and beyond the Defence organisation.

(3) *Create a Defence GIS Policy and Planning Committee*. There is a need for a defence committee chaired by the abovementioned senior officer to bring together the service and civilian organisations with direct interests in the field. The primary roles of this committee should be as follows:

- The Definition of Defence GIS Requirements and Priorities.
    - This would require the identification and examination of many Defence GIS options and probably the commissioning of cost-benefit analyses.
    - The establishment of geographic priorities for Defence GIS effort.
- Coordinate Defence GIS Activity.
    - Review existing Defence GIS responsibilities and activities.
    - Coordinate the planning of Defence GIS activities.
    - Periodically review the development of Defence GIS.
- Develop Strategies for Defence GIS Development.
    - The development of computerised GIS within Defence will inevitably be gradual, with the range of available products expanding with the growth of system development and coordination.

— The introduction of computerisation to an information process function requires movement from low- to medium- or high-level skills for most participants. Training requirements for operators and management should be an early priority.
— Standards and procedures would need to be established to maximise system compatibility within Defence and beyond.
— The establishment of adequate security procedures.
— Determine the level of reliance that should be placed on civil databases and negotiate access to such data sources.
— Identify those data sets not available from civil sources that are important for defence activity. In these cases it would be necessary to determine whether existing data can be interpolated to provide a satisfactory product at low cost or whether active defence collection is necessary.
— Where data collection in unavoidable, determination of the most cost-effective means of data gathering and the establishment of procedures for maintaining data currency.
— Determine policy and practices for external access to Defence databases, including revenue collection.
— Resolve legal issues concerned with the external use of Defence databases — especially copyright, privacy, and indemnity.
— Oversight the development of priority bids for resources.
● Secure Defence's External GIS Interests.
— Develop policy and strategy for the furthering of Defence GIS interests with external agencies.

## CONCLUSION

The conjunction of Australia's changed strategic priorities, the arrival of new technologies, and the rapidly expanding use of these technologies in the civil community provides the Defence organisation with great opportunities. There is scope to acquire immensely valuable geographic intelligence that has the potential to be a real force multiplier for defence planning and operations in the Australian environment.

Strong central management of Defence GIS activity could rapidly bring substantial benefits. The scope for duplication would be reduced, databases already held would become more accessible to priority users, some valuable new products could be produced and Defence's priority interests could be secured through the national GIS coordination machinery.

In the medium to long term the potential for greatly improved tailor-made products, generated very rapidly and at low cost, could be expected to grow substantially. This should occur as Defence devises methods for successfully accessing a wide range of external databases, develops confidence in the skills required for GIS system networking, and becomes more practised and creative in manipulating data to meet the priority needs of defence personnel.

In the final analysis, however, the success of geographic information systems in Defence will depend not so much on the advanced technologies they use or even on the level of funding they attract. The critical factor in all geographic information systems is the quality and skills of the personnel. Management needs to be of a very high quality and specialised staff need to be trained and fostered with the requisite advanced technology skills.

The trend of rapid Australian GIS development is predictable and largely inevitable. The potential for Defence is substantial. The benefits will not, however, flow automatically into the Defence organisation. The corporate development of Defence GIS is deserving of early high-level attention.

# NOTES

1  The fundamental reordering of Australia's priorities is discussed at greater length in Ross Babbage, 'Australian Foreign Policy: The Security Objectives' in F.A. Mediansky and A.C. Palfreeman (eds), *An Introduction to Australia's Foreign Policy* (Pergamon Press, Sydney, 1987).

2  Department of Defence, *The Defence of Australia 1987*, White Paper presented to Parliament by the Minister for Defence, the Hon. Kim C. Beazley, March 1987 (Australian Government Publishing Service, Canberra, 1987), p. 40.

3  Australian Advisory Committee on Land Information, *Recent Developments in Land Information System, Australasia* (Australian Government Publishing Service, Canberra, 1987), p. 3.

4  This was the consensus of civilian and defence GIS experts that assembled for the Geographic Information Systems and the Defence of Australia Workshop, 20–21 August 1987, at the Australian National University.

5  The potential uses of geographic information systems in natural disasters is argued persuasively by Ken Granger in The Rabaul Volcano: An Application of Geographic Information to Comprehensive Crisis Management. Draft MA Thesis, Department of Geography, Australian National University, 1987.

6  These details were contributed by the Office of the Australian Surveyor-General, Canberra.

7  Department of Defence, *Functional Directory*, DRB6 (Department of Defence, Canberra, 1987), p. 67.

8  ibid., p. 10.

9  ibid., p. 164.

# BIBLIOGRAPHY

## OFFICIAL SOURCES

Australia, Parliament, Joint Committee on Foreign Affairs and Defence, *The Australian Defence Force: Its Structure and Capabilities* (Australian Government Publishing Service, Canberra, 1984).

Australian Advisory Committee on Land Information, *Recent Developments in Land Information Systems, Australasia* (Australian Government Publishing Service, Canberra, 1987).

Australian Bureau of Statistics, 1976 Census of Population and Housing, LGAO Summary Data Computer File, Tables LG002 to LG049.

Australian Bureau of Statistics (ABS), *Exports, Australia — Annual Summary Figures 1985–86*, Cat. No. 5424.0 (ABS, Canberra, 1987).

Australian Defence Force, Joint Services Administration, *Division of Administrative Responsibility of the Services in Operations (DARSO)*, JSP(AS)201 (Department of Defence, Canberra, 1970).

Australian Defence Force, Joint Services Administration, *Directory of Service Responsibilities for Australian Infrastructure Information*, JSP(AS)205(A) (Department of Defence, Canberra, 1983).

Australian Key Centre in Land Information Studies, *Airborne Multispectral Scanner Joint Research Project — Gold Coast* (Australian Key Centre in Land Information Studies, University of Queensland, St Lucia, Queensland, September 1987).

Australian Survey Office, *A Pilot Geographic Information System (GIS) for Jervis Bay* (Brochure prepared by the Australian Survey Office, Department of Local Government and Administrative Services, Canberra, 1986).

L.L. Belbin, D.P. Faith and P.R. Minchin, *Some Algorithms in the Numerical Taxonomy Package NTP*, Technical Memorandum No. 84/23 (CSIRO Division of Water and Land Resources, Canberra, 1984).

P. Burden, Application of Statistical Data to a GIS, Queensland Department of Mapping and Surveying, PRP 87/004, 1987.

P. Burden, Application of Road Network Infrastructure Data to a GIS, Queensland Department of Mapping and Surveying, PRP 87/005, 1987.

H.W. Calkins and R.F. Tomlinson (eds), 'Geographic Information Systems, Methods, and Equipment for Land Use Planning, 1977'. Report prepared by International Geographical Union, Commission on Geographical Data Sensing and Processing, for US Department of the Interior, Geological Survey MS-750, Resource and Land Investigations Program, August 1977.

Centre National d'Etudes Spatiales (CNES), *SPOT Simulation Applications Handbook* (CNES, Paris, 1984).

K.D. Cocks, Representativeness of the Proposed Army Training Area at Cobar. CSIRO Division of Water and Land Resources, Land Use Planning Group Working Document No. 86/3, Canberra, 1986.

K.D. Cocks, Using ARIS to Map Rainforest Formations. CSIRO Division of Water and Land Resources, Land Use Planning Group Working Document No. 86/7, Canberra, 1986.

K.D. Cocks, G. McConnell and P.A. Walker, *Matters for Concern — Tomorrow's Land Use Issues*, Divisional Report No. 80/1 (CSIRO Division of Land Use Research, Canberra, 1980).

K.D. Cocks and P.A. Walker, *An Introduction to the Australian Resources Information System*, Technical Memorandum No. 80/19 (CSIRO Division of Land Use Research, Canberra, 1980).

K.D. Cocks and P.A. Walker, Using ARIS to Identify Soils Suitable for Guayule. CSIRO Division of Water and Land Resources, Land Use Planning Group Working Document No. 86/1, Canberra 1986.

K.D. Cocks and P.A. Walker, *Using ARIS to Evaluate the Biogeographical Spread of Australia's Biosphere Reserves*, Technical Memorandum No. 86/22 (CSIRO Division of Water and Land Resources, Canberra, 1986).

Department of Defence, Army Office, *Australian Infrastructure Information*, DI-(A)OPS 21.1, No. 10/78 (Department of Defence, Canberra, 1978).

Department of Defence, Army Office, *Defence Land Information*, Staff Instruction No. 22/86 (Department of Defence, Canberra, 1986).

Department of Defence, Army Office, The Army Logistic Infrastructure Data System, Departmental Working Paper, Canberra, February 1983.

Department of Defence, Navy Office, *Oceanography in the RAN — Policy, Responsibilities and Ship Programming*, DI(N) OPS 45–1, No. 12/80 (Department of Defence, Canberra, 1980).

Department of Defence, Navy Office, *Organisation of the Office of the Deputy Chief of Naval Staff*, DI(N) ADMIN 2–2, No. 16/83 (Department of Defence, Canberra, 1983).

Department of Defence, *The Defence of Australia 1987*, White Paper presented to Parliament by the Minister for Defence, the Hon. Kim C. Beazley, March 1987 (Australian Government Publishing Service, Canberra, 1987).

Department of Defence, *Functional Directory*, DRB6 (Department of Defence, Canberra, 1987).

Paul Dibb, *Review of Australia's Defence Capabilities*, Report to the Minister for Defence (Australian Government Publishing Service, Canberra, 1986).

Director of Military Survey, United Kingdom, *United Kingdom Five Nations Report*, North Atlantic Treaty Organisation Report, 1985.

Division of National Mapping, Department of Minerals and Energy, *Australia 1:250 000 Map Series Gazetteer* (Australian Government Publishing Service, Canberra, 1975).

R. Duffy, AUTOMAP and its Inclusion in the Crown Lands Project, Queensland Department of Mapping and Surveying, PRP 87/002, 1987

R. Duffy, The DCDB and its Incorporation in the Crown Lands Project, Queensland Department of Mapping and Surveying, PRP 87/003, 1987.

ESRI-Australia Pty Ltd, Terrain Studies for Army. Report prepared for Director of Operational Analysis (Army), Department of Defence, Canberra, Authority CAPO W.180168, January 1983.

W.E.Gabrau, J.K. Stoll and B.G. Stinson, *A Plan for Quantitative Evaluation of the Cross Country Performance of Prototype Vehicles*, Miscellaneous Paper M–70–7 (US Army Corps of Engineers, Waterways Experiment Station, Vicksburg, Mississippi, 1970).

R.W. Galloway, R. Story, R. Cooper and G.A. Yapp, *Coastal Lands of Australia*, Natural Resources Series No. 1 (CSIRO Division of Water and Land Resources, Melbourne, 1984).

K. Grant, J.R. Davis and C. de Visser, *A Geotechnical Landscape Map of Australia*, Divisional Report No. 84/1 (CSIRO Division of Water and Land Resources, Canberra, 1984).

K. Grant, A.A. Finlayson, A.P. Spate and T.G. Ferguson, *Terrain Analysis and Classification for Engineering and Conservation Purposes of the Port Clinton Area, Queensland*, Technical Paper No. 29 (CSIRO Division of Applied Geomechanics, Canberra, 1979).

G.N. Harrington, A.D. Wilson and M.D. Young (eds), *Management of Australia's Rangelands* (CSIRO, Melbourne, 1984).

D. Hebblethwaite, *Draft Execution Plan — Regional Geographic Information System Program* (Australian Key Centre in Land Information Studies, University of Queensland, St Lucia, Queensland, February 1987).

M.F. Hutchinson, *MAPROJ — A Computer Map Projection System*, Technical Paper No. 39 (CSIRO Division of Land Use Research, Melbourne, 1981).

J.R. Ive, *LUPLAN: MICROSOFT BASIC, CP/M User's Manual*, Technical Memorandum No. 84/5 (CSIRO Division of Water and Land Resources, Canberra, 1984).

D. Jupp, P. Guerin and W. Lamond, 'Rectification of LANDSAT Data to Cartographic Bases with Application to the Great Barrier Reef Region', in D.L.B. Jupp et al., *Collected Workshop and Conference Papers from the Great Barrier Reef Marine Park Project*, Technical Memorandum No. 84/8 (CSIRO Division of Water and Land Resources, Canberra 1984).

K.J. Lyons and R.J. Eden, 'Which LIS Concept?' in *Proceedings*, Queensland Land Information Systems Seminar, Bardon, Brisbane, May 1984 (Department of Mapping and Surveying, Brisbane, 1984).

D. Marlow, *Project Proposal for the Q-NET Satellite Network — Regional Geographic Information System (REGIS) Project* (Australian Key Centre in Land Information Studies, University of Queensland, St Lucia, Queensland, February 1986).

D. Marlow, The Regional Geographic Information System Project. Paper presented to LIS Seminar, Queensland Department of Mapping and Surveying, May 1986.

D. Marlow, *Q-NET, Data Communication by Satellite* (Australian Key Centre in Land Information Studies, University of Queensland, St Lucia, Queensland, October 1986).

D. Marlow, The Regional Geographic Information System Program — An Executive Summary, Queensland Department of Mapping and Surveying, January 1987.

J.A. Messmore, T.C. Vogel and A.R. Alexander, *Terrain Analysis Procedural Guide for Vegetation*, ETL–0178 (US Army Corps of Engineers, Engineer Topographic Laboratories, Fort Belvoir, Virginia, March 1979).

P.M. Nanninga and P.A. Walker, *Regionalisation of Grid Cell Data: REGION — a Maximally Connected Components Algorithm*, Technical Memorandum No. 83/19 (CSIRO Division of Water and Land Resources, Canberra, 1983).

G. Newman, A. Klason and C.A. Parvey, *1981 Electoral Atlas* (Department of the Parliamentary Library, Canberra, 1983).

S.M. Odle, *Bibliography of In-House and Contract Reports*, Supplement 6, ETL–0143 (US Army Corps of Engineers, Engineer Topographic Laboratories, Fort Belvoir, Virginia, February 1978).

C.A. Parvey, *The Federal Electorate Divisions Information System: Its Spatial Base and Mapping System*. Technical Memorandum No. 82/6 (CSIRO Division of Land Use Research, Canberra, 1982).

C.A. Parvey, *Grid Cell Data Capture for a National Resources Information System*, Technical Memorandum No. 86/16 (CSIRO Division of Water and Land Resources, Canberra, 1986).

C.A. Parvey, H.D. Blain and P.A. Walker, *A Register and Atlas of Local Government Land Use Issues*, Technical Memorandum No. 83/21 (CSIRO Division of Water and Land Resources, Canberra, 1983).

C.A. Parvey and N.H. Wood, *Spatial Units in the Australian Resources Information System*, Technical Memorandum No. 80/27 (CSIRO Division of Land Use Research, Canberra, 1980).

A.R. Pearson and J.S. Wright, *Synthesis Guide for Cross-Country Movement*, ETL–0220 (US Army Corps of Engineers, Engineer Topographic Laboratories, Fort Belvoir, Virginia, February 1980).

Queensland, Department of Mapping and Surveying, Towards an LIS. Paper prepared by Non-Urban LIS Project Team, June 1985.

Queensland, Department of the Valuer-General, Land Data Bank Project: Report 1982. Report to Cabinet by Land Data Bank Steering Committee, accepted by Cabinet Decision No. 38854, Brisbane, 1 November 1982.

Queensland, Office of the Minister for Survey and Valuation, Land Data Bank Report. Report to Cabinet by a Delegation sent overseas to investigate the establishment of a Land Data Bank, accepted by Cabinet Decision No. 29409, Brisbane, 30 October 1978.

G. Stanton, *The Atherton-Mareeba Project — Execution Plan* (Australian Key Centre in Land Information Studies, University of Queensland, St Lucia, Queensland, February 1987).

G. Stanton and A. Lee, The Crown Lands Project, Queensland Department of Mapping and Surveying, PRP 87/001, 1987.

J. Tazelaar, *Terrain Analysis Procedural Guide for Geology*, ETL–0207 (US Army Corps of Engineers, Engineer Topographic Laboratories, Fort Belvoir, Virginia, November 1979).

US Department of the Army, *Military Geographic Intelligence (Terrain)*, FM 30–10 (US Department of the Army, Washington DC, March 1972).

T.C. Vogel, *Terrain Analysis Procedural Guide for Roads and Related Structures*, ETL–0205 (US Army Corps of Engineers, Engineer Topographic Laboratories, Fort Belvoir, Virginia, October 1979).

P.A. Walker, *GRIDBANK: A Guide to the Database Using DEC VAX–11 DATA-TRIEVE*, Technical Memorandum No. 85/10 (CSIRO Division of Water and Land Resources, Canberra, 1985).

P.A. Walker and J.R. Davis, *The Nelligen Geographic Processing System: System Design*, Technical Memorandum No. 78/11 (CSIRO Division of Land Use Research, Canberra, 1978).

K.F. Wells, N.H. Wood and P. Laut, *Loss of Forests and Woodlands in Australia*, Technical Memorandum No. 84/4 (CSIRO Division of Water and Land Resources, Canberra, 1984).

N. Wood, *Procedures for Selectively Listing Data from the Australian Resources Data Bank*, Technical Memorandum No. 83/12 (CSIRO Division of Land Use Research, Canberra, 1983).

N.H. Wood and K.D. Cocks, *Microfiche of Data held against Basic Mapping Units in the Australian Resources Data Bank*, Technical Memorandum No. 84/31 (CSIRO Division of Water and Land Resources, Canberra, 1984).

N.H. Wood and K.D. Cocks, *GRIDLIST: A Procedure for Accessing GRIDBANK on the VAX 11–750*, Technical Memorandum No. 85/20 (CSIRO Division of Water and Land Resources, Canberra, 1985).

M.D. Young, P.A. Walker and K.D. Cocks, 'Distribution of Influences on Rangeland Management', in G.N. Harrington, A.D. Wilson and M.D. Young (eds), *Management of Australia's Rangelands* (CSIRO, Melbourne, 1984).

## BOOKS AND MONOGRAPHS

Australian Urban and Regional Information Systems Association (AURISA), *Report of the Working Group on Statewide Parcel-based Land Information Systems in Australasia*, Technical Monograph No. 1 (AURISA, Sydney, 1985).

Ross Babbage, *Rethinking Australia's Defence* (University of Queensland Press, St Lucia, Queensland, 1980).

Ross Babbage, 'Australian Foreign Policy: The Security Objectives', in F.A. Mediansky and A.C. Palfreeman (eds), *An Introduction to Australia's Foreign Policy* (Pergamon Press, Sydney, 1987).

A. Barr and E.A. Feigenbaum, *The Handbook of Artificial Intelligence*, Vol. 1 (Heuristech Press, Stanford, California, 1981).

Eric C. Barrett and Leonard F. Curtis (eds), *Environmental Remote Sensing 2: Practices and Problems* (Edward Arnold, London, 1977).

L. Breiman, J.H. Friedman, R.A. Olshen and C.J. Stone, *Classification and Regression Trees*, Wadsworth Statistics/Probability Series (Wadsworth, Belmont, California, 1984).

K.R. Bullock, *Design Principles for Land Information Systems*, UNISURV Report S–24 (School of Surveying, University of New South Wales, Sydney, 1984).

P.A. Burrough, *Principles of Geographical Information Systems for Land Resources Assessment* (Clarendon Press, Oxford, 1986).

Carl von Clausewitz, *On War*, ed. and tr. Michael Howard and Peter Paret (Princeton University Press, Princeton, New Jersey, 1976).

Robert N. Colwell (ed.) *Manual of Remote Sensing*, 2 vols. 2nd edn (American Society of Photogrammetry and Remote Sensing, Falls Church, Virginia, 1983).

Paul J. Curran, *Principles of Remote Sensing* (Longman, London and New York, 1985).

J. Dangermond, 'Selecting New Town Sites in the United States Using Regional Data Base', in E. Teichoz and J.L. Berry (eds) *Computer Graphics and Environmental Planning* (Prentice-Hall, New York, 1983).

R. Davis and J. King, 'An Overview of Production Systems', in E.W. Elcock and D. Michie (eds), *Machine Intelligence* (John Wiley and Sons, New York, 1977).

Digital Equipment Corporation (DEC), *VAX–11 Datatrieve Reference Manual* (Digital Equipment Corporation, Maynard, Massachusetts, 1981).

J.E. Estes and L.W. Senger, *Remote Sensing: Techniques for Environmental Analysis* (Hamilton Publishing Company, California, 1974).

European Software Contractors, *GEOPAK Users Manual*, Version 83.1 (European Software Contractors A/S, Gentofte, Denmark, 1982).

P.J. Greville, 'National Defence and National Infrastructure' in Robert O'Neill and D.M. Horner (eds) *Australian Defence Policy for the 1980s* (University of Queensland Press, St Lucia, Queensland, 1982).

Harvard University, Laboratory for Computer Graphics and Spatial Analysis, *POLYVRT: A Program to Convert Geographic Base Files, Manual* (Laboratory for Computer Graphics and Spatial Analysis, Harvard University, Cambridge, Massachusetts, 1974).

R.K. Holz, *Remote Sensing of the Environment* (Houghton Mifflin, Boston, 1973).

Institution of Engineers, Australia, Construction Industry Committee, Guidelines for the Provision of Geotechnical Information in Construction Contracts, Mimeo, 3 December 1986.

J.T.M. Kennie and M.C. Matthews, *Remote Sensing in Civil Engineering* (John Wiley and Sons, New York, 1985).

J.O. Langtry, *The Status of Australia's Defence Preparedness*, Working Paper No. 22 (Strategic and Defence Studies Centre, Research School of Pacific Studies, Australian National University, Canberra, 1981).

J.O. Langtry and Desmond Ball (eds), *A Vulnerable Country? Civil Resources in the Defence of Australia* (Australian National University Press, Canberra, 1986).

T.M. Lillesand and R.W. Kiefer, *Remote Sensing and Image Interpretation* (John Wiley and Sons, New York, 1979).

Joseph Lintz, Jr and David S. Simonett (eds), *Remote Sensing of Environment* (Addison-Wesley, Reading, Massachusetts, 1976).

Pamela McCorduck, *Machines Who Think: A Personal Inquiry into the History and Prospects of Artificial Intelligence* (W.H. Freeman, San Francisco, 1979).

James Martin, *Principles of Data-base Management* (Prentice Hall, Englewood Cliffs, New Jersey, 1976).

K.H. Northcote, R.F. Isbell, G.G. Murtha and A.A. Webb, *Atlas of Australian Soils*. Sheet 7: Townsville-Normanton-Cooktown-Mitchell River-Torres Strait Area (CSIRO and Melbourne University Press, Melbourne, 1968).

Desmond O'Connor, *Problems of Research and Development Relating to the Defence of Northern Australia*, Working Paper No. 43 (Strategic and Defence Studies Centre, Research School of Pacific Studies, Australian National University, Canberra, 1981).

Desmond O'Connor, *The Future of Defence and Technology in Australia: General Considerations*, Working Paper No. 44 (Strategic and Defence Studies Centre, Research School of Pacific Studies, Australian National University, Canberra, 1981).

Robert O'Neill (ed.), *The Defence of Australia — Fundamental New Aspects* (Australian National University, Canberra, 1977).

Patrick O'Sullivan and Jesse W. Miller Jr, *The Geography of Warfare* (Croom Helm, London, 1983).

Louis C. Peltier and G. Etzel Pearcy, *Military Geography* (D. Van Nostrand and Company, Princeton, New Jersey, 1966).

T.A. Ryan, B.L. Joiner and B.F. Ryan, *Minitab Reference Manual* (Statistics Department, Pennsylvania State University, Pennsylvania, 1982).

F.F. Sabins, *Remote Sensing: Principles and Interpretation* (W.H. Freeman, San Francisco, 1978).

J. Walker and M.S. Hopkins, 'Vegetation' in R.C. McDonald et al. (eds), *Australian Soil and Land Survey: Field Handbook* (Inkata Press, Melbourne, 1984).

# CONFERENCE PAPERS, JOURNAL AND NEWSPAPER ARTICLES, THESES

D.J. Abel, 'Some Elemental Operations on Linear Quadtrees for Geographic Information Systems', *Computing Journal*, Vol. 48, No. 1, 1985.

K. Bell, LIS Information Available from State Government Departments. Paper presented at AURISA Seminar on LIS Development in Queensland: The Queensland HUB Concept, Brisbane, April 1987.

J. Blackburn, A. Nairn and G. Bisshop, 'A GIS Joint Venture — the Jervis Bay Pilot Project', in S.D. Hunter (ed.), *Proceedings* URPIS 14 Conference, Melbourne, 1986 (AURISA, Sydney, 1986).

K.D. Cocks and P.A. Walker, 'Estimating Proximate Populations for an Extensive Set of Locations in Australia', *Australian Geographer*, Vol. 16, 1985.

K.D. Cocks and P.A. Walker, 'Using the Australian Resources Information System to Describe Extensive Regions', *Applied Geography*, Vol. 7, No. 1, January 1987.

K.D. Cocks, P.A. Walker and C.A. Parvey, 'Using Information Technology to Examine the Location of a High Speed Ground Transport System for Australia', Australian Institution of Engineers, Civil Engineering Section, *Transactions*, Vol. 27, No. 3, 1985.

K.D. Cocks, P.A. Walker and C.A. Parvey, Evolution of a Continental-scale Geographic Information System, Part 1: System Development. Paper submitted to *International Journal of Geographical Information Systems*.

K.D. Cocks, M.D. Young and P.A. Walker, 'Mapping Viability Prospects for Pastoralism in Australia', *Agricultural Systems*, Vol. 20, 1986.

R.N. Colwell, 'The Remote Sensing Picture in 1984', Keynote Address, in *Technical Papers*, American Society of Photogrammetry and Remote Sensing, Fall Convention, San Antonio, Texas, 1984 (American Society of Photogrammetry and Remote Sensing, Falls Church, Virginia, 1984).

Robert N. Colwell and Charles E. Poulton, 'SPOT Simulation Imagery for Urban Monitoring: A Comparison with Landsat TM and MSS Imagery and with High Altitude Colour Infrared Photography', *Photogrammetric Engineering and Remote Sensing*, Vol. 51, No. 8, August 1985.

P.F. Crapper, P.A. Walker and P.M. Nanninga, 'Theoretical Prediction of the Effect of Aggregation on Grid Cell Data Sets', *Geoprocessing*, Vol. 3, No. 2, 1986.

J.R. Davis, K. Grant and C.A. Parvey, 'Assessing the Geotechnical Component of Road Construction Suitability Across Australia', *Australian Geographical Studies*, Vol. 24, No. 2, 1986.

J.R. Davis, J.R.L. Hoare and P.M. Nanninga, 'Developing a Fire Management Expert System for Kakadu National Park, Australia', *Journal of Environmental Management*, Vol. 22, 1986.

J.R. Davis and C.A. Parvey, 'Local Government Perceptions of Water Related Issues in Rural Australia', *Australian Geographical Studies*, Vol. 24, No. 1, 1986.

F.J. Doyle, 'A Large Format Camera for Shuttle', *Photogrammetric Engineering and Remote Sensing*, Vol. 45, 1979.

R.J. Eden, 'Queensland Multi-Purpose Cadastre', in *Proceedings*, URPIS 12 Conference, Wollongong, 1984 (AURISA, Sydney, 1985).

R.J. Eden, Modelling for Land Information Systems Development in Australia and Particularly Queensland, Draft PhD thesis, Department of Geographical Sciences, University of Queensland, 1987.

Ken Granger, The Rabaul Volcano: An Application of Geographic Information to Comprehensive Crisis Management. Draft MA thesis, Department of Geography, Australian National University, 1987.

D. Hebblethwaite and R.J. Eden, 'The Corporate Working Map', in S.D. Hunter (ed.), *Proceedings*, URPIS 14 Conference, Melbourne, 1986 (AURISA, Sydney, 1986).

M.O. Hill, 'Correspondence Analysis: A Neglected Multivariate Method', *Applied Statistics*, Vol. 23, No. 3, 1974.

G.J.F. Holden, 'Future Topographic Mapping Programme for Australia', in International Cartographic Association (ICA), *Technical Papers*, 2 vols, 12th International Conference of the International Cartographic Association (12th ICA Conference Committee, Perth, 1984).

L.D. Hopkins, 'Methods for Generating Land Suitability Maps', *Journal of the American Institute of Planners*, Vol. 43, 1977.

J.R. Ive and K.D. Cocks, 'SIRO-PLAN and LUPLAN: An Australian Approach to Land-use Planning. 2. The LUPLAN Land-use Planning Package', *Environment and Planning B: Planning and Design*, Vol. 10, No. 3, September, 1983.

Colonel P.M. Jeffrey, 'Initial Thoughts on an Australian Land Surveillance Force', *Defence Force Journal*, No. 21, March–April 1980.

P. Laut, 'Land Evaluation for Bovine Tuberculosis Eradication in Northern Australia', *Australian Geographical Studies*, Vol. 24, No. 2, October 1986.

Air Vice-Marshall J.D.G. Lessels, 'Counter Disaster Organisation in Australia' in *Natural Disasters in Australia*, Proceedings of the Ninth Invitation Symposium of the Australian Academy of Technological Sciences, Sydney, 1985 (Australian Academy of Technological Sciences, Parkville, Melbourne, 1985).

Major K.J. Lyons, 'That Factor — Terrain', *Defence Force Journal*, No. 6, September/October 1977.

K.J. Lyons, 'Environmental Characteristics and Defence in Mapping the Environment: The Need for a Data Bank', in *Proceedings*, Symposium on Environmental Characteristics and Defence, Murdoch University, Perth, March 1978 (Australian Institute of Cartographers (WA) and School of Environmental and Life Sciences, Murdoch University, Perth, 1978).

K. Lyons, R. Divett, P. Guerin, R. Gerber, S. Jones, T. Danaher and W. Bateman, 'Shallow Water Mapping Pilot Project: Papua New Guinea', in *Proceedings*, 20th Survey Congress, Association of Surveyors of Papua New Guinea (ASPNG), Rabaul, 1985 (ASPNG, Port Moresby, 1985).

K.J. Lyons and R.J. Eden, 'Multipurpose Cadastre and LIS Considerations for Australia', in *Proceedings*, International Federation of Surveyors (FIG) Commission 3 Symposium, Edmonton, Canada, October 1984 (Canadian Institution of Surveyors, Edmonton, 1985).

C.R. Margules, D.P. Faith and L. Belbin, 'An Adjacency Constraint in Agglomerative Hierarchical Classifications of Geographic Data', *Environment and Planning A*, Vol. 17, No. 3, March 1985.

M. O'Brien, 'Geographic Information Systems in Australia', *AURISA News*, December 1984.

C.A. Parvey, K.C. Hynson and P.A. Walker, 'The Potential of Space Shuttle Photography for Regional Resource Mapping and Evaluation', in P.J. Hocking (ed.), *Proceedings*, URPIS 13 Conference, Adelaide, 1985 (AURISA, Sydney, 1986).

C.A. Parvey and P.A. Walker, 'Coverage of Australia by Large Format Camera Space Shuttle Photography', *Cartography*, Vol. 14, No. 2, 1985.

C.A. Parvey, P.A. Walker and H.D. Blain, 'Local Government Land Use Issues: A Data Set for a Geographic Information System', in B. Pathe (ed.), *Proceedings*, URPIS 11 Conference, Brisbane, 1983 (AURISA, Sydney, 1984).

J.K. Payne and P.G. Lawler, 'Revision of 1:1 Million Scale Topographic Maps Using Satellite Imagery' in International Cartographic Association (ICA), *Technical Papers*, 2 vols, 12th International Conference of the International Cartographic Association (12th ICA Conference Committee, Perth, 1984).

M. Phillips and K. Bell, 'National Coordination in Land Information — Can it Really Work?', in P. Zwart (ed.), *Proceedings*, URPIS 15 Conference, Hobart, 1987 (AURISA, Sydney, 1987).

M. Phillips and P. Holland, 'Land Information Management in the Australian Survey Office — the Role of Remote Sensing and Geographic Information Systems' in *Proceedings*, 4th Australasian Remote Sensing Conference, 2 vols (South Australian Centre for Remote Sensing, Adelaide, 1987).

D.J. Puniard, 'Australian Defence Force Requirements for Land Related Information', in P.J. Hocking (ed.), *Proceedings*, URPIS 13 Conference, Adelaide, 1985 (AURISA, Sydney, 1986).

D.J. Puniard, The Vegetation Element in Military Terrain Intelligence: Its Acquisition and Integration into Military GIS. Master's Project, Department of Surveying, University of Queensland, 1986.

D. Rhind and H. Mounsey, 'The Land and People of Britain: A Domesday Record', *Transactions*, Institute of British Geographers, New Series 11, 1986.

C.D. Tomlin and J.K. Berry, 'A Mathematical Structure for Cartographic Modelling in Environmental Analysis', in *Proceedings*, 39th American Congress on Surveying and Mapping, Washington DC, 1979.

P.A. Walker, ARIS — A Guide to the Database Using DEC Datatrieve. In preparation.

P.A. Walker and K.D. Cocks, 'Computerised Choropleth Mapping of Australian Resource Data', *Cartography*, Vol. 13, No. 4, 1984.

P.A. Walker, K.D. Cocks and C.A. Parvey, Evolution of a Continental Scale Geographic Information System, Part 2. Applications and Research Projects submitted to *International Journal of Geographical Information Systems*.

P.A. Walker, K.D. Cocks and M.D. Young, 'Regionalising Continental Data Sets', *Cartography*, Vol. 14, No. 1, 1985.

P.A. Walker and I.W. Grant, 'Quadtree: A Fortran Program to Extract the Quadtree Structure of a Raster Format Multi-coloured Image', *Computers and Geosciences*, Vol. 12, No. 4, 1986.

R. Welch, 'Cartographic Potential of SPOT Image Data', *Photogrammetric Engineering and Remote Sensing*, Vol. 51, No. 8, August 1985.

Ian P. Williamson, 'Trends in Land Information System Administration in Australia', in *Proceedings*, Auto-Carto Conference, London, September 1986.

# INDEX